FORENSIC
INVESTIGATOR

Esther Mckay served seventeen years in the New South Wales Police Force, attaining the rank of Detective (technical) Senior Constable. She worked in the area of Forensic Services for fifteen years, attaining expert status in crime-scene examination and vehicle identification. She also worked in Training and Research, as well as Document Examination. She has a Diploma of Applied Science in Forensic Investigation (NSW Police), and was awarded the National Medal for service in 2001 and the Ethical and Diligent Police Service medal with fifteen-year clasp in 2008.

She was discharged from the force in 2001 with post-traumatic stress disorder as a direct result of her forensic work. Her best-selling autobiography, *Crime Scene: True Stories from the Life of a Forensic Investigator*, was published by Penguin in 2005.

She works actively in supporting traumatised serving and former police and is the President of the Police Post Trauma Support Group. She was awarded the Pride of Australia Medal in 2007 for Community Spirit for her work with traumatised police, and regularly speaks to various groups and schools about her life experience, writing and former forensic work. Esther is patron of the Australian Missing Persons Register and has been an Australia Day Ambassador since 2007. She lives in the Southern Highlands with her husband and two children.

FORENSIC
INVESTIGATOR

ESTHER MCKAY

MICHAEL JOSEPH
an imprint of
PENGUIN BOOKS

MICHAEL JOSEPH

Published by the Penguin Group
Penguin Group (Australia)
250 Camberwell Road, Camberwell, Victoria 3124, Australia
(a division of Pearson Australia Group Pty Ltd)
Penguin Group (USA) Inc.
375 Hudson Street, New York, New York 10014, USA
Penguin Group (Canada)
90 Eglinton Avenue East, Suite 700, Toronto, Canada ON M4P 2Y3
(a division of Pearson Penguin Canada Inc.)
Penguin Books Ltd
80 Strand, London WC2R 0RL, England
Penguin Ireland
25 St Stephen's Green, Dublin 2, Ireland
(a division of Penguin Books Ltd)
Penguin Books India Pvt Ltd
11 Community Centre, Panchsheel Park, New Delhi – 110 017, India
Penguin Group (NZ)
67 Apollo Drive, Rosedale, North Shore 0632, New Zealand
(a division of Pearson New Zealand Ltd)
Penguin Books (South Africa) (Pty) Ltd
24 Sturdee Avenue, Rosebank, Johannesburg 2196, South Africa

Penguin Books Ltd, Registered Offices: 80 Strand, London WC2R 0RL, England

First published by Penguin Group (Australia), 2009

10 9 8 7 6 5 4 3 2 1

Design by Cameron Midson © Penguin Group (Australia)
Cover photographs – dead woman in woods: Karen Moskowitz/GettyImages; blue police tape © Newspix/News Ltd
Photograph of Geoff Bernasconi on p. 261 courtesy of the *Daily Advertiser*, Wagga Wagga
Typeset in Minion by Post Pre-press Group, Brisbane, Queensland
Printed and bound in Australia by McPherson's Printing Group, Maryborough, Victoria

National Library of Australia
Cataloguing-in-Publication data:

Mckay, Esther Mary.
Forensic investigator: True stories from the life of a country crime scene cop / Esther Mckay.
9781921518218 (pbk.)
Bernasconi, Geoff. Police – Australia – Biography. Crime – Australia – Case studies. Forensic
sciences – Australia – Case studies. Criminal investigation – Australia – Case studies.

363.2092

penguin.com.au

CONTENTS

FOREWORD

You have either bought this book, or you have taken it off a bookshelf, probably because, like me, you are fascinated by police work. This is an appetite you share with millions of Australians who every week tune their television in to police and crime dramas. Many of these involve forensic investigation. It seems that these fictionalised cases are mostly solved by what seems to be access to unlimited manpower, infinite resources and scientific techniques (some of which haven't been invented yet). The reality is somewhat different and this book is blunt and confronting in its reality.

Esther and I met through a mutual friend, Greg Chilvers of the NSW Police Association. Our immediate connection stemmed from the work I do with police as a psychotherapist and the fact that Esther had her own psychological legacy from years of working in the often brutally confronting field of forensics. Like Geoff Bernasconi, the subject of this book, Esther herself had years of being involved in investigations that exposed her to heinous crimes. These tragedies illustrated the ability some humans have to inflict intolerable cruelty on others. As a result of those experiences she wrote her first book, *Crime Scene*. Following publication of that book, Esther tried to find ways to assist others who, like her, had become damaged by operational police work.

We corresponded and discussed my own work, and we found several matters we sensed we could collaborate on. At the time, Esther was developing a trauma support group for both serving and retired officers, especially those who suffered post-traumatic stress disorder. In just three years Esther has been able to start six support groups throughout New South Wales. Her work has been recognised by awards and certainly affirmation, the most obvious of which came when former Commissioner, and much respected police officer, Ken Maroney agreed to be patron of these support groups.

I have taken this diversion from the normal content of writing a foreword because, as I indicated earlier, this book is not just another story; it springs deeply from Esther's passion for caring and compassion. It's transparent that as a forensic investigator she aimed to find answers for the dead. Esther now tries to help find answers for the living, a pursuit that has proved integral to how she herself became healed.

Television especially is the world of fiction, yet behind our fascination is, as always, a starker, at times even more compelling reality. *Forensic Investigator* is a book about Geoff Bernasconi, a man committed to but also damaged by the work he was dedicated to. This is a powerful story as told and written by Esther Mckay. While it's a story about a colleague, it's also a story that reflects the exceptional calibre and compassion of the author, herself an ex-forensic investigator.

For more than two decades I have been working with police, and clearly this book is an outstanding achievement that adds to our understanding of those who serve us. *Forensic Investigator* demonstrates the commitment and dedication of just one officer, but clearly shows that this work is not without its emotional, psychological and physical cost to all who work in this field.

Almost anyone can write a book; few can tell a story. Esther gives a moving account of what forensic investigation is about. Yet this is also a book and a story that is highly relevant to police, their administrators, families of police and certainly those whose lives have been touched by traumatic incidents – the human cost and currency of day-to-day policing.

If you expect this book to be about the tragic, even gruesome events and the reality of what forensic investigations are about, you will not be disappointed. The stories, as I said at the beginning of this foreword, are real, brutal and confronting. *Forensic Investigator*, through the life of this exceptional man Geoff Bernasconi, not only reveals the ugliness of many terrible and tragic events, but the ability of humans to show compassion. *Forensic Investigator* goes beyond just the factual events and clearly emphasises the psychological cost to our police officers and everyone involved in their lives.

Forensic Investigator bravely directs criticism at administrators who fail to serve and protect their own. It would be easy for police agencies to say that things have changed, but what Esther McKay has achieved in *Forensic Investigator* is to show that the issues of welfare are not just about yesterday, but remain relevant today and undoubtedly will continue to do so into tomorrow.

Roger F. Peters PhD
Newcastle, New South Wales
Winter 2008

1

FROM THE GRAVE
2004

Sitting at my desk in Sydney's south-western suburbs on a hot December day in 2004, my attention was momentarily stolen from my work. Pausing to listen to the radio broadcast, I sat motionless.

Former forensic investigator with the New South Wales Police, Detective Sergeant Geoff Bernasconi, 48, sits by a grave at Wagga in far southern New South Wales while a Sydney judge hands down the maximum compensation for his suffering and lost career as a direct result of repeated exposure to trauma culminating in post-traumatic stress disorder.

As the words sank in, my hand instinctively went to my forehead, pushing down hard and rubbing back and forth in a painful but still mesmerising motion. Sadness consumed me as I realised that yet another of my former workmates had succumbed to the overwhelming emotional and spiritual burden of forensic work.

Then, in that instant, I was gripped by a familiar pounding of my heart as I visualised Geoff standing in that lonely Wagga graveyard.

I felt the irony of his isolation. Throughout his career he had often worked by himself. On this day, when his career had finally come to an end, again he stood alone, this time taking solace through being only with the dead. Over the seventeen years he'd spent committed to forensic work, he'd endured, day after day, horrible realities in order to serve the people of New South Wales. I longed to stand by his side, and place my hand on his shoulder, to reassure him that he was no longer alone, to tell him he had done a good job and that I cared.

Many years before, when I, too, worked as a forensic investigator with the NSW Police, I'd become burdened by the constant reminders of death as I went about my work. Day after day, my life was consumed by killings, distress and gruesome sights, each one adding another piece to an ever-growing mosaic that seemed to be made up of bloodied disposable gloves, plastic bags and human waste. It was what my life had become in the late 1980s, as I struggled with the reality of crime-scene work. Now, a momentary flashback made me cringe – suddenly, I was standing by the hacked-up body of a young woman lying dead among the pretty pink decor of a child's bedroom in a terrace house in Airds. The sound of the swaying branches of a rubber tree that had been at the window and the smell of drying blood filled my mind as though it had happened yesterday.

I joined the NSW Police in 1984, as a twenty-one-year-old. After serving seventeen years, mostly attached to forensic services, I'd suffered my own breakdown after repeated exposure to traumatic scenes when working as a crime-scene examiner. I was discharged from the force, classified as hurt on duty and with post-traumatic stress disorder (PTSD) in 2001. On the day of my medical discharge, I began writing my story, *Crime Scene: True Stories From the Life of a Forensic Investigator*, which was published by Penguin in 2005.

I was convinced that through my own experiences with tragedy and learning to deal with its aftermath, I was now well equipped to support Geoff in his battle with PTSD, depression and anxiety. I would soon also realise that Geoff had a powerful story to tell – and it would be my job to tell it.

In 1999 while I was undergoing treatment for PTSD at St John of God Hospital in Burwood, a Sydney suburb, I learnt that Geoff was also a patient there. Keen to speak to another former crime scene investigator, I asked after him at the front desk, only to be told he'd been discharged the day before. I was disappointed to have missed him, as I wondered how he was coping and if he had started the long road to recovery, but, most of all, I was curious if he would return to forensic work.

Listening to the radio broadcast, I again felt Geoff's presence. I had no contact details for him except that I knew he lived in Wagga Wagga, a large town some five hours south of Sydney. I made a few phone calls to try to find out his whereabouts but then I felt unsure whether he'd want to talk to me. Perhaps, I thought, my intrusion into his life at this point might make matters worse. But still, I had a burning desire at least to give him my support and tell him that I understood.

Although I'd heard of Geoff during my early days as a crime-scene examiner at Macquarie Fields police station, in Sydney's south-western suburbs, it wasn't until 1994 that we actually met. He and I were among thirty police selected for the first intake of the Diploma of Applied Science in Forensic Investigation (NSW Police). The first two-week block of residential study was held at the Canberra Institute of Technology, where forensic police came from all over the state to attend lectures and participate in field studies. Geoff, then with thirteen years' crime scene experience and holding the rank of Detective (Technical) Sergeant, was the most experienced member of the group. For him, and for myself and other seasoned forensic investigators, this course had been introduced years too late; even though some of these people were already classed as experts, they were encouraged to undertake the diploma in order to keep up with the new and younger police joining the section.

During his time with the force, Geoff also took on the roles of union representative and peer support officer, and was active as an advocate for improving conditions for the 130 statewide forensic contingent. It was obvious from the first time we met that Geoff, as a detective sergeant and an experienced investigator, had not only earned respect from his peers but that the section as a whole regarded him highly and relied upon him.

I immediately felt a connection with him, having worked in the 1980s at a suburban crime-scene unit in Sydney's south-west. We suffered under similar conditions as those in which he worked, although they were nowhere near as bad as those of the unit at Wagga at which Geoff had been for his whole forensic career. Understaffing, lack of equipment, little supervision and long hours working on twenty-four hour call-out created hardened forensic investigators who existed on little sleep and pure adrenaline. It was a comparable situation in many of the thirty or so outsourced crime scene units throughout NSW, and it wasn't until so many country police came together for the Diploma of Applied Science in Forensic Investigation that the appalling conditions were compared and discussed.

Until 1998, I saw Geoff a couple of times a year when our diploma group met in Canberra or Sydney for the residential component of the course. Each time, I found him to be a key member of the group, who went out of his way to help other class members.

He also encouraged everyone to become involved in the social side of doing the course, seeking out those who'd been left out to make sure they weren't forgotten.

But it was his boyish good looks and almost cheeky and mischievous manner that most caught my eye. Geoff always had a funny story to tell, and I'd often stop and chat with him between lessons or over a meal. I also observed a kindness in him that I'd never really seen in a colleague before and, although we never discussed his personal situation or family life, I felt a deep bond with him.

The police network works in mysterious ways. Since being discharged from the force in 2001, I've kept in contact with many of my former colleagues, and one of my dearest friends is Suzana Whybro, whom I met at the Sydney district crime-scene unit in 1991. Suzana was a crime-scene examiner too and part of the first intake of the Diploma of Applied Science in Forensic Investigation. Suzana and I became close friends while doing the course, sharing a room during the residential phase and studying together. She was also, as a direct result of her crime-scene work, medically discharged from the force with PTSD, and we continued to give each other emotional support as we worked through our trauma.

I'd mentioned Geoff to Suzana a couple of times and we'd discussed his possible whereabouts, although she had no idea where Geoff was living or what had become of him. Around mid-2006, though, Suzana connected with him through a member of his family and passed on my details. That very same day I received an email from Geoff, and the journey began.

From our first correspondence, Geoff expressed a desire to tell his story. I thought about this and found myself thinking about what had happened to him during all those years of crime-scene work in country New South Wales. There was something unfinished about our conversations and this haunted me even after speaking to Geoff on the phone. Just as I had felt when I was writing *Crime Scene*, I instinctively knew this was a story that had to be told.

In late July 2006 I made the journey by car to Wagga. When I arrived, Geoff was waiting on his front lawn, and we embraced and said hello. After such a long time, we were meeting as ex-police and our former association as crime scene examiners was over – we now had a new and profound reason to come together.

Geoff still had his boyish good looks but didn't appear quite the way I'd remembered him: although we had both aged, it was more than that; it was a deep inner sadness. Geoff had told me in an earlier email that he was taking medication to help him control the intrusive thoughts from his past and I could see the effects immediately. It had obviously changed his demeanour and I also noticed a slight tremor in his hands. Still, although the brightness was gone from his eyes, I could even now see some of the old Geoff lingering in the morning light as just a hint of that cheeky grin hid beneath the surface.

His warmth and kindness were still there too and we quickly renewed our friendship as he welcomed me into his lovely home. Once inside he showed me around, and over a cup of tea we caught up on family and past experiences, but it was on my mind that we both knew I'd come to hear his story. After we'd finished catching up, he led me into the upstairs dining room and swept his hand towards a coffee table with a glass top that was in the centre of the room.

'Have a look at that and come downstairs into the bar when you're finished; it's my reflection table, I made it in St John of God

Hospital,' he said as he left the room.

As I bent down to see what it was, my eyes focused on the small objects under the glass. Suddenly, I realised they were a miniature church and cemetery, with people and tombstones. I caught my breath as I realised what the table represented. Looking closer, I started to read the collage of newspaper articles pasted around the perimeter: 'Twins drown'; 'Four die in plane crash horror'; 'Split second that wiped out a family'; 'Wagga man murdered'. Just then the room seemed to become dark and I sensed a sombre mood invading my mind as I read through the clippings in deathly silence.

A plaque in the centre of the table read, 'For my precious family. In memory of those that have touched our lives . . . Geoffrey/Dad, 14/5/2000'.

My eyes welled and it took all my strength to remain composed. I knew it would be okay to cry but I didn't want to let go, for fear I wouldn't be able to stop. No one understood better than I what this table represented and why Geoff had felt the need to make this memorial; in a way it prepared me for what was to come. I hoped I could do Geoff's story justice.

In the late afternoon, sitting in a room downstairs, with a beer for him and a glass of wine for me, and the soothing sounds of the Dixie Chicks in the background, he took a long drag on his cigarette, paused and, with eyes downcast, began to tell his story.

2

JOINING THE RANKS

Geoff is the youngest of three children born to fifth-generation Australians; his parents had a strong Catholic faith and were country people at heart. He was born on the 14th of May 1956 at Parkes, and grew up on the south coast of New South Wales, approximately an hour and a half south of Sydney, in the small working-class suburb of Warilla. His dad worked as an accountant at the local steelworks and his mum earnt extra cash cleaning. Geoff and his siblings all went to Catholic schools, and his sister became a nurse, while his brother followed in their father's footsteps, eventually taking a position at the steelworks.

Geoff's childhood was happy and carefree. He has fond memories of his best mate and neighbour, a Koori boy named 'Cracker', and would later be best man at his wedding. They went everywhere together, and spent many hours playing in the backyard or around the neighbourhood, riding their bikes and making their own fun. Geoff would catch the bus to and from school, and in the afternoons rode his bike the three kilometres to the beach to surf and swim. As long as he was home by tea, he could pretty much do as he liked. At school, Geoff excelled in athletics; he loved a game of footy and would get involved in whatever sport was going. Academically, he cruised along, getting good marks and never really worrying too much about his education.

Geoff and Cracker had a mutual love of music, and one year Geoff's parents bought a Hanimex tape recorder. The two boys spent hours writing songs, playing their guitars and singing together while making amateur recordings, and then doubling over with laughter as they listened to themselves on tape. Geoff was never fortunate enough to have guitar lessons but was content with teaching himself to play. He mostly played country rock and by the time he was fifteen, he was singing and playing guitar at parties. This eventually led to the formation of a three-piece band that played mostly at restaurants and weddings.

Geoff describes his family's house as a basic housing-commission cottage, surrounded by working-class neighbours who all knew each other and wouldn't hesitate to give each other a hand if the need arose. It was a happy and close-knit neighbourhood, in which the man of the house typically put in a good day's work. This helped shape Geoff into a young man with a strong work ethic and a solid sense of justice.

As Geoff grew up, he started to think about a vocation; he'd always felt a deep connection to the Catholic church and toyed with the idea of entering the priesthood. As well, he had an aunt who was a nun, which reinforced his family's strong ties to the church. But any idea of becoming a priest was abandoned when he met Annette through a school friend at the rollerskating rink at Thirroul, who he would marry in 1976.

When Geoff was about fourteen, an incident occurred that changed his outlook on life and led to his early thoughts of pursuing a career in the police force. One evening he was visiting the local library, where he'd often spend time reading and listening to classical music. He went to use the toilets and walked the short distance to the nearby amenities block. As he left the building, a man spoke to him from what looked like a Commonwealth or local government car, with Z number plates. He said, 'You shouldn't be walking around on your own at this time of night'.

Geoff explained that he'd been at the library and was about to walk home after using the toilets. The man offered Geoff a lift, which he naively accepted. When he was in the car, the man was friendly enough and the two of them chatted until suddenly the man reached over and placed his hand on Geoff's crotch. Shocked and angry, Geoff yelled at him to stop the car, desperately clambered out and ran off to get as far away as possible from this predator.

Over the next few days, Geoff did his best to make sense of what had happened, but found himself harbouring a deep-seated hatred of the man and what he represented. He didn't report the incident, nor did he tell anyone what had happened, and eventually he put it out of his mind. A few years after the incident, Geoff was attending a social function with Annette and her Ambulance Service colleagues when he saw the man again. Geoff was sickened to see him at the function but this was before paedophilia issues were discussed publicly and he felt helpless to do anything about it. He was sure this man could make things very uncomfortable for him if he went to the police, as it would be Geoff's word against his, but Geoff vowed then that he'd do anything in his power to prevent the type of assault he'd experienced happening to anybody else. It was at this time that he began seriously to consider a career in the police force.

Also around the time of the incident with the man at the toilets,

Geoff noticed a vagrant living in a shack next to the railway tracks. He would often walk home along the railway line after visiting his aunt, and Geoff liked to chat to the old man, who was lonely and obviously down-and-out. He told Geoff that he'd been in trouble with the law, lost his family and become an alcoholic. He was now destitute with no friends, not having even a proper roof over his head. Geoff wished he could help this poor man, but was at a loss as to what he could do. It stuck in his mind that people can find themselves in a rut and that, perhaps, joining the police force would enable him to influence how things turned out for them.

When Geoff left school, he became an accountant in the transport industry, but although he earned good money, he never really settled in the job. One day in 1977, he was chatting to a friend he'd met through the local youth club who mentioned he was joining the NSW Police as a cadet. This brought back to Geoff his earlier thoughts of joining the force and would later lead to him answering a recruitment advertisement in the local paper for young people to join the ranks. Having decided to find out more about policing, he paid a visit to the local station, where a rather overweight and burly sergeant behind a desk greeted him. Upon seeing Geoff's somewhat tall and lanky physique, he barked, 'When you put five or six stone on, son, come back and see us!'

Geoff was a bit taken aback but it didn't deter him; he just thought that obviously he would have to bulk up a bit before presenting himself to the recruitment office, needing a bit more weight in order to fit the mould of a police officer as it was in the late 1970s.

Around this time, Geoff's sister married an ambulance officer and a couple of his friends joined the police force, so becoming a police officer increasingly seemed the right thing to do. With

Annette's blessing, at the age of twenty-one Geoff resigned from his accounting job, took a large pay cut and joined the ranks.

In 1978, Geoff was posted to Sutherland police station after graduating in class 158, the biggest class ever to pass through the Redfern Police Academy. Geoff worked in the Sutherland shire, twenty kilometres south of Sydney, for thirteen months before securing a transfer to Wollongong.

One of his first memories of working as a new probationary constable was of being shown the 'Stud Book', which listed in order of seniority those police waiting for promotion. Every now and again, Geoff had a strange feeling when he saw the station sergeant pull the book out of the safe and rule a neat line through the name of an officer who'd died.

You're not going to rule me out! he thought.

It was confronting to realise that the death of a workmate could be treated as a number, but he would soon realise that policing was very much a numbers game and that there was nothing he could do to change it.

In 1980, while working as a young constable on highway patrol, Geoff was involved in an accident that would affect him deeply. An elderly man in his eighties, driving a Mini Minor, made a right-hand turn across the path of Geoff's patrol car. Geoff slammed on the brakes as hard and fast as he could, but it was too late and his vehicle slammed head on into the small car. Geoff was so close to the other car that he could see the look of horror on the other man's face when he realised they were about to collide. The man, who was suffering from cancer, was critically injured. Geoff went straight to the man's bedside in hospital, but, soon after, he died of his injuries.

Even though the accident wasn't Geoff's fault and he couldn't have done anything to avoid the collision, it still weighed on his mind. He began to have nightmares in which he could clearly see the man's face, and in which he would slam on the brakes to try to avoid the crash. As a result, Geoff would wake from a deep sleep with his legs pushed down hard, as he would when braking. He later came to realise that the man's injuries had probably not been life threatening and his death had had more to do with his advanced age and unstable health, but he still thought of it often and with regret.

In 1981, Geoff began looking for a change of career. He enjoyed highway patrol but couldn't adjust to the numbers game and the attitude of his colleagues, who would sit on an intersection and spend all shift handing out tickets. It seemed that the more drivers you fined the more respect you earnt, which wasn't the way Geoff saw things. It annoyed him when he was criticised for making too many arrests, and constantly told to concentrate on fining drivers and handing out traffic infringement notices. As far as Geoff was concerned, he hadn't joined the police force for that and, after discussing with Annette the possibility of becoming a country cop, he made a phone call to the country superintendent's office. He was told that a position was available at Enngonia and that the transfer was his if he wanted it.

Having no idea where Enngonia was or what the town was like, he decided to go and have a look. He caught a lift to Dubbo with the early-morning paper truck and then hitchhiked to Bourke, finally arriving in Enngonia after a day-long trip. The town appeared to be quiet and, as he looked around, Geoff's mind was full of ideas about the great things he could achieve. What he didn't know about was the surge in alcohol-fuelled violence that occurred during 'pay week', when the local Aboriginal people would spend their dole money on alcohol. Had Geoff arrived a week earlier, his view of the town would have been very different. Now, though, his only worry was the town's obvious isolation and whether it would be suitable for him, Annette and Scott, their baby son, who had just been born. His main worry at that point was whether Annette, with a new baby, would cope with the lack of facilities and infrastructure. After a quick look around, and satisfied with what he'd seen, he hitchhiked all the way back to Sydney.

When he arrived, he talked it over with Annette, who was happy to go along with whatever decision he made. After thinking it through, he still had some doubts about going ahead with the transfer. He discussed it with his father, who promptly told him he was mad to consider such a move. Having worked at Brewarrina on the railways, he knew full well what it was like to live in such an isolated town, and told Geoff to forget it.

Geoff rang the country superintendent's office to tell him he'd decided that Enngonia was too isolated and not suitable for Annette and the baby. The super's reaction completely took him by surprise. The man barked down the phone, 'Too bad. The decision has already been made, and you better take the posting or else you'll be transferred to Sydney!'

Geoff couldn't believe it. He'd had no idea the mere mention of a country posting would see him locked into a major move without his even having seen the town or considered the impact on his family. He found out later that positions such as the one in Enngonia were so hard to fill that he'd pretty much signed his own death warrant simply by making the inquiry. Having no choice but to take the position, he thought that at least it would be better than the threatened transfer to Sydney, which would most likely be to the central business district; he'd been told he definitely wouldn't get Sutherland, which was, at least, on the Wollongong rail line.

As luck would have it, one of the sergeants he'd worked with had just received notification of his promotion to inspector, at Bourke. Inspector Hardman was more like a father figure than a boss to Geoff, who had tremendous respect for him. He asked him about the transfer to Enngonia and mentioned his reservations regarding the move but, after hearing how positive his superior officer was about the transfer, he decided he'd make the best of it. From that moment on, things moved quickly, with the transfer taking effect immediately. Within days, the paperwork was filed and, along with Annette and baby Scott, Geoff set off for a new life in the country.

Enngonia was managed by a two-man police station in a remote Aboriginal settlement located 100 kilometres north-west of Bourke and forty kilometres south of the Queensland border. As Annette and Geoff drove into town together for the first time, tears filled Annette's eyes; she was dumbfounded at how isolated it was. They drove past the tennis courts, the hotel (aptly named The Oasis) and the town hall, before seeing a few demountable homes and buildings. Next was the school, which was quite modern with a swimming pool at the back of it, and the Country Women's Association building across the road. Close by was the police station, a modern building with a welcoming garden, and next door a large police residence, with wide verandahs all around. Geoff and Annette started to think that perhaps Enngonia wasn't that bad after all – the town seemed quite modern as well as quaint, and had a welcoming air. That was until they caught sight of their new home: beside the grand police residence was a tiny transportable building sitting in an unkempt and barren garden. Annette's heart sank.

Inside, the house was basic but clean and, as he and Annette stood there drenched in perspiration from the humidity, Geoff's mind turned to the wall-mounted airconditioner he'd purchased from the previous tenant. His first priority was to get it going and then at least one room in the house would give some relief from the searing heat. The house was also equipped with its own fresh water tanks, which Geoff located and turned on before setting about organising their furniture and making the house a home. The television reception was non-existent, except for a snowy picture on the ABC, so Geoff bought a VHS video recorder for the exorbitant amount of $700. For entertainment at home they would swap movies with the locals and hire limited titles from the local shop, which was manned by the Enngonia Aboriginals and had basic supplies. For anything else, it was a 100-kilometre trip to Bourke.

Annette soon met the local community nurse and school staff, and, being resourceful, before long offered to care for the school principal's newborn baby to earn extra cash. She also got to know the women at the CWA, where she became involved in local activities and fundraisers. Luckily for Annette, the town was sociable, always with people about and someone to talk to. As well, the police from Bourke introduced themselves and became part of Geoff and Annette's social circle, coming over for barbecues and offering support.

Annette made the most of this and settled in quickly, always taking part in local functions such as the Melbourne Cup Day luncheon in the police station yard or the regular get-togethers at which the local farmers culled sheep in order to divvy up the meat among the townsfolk. Once, Geoff was cutting up meat with a very sharp knife, which he accidentally sliced through his hand. With blood pouring from the wound he rushed straight to the community nurse, who immediately exclaimed, 'I can't do anything with that! You'll have to go to Bourke.' Not realising how deep the cut was, Geoff promptly jumped into his car and rushed to Bourke, where he received fourteen stitches.

It was occasions like this that really rammed home to Geoff and Annette how isolated Enngonia was. As time went on, though, and they continued to get to know the locals, they settled into their new lifestyle and came to feel part of the town.

Geoff found the work challenging, especially the alcohol and abuse problems of the Aboriginal settlement. He had thought he could make a difference in the town but he came to realise it was best just to stick to enforcing the law, and keeping peace and order. Geoff did, however, feel supported by the boss, Inspector Hardman from Bourke, who was tough but fair, and always available for a chat. He really cared about the troops but, at the same time, wasn't afraid to put on his gun and handcuffs and get into a fray. He always supplied the Christmas drinks and made every effort to be involved with the officers' families.

One of the local landmarks Geoff was drawn to was the local cemetery, which was located at a place known as 'red dirt plane'. He first went there not long after he and Annette moved to Enngonia, but his real introduction to it was assisting with the marking out of a grave for an Aboriginal burial. He was supervising the Kooris and making sure they dug the grave square, but decided to pitch in because it was so hot that he just wanted to get the job finished. After spending most of the day in the cemetery he felt a connection, and often went back just to walk around and read the inscriptions on the headstones, which contained a great deal of local history. Parts of the cemetery were in disrepair and Geoff wished it were better maintained, but he still felt it was hallowed ground and found solace in wandering among the tombstones.

About a year after Geoff arrived in Enngonia, he was patrolling the town alone one afternoon when he came across a group of intoxicated young Aboriginals. He asked them to move on, but they became abusive and, instead of doing as he asked, challenged his authority. Things quickly deteriorated to the point that an arrest was necessary. One young man became violent and Geoff struggled with him as he attempted to place him under arrest. A scuffle broke out and suddenly Geoff was surrounded by an angry mob jeering and protesting that he release their mate. His alarm grew as he realised he was outnumbered and couldn't defuse the situation. Within minutes a riot erupted, forcing Geoff to retreat to the police residence, where he was holed up while an angry mob of 100 or so locals congregated outside. They soon surrounded the house, and threatened Geoff and his family. As the other local police officer was on holiday, Geoff had to call for backup from Bourke. The threats continued for several hours until, eventually, eight police from the closest station arrived.

The incident affected Annette profoundly. It also had a severe impact on Geoff, who was fearful for his safety and felt he was constantly on duty, as he was often left to deal with episodes of violence on the Aboriginal reserve by himself. This wasn't what he'd expected and it placed a huge strain on his marriage.

Having considered his future, Geoff, after much discussion

with Annette, made a phone call to the country superintendent's office. He was told that an officer from Bourke was interested in taking over his position and, as he'd done his tenure at Enngonia, which was classified as a disadvantaged station, he was offered one of two possible transfers. One was at Gwabegar, up in the mountain country in the northern tablelands, and the other, a position of lockup keeper, was at Urana, a one-person station located 578 kilometres south-west of Sydney and 107 kilometres west of Wagga. As Annette was pregnant with their second child, Urana's closeness to a regional centre made them favour it. As well, Geoff rang the sergeant at Lockhart, which was clustered with Urana, and learnt that the town had a doctor and a hospital, as well as a preschool.

On 17 December 1982, Geoff and Annette set off for a fresh start. For Annette the move was bittersweet – she'd made close friends in Enngonia she knew she'd dearly miss. She cried as they drove out of town, but after the riot she'd essentially lost her sense of belonging and, staring straight ahead at the dry and parched land, she didn't look back.

After a long journey through drought-ridden country, they finally drove into town. As they did so, the first thing they saw was the town's Catholic church and just up the road from it was the police station, with the residence on the corner and the courthouse next to it. They came across businessses that included a little supermarket, a cafe/newsagent and a bank, and also checked out the hospital, netball courts and football oval. Geoff and Annette agreed that, compared with Enngonia, Urana was paradise!

Pulling up outside the police residence, they saw the furniture delivery truck awaiting their arrival. They stepped out into the full force of the over-forty-degree afternoon heat. Geoff and the removalists began unloading the furniture and other belongings and, within the hour, a stream of locals dropped by asking if they could help. That evening, Geoff and Annette watched colour television, which was a luxury after the scratchy ABC-only reception they'd had at Enngonia.

Geoff and Annette's daughter Kate was born in July 1983 in Corowa, down near the Victorian border. By this time, they had settled into Urana, and Geoff embraced the sense of community that came with policing in a small country town. The wool and wheat graziers and lamb and beef growers gave the townspeople a good livelihood. As well, the locals worked in the council office, and the local businesses, school and preschool. Most people knew each other and would lend a hand when the need arose. Geoff became well-known in the town, as he took on positions such as secretary of the football club and treasurer of the bowling club. This meant he spent most of his spare time serving the community.

One of the first places Geoff visited after he started working in Urana was the cemetery. It had a Returned Services League memorial that had obviously seen better days, and, after joining the Apex Club, which services community needs, he helped out with restoring the monument to its original condition. After that, Geoff visited the cemetery from time to time, wandering among the headstones and reading their inscriptions, pausing to reflect on the lives they recorded. On special days, such as Mother's Day or Father's Day, he'd see lots of flowers adorning the graves, some many decades old, which showed that even with the passage of time there were still those who cared. He felt peaceful during these visits, which reminded him of his own mortality and of the gift of life.

Geoff believed that it was because Urana was a little off the beaten track that the town had very little crime. The community preferred trouble to be sorted out locally, rather than a fuss being made, and were happy as long as they perceived justice to have been done. Geoff's policing style was described as 'justice Urana-style', and an example of it occurred one New Year's Eve. After patrolling the town until around 2 a.m., he decided to knock off and get some sleep as things were dead quiet. The next morning he left home only to see that every shop and building had been painted white! On hearing the news, the locals came rushing into town to inspect the damage to their businesses and property. They banded together and wanted to know what Geoff was going to do about it.

'If I find out who's done it, they can clean it,' he promised.

All Geoff had to do to find the culprits was follow a trail of white paint down the road, which led straight to the offender's house. He knocked on the door and, a few minutes later, a number of tired and guilty-looking kids streamed out, all covered in white paint. That day Geoff supervised the kids systematically cleaning every inch of the town until there wasn't a trace of white paint anywhere. The locals were happy with Geoff's summary justice approach and nothing more was said about the incident.

Annette had also settled quickly into Urana and made friends through the preschool and the local church group. She and Geoff loved the town. However, a significant event was about to occur.

3

NO MAN'S LAND
1984

It was dusk on 14 May 1984, and Geoff was looking forward to celebrating his twenty-eighth birthday with his mates and a few quiet beers. First, though, he had a football meeting in Urana, to be followed by a family dinner at home. The meeting had just got underway when he got a phone call from Annette, who had received a call for assistance at the police residence. She told him there'd been an accident out on the Newell Highway, near Widgiewa Siding and about fifty kilometres north of Jerilderie, and that there was at least one person dead. Geoff rushed home, collected the police sedan and sped to the address.

When he arrived at the scene of the accident, he realised he was in a lonely place he called 'No Man's Land'. It was a semi-arid cropping belt, with very few trees, shrubs or vegetation. Geoff was immediately struck by the absence of bush noise: there were no birds chirping or other sounds of wildlife. In the still night air, a heavy atmosphere of diesel fumes had settled over the road, instantly attacking Geoff's sense of smell. He saw, some metres off the road surface on the northern side of the highway, the twisted state of the vehicles, one on top of the other. Wedged underneath a 'MAN' pantech truck was a Valiant sedan, unrecognisable except for the boot, which he could identify from the tail lights. The enormity of his task weighed heavily upon him as he digested the extent of the carnage. There were a number of people about, walking around aimlessly or standing in groups, but what struck him immediately was the lack of urgency.

But, within minutes, ambulances and fire trucks pulled up simultaneously, and the scene quickly developed into chaos as the traffic increased and more people gathered. The full moon gave the scene a shadowy glow and, in the dim light, Geoff noticed some nappies among the debris. He went straight to the truck driver, Robin Condor, and his passenger, Mary Ryan, who were obviously distressed and suffering from shock. They walked around the right side of the vehicles to show Geoff the wreckage. Torch in hand, he bent and peered in through the squashed remains of the car.

Oh, shit, he thought, *here I am in 'No Man's Land', in charge of this!*

Staring straight back at him were the smashed skulls of two dead bodies, one behind the other, indicating where they had been sitting when the crash occurred. Geoff flinched at the sight. Looking beyond them into the darkness of the mangled wreck, he realised there appeared to be more skin, blood and hair, but it was just a mass of human tissue. He thought that surely there couldn't be any survivors, but what if someone were still alive in there? His mind started to race; there was so much to do. *Where to start? What should I do? Got to take charge. My God, there could be kids in there!*

Taking it one step at a time, Geoff started with Robin Condor.

'How did this happen'? he asked him.

Robin solemnly began to speak. 'I saw a green light coming

towards us and then I knew I'd hit something, even though there was no sound or sensation. I thought the car had spun off to the left, but then I went to get out of the truck and realised we were too high, that the car was beneath me. I didn't see them until it was too late. They just came straight at me – there was nothing I could do. I couldn't go anywhere. My God, why? How are we gonna get them out?'

As Geoff nodded, he noticed Robin trembling; then the sobbing began. *God, I've got to get him out of here. He's losing it*, he thought.

'It's okay. Calm down. Don't worry,' he said to him gently.

Shortly after this, Robin again became calm and coherent but his mind seemed to be somewhere else. Geoff knew that he had to get him out of there quickly.

Mary Ryan, an elderly woman, was standing beside Robin and was quite talkative and agitated.

'I was blinded by headlights in the time it takes you to click your fingers,' she said as her voice quavered. In a whisper, she went on: 'We looked into the car with a torch and there was nothing, no sign of life. We realised they were all dead.'

As they stood talking by the side of the road, the silence was intermittently interrupted by a gust of wind and the rumble of passing traffic. Geoff moved the couple to the police vehicle, as he wanted to remove them from the devastation, which was obviously taking its toll.

Geoff then walked along the roadway looking for physical evidence, having decided not to close the road but instead to allow the traffic to flow; the last thing he wanted was more of a crowd. He was then approached by a local property owner, Linton Gooden. They stood talking for a minute but Geoff could see that Linton was struggling, his agitation obvious. He needed to keep busy. Linton offered assistance, and later he and his wife supplied the workers with hot coffee and sandwiches, which was much appreciated, although most had no stomach for food. With the possibility of multiple fatalities and the difficult job of identification, Geoff knew that this was a job for the Scientific Investigation Section. A trained forensic investigator would take over all aspects of recording the scene: taking photographs and measurements, reconstructing how the accident occured, and ultimately determining the point of impact. He desperately needed the scientific section to attend, take control and look after the lengthy identification process of each body using disaster victim identification (DVI).

Geoff returned to his vehicle and picked up the radio handset to request assistance from Wagga. He was alone, out of his depth and trying to stay calm. As the radio wasn't working too well, he struggled to get his message across. The radio operator said that Scientific weren't coming, as the deceased was at fault. *The hell they won't!* Geoff thought. His outrage obvious, he argued with the radio operator: 'How the hell can they make a call like that without seeing the scene?' Finally, Geoff won out.

In the meantime, the people at the scene were becoming increasingly tense and an air of unease descended as the temperature dropped. The minutes ticked by slowly, seeming like an eternity.

Finally, a man from Scientific arrived, and begrudgingly took a number of photographs of the roadway and a single shot of the car. Apparently angry, as well as stand-offish, he took his time going about the job before leaving without a word.

Now, what to do with the bodies; got to get them out, Geoff thought. He crawled under the wreck – *Yep, two dead.* He could smell death and it was colder now. *More people turning up, rescue, media, tow trucks, got to get some order, take control, put that bloody smoke out! This isn't right – I'm normally the helper, not the main player. Keep calm, you can do it.*

Next, the detectives arrived and, after a short discussion, left, taking Robin and Mary to the station to give a statement. Geoff was relieved to see the truck driver and his passenger go, as their distress was growing. *Thank God they won't see the bodies once the vehicles are separated.* As they were leaving, the heavy salvaging and lifting equipment arrived, along with rescue lighting and personnel.

Once all the emergency workers were assembled and under the control of the salvage operators, Herbie Fisher and Kevin Barber from the Narrandera rescue squad, they discussed the best possible method of lifting the truck off the Valiant before starting the painstaking job of prising the two vehicles apart using a crane and heavy lifting equipment. A screen was erected to shield the carnage beside the road from the passing traffic, and rescue lights were directed towards the flattened Valiant. During the next five hours, the rescue crew worked to release the Valiant from underneath the bogey steer of the 'MAN' truck. Using power jacks and cutting tools, they worked until the truck was finally lifted from the twisted and crushed Valiant, and then the operation focused on separating the car from the truck's twin steering system. Geoff was relieved that everything was going to plan: although it was a slow process, he was getting closer to freeing the bodies.

Once the two vehicles were separated, the team sliced the roof from the body of the car, eventually peeling it back like a lid from a can of beans. Meanwhile, the bodies inside were heating and fermenting under the weight of the twisted metal. A deathly shot of steam permeated the still air as the roof was peeled back, shocking those present as the horror contained within was revealed.

The pungent odour invaded Geoff's senses before he could stop it. At first he didn't know what exactly he was looking at: it appeared to be a car full of twisted and broken bodies, but then, as he moved closer, he saw two, four or possibly five dead as the awful picture became clearer. He looked around him and saw even the rescue men backing off in horror. Geoff had never seen anything like it before and it took him a few minutes to digest the mass of bodies twisted in the wreckage. *Where do we begin?* There was no easy way; it just had to be done. With the help of the ambulance officer, Geoff began the grim task of pulling the victims from the wreckage.

It was at this point he witnessed the most terrible image he had ever seen. As he pulled one of the broken bodies out, he unearthed the remains of a baby still strapped into its harness in a car seat at the back of the wreck. His head was so squashed that he looked like a cartoon character. *Oh my God*, Geoff thought, *he's a similar age to Scott.* Grown men openly wept at the sight of the baby, and consoled each other, all the time knowing they had to get back to the job at hand. In total, Geoff saw what appeared to be the remains of five adults and one child, all smashed to a pulp. He'd never seen such carnage.

Geoff, a young constable first class, was left to sort through the mangled wreck and somehow extricate the bodies in one piece. He by now had the assistance of Sergeant Potter from Jerilderie, who'd come out to lend a hand. The two of them, with the assistance of the volunteer rescue squad and the ambulance officers, set about the grim task of removing the remains from the wreckage and placing them into body bags. Geoff and the others tried to make sense of what belonged where, but they finally came to the conclusion that it was impossible. The bodies were so smashed up that all six were placed into three body bags. An ambulance then ferried the bodies away to Wagga Base Hospital so that life could be pronounced extinct.

With Scientific gone, and no expert there to take further control, Geoff realised he had to take possession of the wrecked car and truck. He organised tow trucks to remove the vehicles from the scene and deliver them to the rear yard of the police residence; he wasn't content with this arrangement but had no other option. Now that the bodies were gone, people started to drift away. Soon, Geoff would be standing alone in 'No Man's Land'. Most were going home to their loved ones, as they'd finished their jobs; his had just begun.

Driving back to the station, Geoff's mind was racing: he knew there were two males and a little boy among the bodies but he wasn't sure of the ages or genders of the other three. His thoughts turned to the deceaseds' families. *How the hell are they going to cope with this?*

Around midnight, Geoff arrived back at Urana to see a flock of people surrounding the station and waiting for a glimpse of the death car. Ignoring them, he set about assisting the tow truck operator to lower the vehicles into the police compound. As soon as the squashed remains of the roofless green Valiant came to rest within the yard, Geoff's German Shepherd, Lucy, went berserk. She barked incessantly at the car and attacked the wreckage, biting and gnawing at the metal panels. It didn't matter what Geoff did, he couldn't stop her continual barking and growling. He wondered if the chunks of flesh that remained entangled in the car's body were the cause of the dog's torment. He was desperate to settle her and the only thing he could think to do was to cover the vehicle with a tarpaulin. He got one from a local and together they strapped it over the car. Lucy settled momentarily before launching into another attack aimed directly at the foreign object in the yard. Defeated, he walked away from her.

Geoff then went straight to the police residence and checked on his kids. Annette had been dealing with the constantly ringing telephone, and doing her best to pass on information and deal with inquiries. Each call came in via the manual exchange and the operator had never had so many. Even as Geoff explained the accident to Annette, the phone continually rang, interrupting them. Annette was clearly exhausted and anxious from lack of sleep and the pressure of fielding inquiries. Geoff told her that he would take over and that he wouldn't be coming to bed tonight. From inside the police station he could still hear Lucy barking; it was getting on his nerves but what could he do? And, anyway, there were more pressing matters on his mind.

While at the scene, Geoff had radioed ahead to Wagga, asking them to get in touch with the relatives of the deceased persons from Victoria, but the station had been having difficulty locating the family and hadn't yet informed them. He rang to check on their progress and then set about typing an occurrence pad entry, which formally documents all major events, and compiling a telex message to notify headquarters of the multiple fatality and sending it to Sydney. Within hours, the media began to arrive, setting up camp outside the station.

At 2 a.m. Geoff received the call he'd been waiting for. Although speaking to the relatives of the dead was an unpleasant task, it was one he felt responsible for. He had vowed three months earlier never to treat a relative the way he'd been treated when his father had died. Geoff's uncle had called him at the station to inform him that his father had passed away on the operating table during heart bypass surgery at St Vincent's Hospital in Darlinghurst. Geoff rang Darlinghurst police station to speak with the officer in charge of the case, explaining to the constable who answered the phone that he was calling to find out the details of his father's passing. The constable asked him to wait while he located the officer involved. Geoff then heard him yell at the top of his voice, 'Who's doin' the Bernasconi dead'un?' Geoff decided at that moment that he would *never* treat a relative with such disrespect. It was for this reason that he always took his responsibility to show compassion to grieving relatives very seriously.

Now, as Geoff picked up the phone in the station, he tried desperately to understand the man on the other end of the line. The words 'Constable Bernasconi' were clear but everything else he said was in Italian. It dawned on him that the man presumed, with a name like Bernasconi, Geoff could speak Italian. It took several minutes for him to realise that Geoff could neither speak nor understand the language.

He then introduced himself as Antonino Aloi; his sister had been killed in the accident. Geoff set about explaining as carefully as he could the horrible details of the smash the night before. Antonino asked Geoff a number of questions; some he answered, some he couldn't and some he didn't want to. Geoff told him that first he would have to come to Urana and take possession of property located in the damaged vehicle, and then he would have to accompany Geoff to the Wagga Base Hospital to identify the bodies. Shortly after they hung up, Geoff realised both that the media would pounce on Antonino when he arrived and that the state of the vehicle would be too upsetting for him. He quickly rang back and asked Antonino to meet him later that morning at a secret location along the highway at Jerilderee, in effect giving the media the slip. Soon after this, Geoff received confirmation from Wagga of the gender of the bodies from the crash, and the identity of the driver. It seemed that a whole family had been wiped out.

The detectives had now finished interviewing the driver of the pantech truck and set off for the return trip to Wagga. Meanwhile, Geoff made up a bed in the interview room for the exhausted truck driver.

The phone rang constantly while Geoff completed the necessary paperwork. Several hours after returning from the accident, he finally slumped back into his chair and put his feet up on the desk. As he expected the phone to continue ringing, it was pointless to go to bed. Even though he was mentally and physically exhausted, his adrenaline continued to pump, and sleep eluded him. He dozed in fractured bursts, waking with a start and feeling disoriented as he grabbed the phone each time it rang.

On waking the following morning, Geoff glanced out the window to see that the media contingent camped outside was growing; more arrived by the minute, until the station was completely besieged. There were groups climbing up and standing on the back fence, trying to get a shot of the wrecked car.

At daybreak, Geoff went outside to check the car. He was shocked by what he saw. There was blood and guts everywhere, and it made him feel physically sick. He secured the tarpaulin, taking care to cover the stark reminder of what had happened to the wreck's occupants, but there was nothing else he could do. The media pounced, and quizzed him on all aspects of the accident. *Fuck them! I'll fix them*, he thought.

Annette, upon rising with the children that morning, was shocked and distressed to see the media surrounding the station. The accident had been headline news and details of it, including footage of the police station, broadcast across the nation. She felt like a virtual prisoner in her own home. Geoff's mother was staying with them after the recent death of her husband and she, too, felt panic at the media frenzy brewing just metres away.

At around 9 a.m. Geoff approached the media camp and told them he was going to the council yard to investigate a theft. Instead, he set off along the highway to Wagga, and stopped at the spot he'd arranged to meet Antonino. When Antonino arrived, the two men solemnly shook hands before setting off to Wagga for the grim task of identifying all six bodies.

At the hospital, Geoff guided Antonino to a quiet area and arranged coffee and lunch for him, while he went to the casualty department to inquire about the bodies. It was the usual practice for life to be pronounced extinct when bodies first arrived at the hospital, but the state of all six victims in this case, and Geoff's inability due to his various duties to get to Wagga on the night of the accident, meant it would be done now, just prior to Antonino attending to each family member's identification. Geoff went to Accident and Emergency as arranged, and spoke to the doctor on duty. At first, Geoff was told to bring the three bags from the morgue into the casualty department, where the doctor would pronounce life extinct, but Geoff refused. He was horrified at the thought of bringing such carnage into the busiest part of the hospital.

'I'm not bringing them in here.'

'I'd prefer to do it in Casualty – it's our normal practice,' the doctor directed.

'No,' Geoff insisted, 'I won't do it. You'll have to come to the morgue and pronounce them dead there; it's not a pretty sight.'

The doctor finally gave in, and followed Geoff and the wardsman along the narrow hallway leading to the morgue. Even after Geoff's warning, he was not prepared for what he was about to see. The doctor was clearly distressed and nearly fainted when the body bags were brought out and unzipped. He quickly pronounced life extinct and left Geoff, the Government Medical Officer (GMO), Dr

Michael Lennon, and the mortuary assistant to prepare the bodies for identification.

Geoff didn't know that this would be the beginning of a long and arduous professional relationship with Doc Lennon: they would work together at many a crime scene and post-mortem, forging a friendship that would last more than a decade. Over the next hour or so, they dragged each broken corpse from its bag and placed them onto separate steel trolleys. They then set about arranging the remains in such a way as to allow for visual identification.

Geoff wanted to spare Antonino the shocking sight of his relatives' disfigured bodies, so he began covering everything bar the section to be used to identify each person. He cleaned and positioned a hand that displayed a ring while shielding the rest of the body from view; he pulled skin together around a section of ear with an earring while covering the rest of the face, and so on, until he had all the bodies ready for viewing. When Geoff got to the little boy, his heart sank; his head was completely flattened, with brain matter exposed. Geoff had never seen such a mess, but he and Dr Lennon got straight to work and did what they could until they were satisfied they'd done their best.

Walking back towards the hospital proper, Geoff felt a wave of exhaustion sweep over him, but he quickly pushed it away and strode purposefully on to collect Antonino. Soon after, the two men stood at the viewing window with curtains drawn on the other side of the glass. Geoff warned Antonino that there wasn't much left of the bodies, and that what he was about to see was extremely distressing. As he spoke, he slid his arm around Antonino's shoulders and stood holding him in readiness for the awful task. One by one, the bodies were wheeled up against the window, the curtain drawn back until Antonino was sure he could positively identify each of his relatives. As he stood and looked at the remains of his sister, two brothers-in-law, Antonino's parents and his little nephew, he held it all together, showing tremendous dignity and strength that not even Geoff could possibly have mustered. The whole process took about half an hour but seemed endless. When it was all over, the two men walked out into the sunlight and stood silently together while tears flowed until there were no more.

Geoff gave Antonino plenty of time to collect his thoughts and work through his grief before leading him back to the car park. Then they drove to Wagga police station, where Senior Constable Ian McKenzie assisted them. Geoff found a quiet room and prepared six separate identification statements, which he handed to Antonino to read and sign. By now, Antonino was very emotional. Geoff didn't know what to say, as his grief was overwhelming, so he just held him. It had been only hours since he and Antonino had met, but so much had passed between the two men.

At the station, Antonino told Geoff that his relatives had been returning to Melbourne from Leeton, where they'd attended their cousin's funeral, when they had been involved in the accident. It made what had happened all the more unbelievable, the fact that this whole family had spent their last day mourning the dead. Geoff, in turn, explained what he'd found at the scene and how he thought the accident had happened. The pantech truck, carrying a full load of clothing, had been travelling north along the Newell Highway when the driver, Robin Condor, saw the green Valiant hurtling towards him head on, on the wrong side of the road. Robin said that he'd just passed a truck going in the other direction on a sweeping bend when the Valiant swerved out onto the wrong side of the road and hit him with full force. It had all happened in an instant, and he'd had no time to brake or to avoid the car. There was nowhere for the truck to go. On impact, the truck bullbar collapsed downward, as it was designed to do, inadvertently pushing the car down and under the truck. The two vehicles then careered out of control, with the Valiant trapped underneath, before stopping sixty metres further north alongside the road. Geoff believed that the Valiant driver was fatigued, although this would be determined at the coronial inquest, during which the cause of the accident would also be determined. Antonino nodded.

Before saying their goodbyes, Geoff promised Antonino that he'd attend the funerals and lend support if required. He'd also be in touch after the post-mortems to let him know when the bodies could be released. He could see that this meant a lot to Antonino; having spent the most difficult day of his life with Geoff, they now shared a unique bond.

After Antonino left, Geoff went to the station to enter the details of property found on the bodies into the miscellaneous property book. One of the policewomen asked him about the prang and then, out of the blue, said, 'Six less wogs.' He couldn't believe it. He looked at her blankly, his mouth open but no words coming out. He was so tired physically and emotionally that he just wanted to crawl into a black hole, to get away from all this somehow. He still had loose ends to tie up, though: he had to see the detectives from Wagga police station and go to the Traffic Office before finally visiting the Coroner.

Sitting alone in the police sedan for the hour-long trip back to Urana, Geoff had time to think. He couldn't understand why Scientific hadn't taken control of the six bodies at the scene and then at the morgue. It was obvious that this incident fitted the criteria of a disaster and that the bodies should have been identified using DVI. Geoff didn't have the experience to perform this task, so why was he left to patch up the bodies in an attempt to identify them visually? Surely DVI would have utilised other avenues of identification, such as dental records, and saved Antonino the heartache of seeing his loved ones' shattered bodies. Geoff went over and over all this in his mind without resolution. He realised he was now faced with witnessing six post-mortems scheduled for the next day. The whole incident seemed like a bad dream but it wasn't, was it?

Geoff was so preoccupied during the trip to Urana that he didn't even remember driving along the road until he suddenly realised he was pulling up outside the police station. Annette rushed out to meet him, distress written all over her face. 'They've jumped over the fence and removed the tarp from the car. I couldn't stop them – they wouldn't listen. They've taken photographs of the car!' she said.

'Bloody media!' Geoff yelled. 'It's okay, love. I'll see to it.'

He rushed into the yard to see the crumpled remains of the Valiant uncovered for all to see. Right by it, the dog stood growling and barking, snapping at the twisted metal in a futile attempt to bite. Geoff pulled the tarp up over the car, and as he leant over one section, he was repulsed by the sight of a clump of human flesh caught in the twisted metal. It was yet another reminder of what he'd just seen at the morgue and what he was scheduled to see the next day. He stood by the car for a minute in a daze; he still couldn't believe what had happened. His stomach churned and he thought he was going to be sick.

Back inside the station, Geoff got straight to work following up on jobs that had come in while he was out and returning phone messages. Before he realised it, day had turned to night and he'd worked a massive eighteen-hour day two days in a row.

When Geoff got home, he grumpily entered the house and

slumped down on the lounge, not wanting to speak to or even acknowledge his family. He didn't want to answer their questions, he didn't want to talk at all; in fact, he didn't even want to think. He had an argument with Annette, and told her to pack up and take his mum and the kids away, get away from this mess, just get the hell out of there. She agreed to leave first thing in the morning, saying she'd return in a week, and then disappeared to pack.

Geoff pulled the top off a stubby of beer and sat back gulping it down. He had taken up smoking again, something he'd been free of for years. He took a long drag on a cigarette and gazed at the smoke as it gently wafted above him. He sat motionless, watching the cigarette die out in the ashtray. Sleep eluded him once again; he tossed and turned all night, until he decided to get up and get back to work.

The next morning, he saw Annette and the kids off as they left to take his mother back to Wollongong. He pleaded with them to travel safely. He was glad his mother was with Annette but, most of all, he was relieved to have peace, as he just wanted to be alone. He prepared to travel back to Wagga for the six post-mortems scheduled to start that morning. He drove there in a daze, still consumed by the accident, exhausted and dreading the day ahead. He was angry about the car in the backyard and the media still camped outside the station. He thought that he must get rid of the car. The constant reminder of the accident the wreck behind the house prompted was agitating him. He made a mental note to get straight onto the paperwork to get rid of it when he got back from the post-mortems.

Striding into the morgue that morning, he went directly to the post-mortem area to assist Doc Lennon. The name 'Carrafa', one that would forever be etched upon his mind, was clearly printed on the trolley on which the first body was being wheeled out in readiness for the autopsy. As soon as the body bag was removed, the smell of death invaded Geoff's senses.

After the twisted and mangled flesh was washed down, the doctor got to work, slicing what was left of the body cavity open, and removing organs to be weighed and placed in bottles for later transportation to a Sydney laboratory for analysis. The doctor collected blood samples and spoke into a dictaphone while he worked, reporting on whether the body was male or female, and whether it had, for example, gross interruptions of the cranio facial region – the head. Finally, the doctor opened the skull with a vibrating saw and examined the brain. This was particularly difficult, due to the fact that the victims' skulls were smashed like eggshells, which made it hard to open the cavities. The doctor told Geoff of his disbelief at the carnage and told him that the number of bodies was something he'd never encountered. After finishing the fourth body he couldn't continue, turning to Geoff and telling him he needed a break. The two men took a short rest outside, drinking coffee in silence. Once they got back to work, the last two bodies were examined and finally wheeled back into the fridge. All the bodies could now be released to the family for the funerals.

It had been several hours since Geoff had seen daylight and his clothes stank of death. He longed for fresh air and was glad to be out of the morgue. Once again, he drove the hour-long trip back to Urana, his exhaustion both mental and physical. He felt numb with fatigue but knew it wasn't over yet. There were still the reports to be finalised and the occurrence pad to be written off, showing that the job had been completed and describing what action he'd taken.

Back at the station, Geoff set about writing a report to the district office, requesting permission to have the car removed from the yard and disposed of. He'd discussed this with Antonino earlier, explaining that there was nothing left of the car and that it wasn't salvageable. Antonino gave permission for the car to be destroyed; he didn't want to see the vehicle or have anything to do with it, as it was all too distressing.

That night Geoff sat in silence at the bar of the local bowling club, a few beers helping him to relax. Afterwards, he returned to an empty house and slumped in front of the television. He fell into a fitful sleep before waking a few hours later. He lay haunted by the memory of the six bodies he'd spent the day with. He thought about the man from Scientific and wondered again why he hadn't helped at the scene of the accident and later with the bodies. In the early hours of the morning, Geoff made the decision to transfer to scientific work. If he were in Scientific, no young constable would *ever* be left in a situation such as the one he had found himself in, he'd make sure of it.

For the fourth day in a row, Geoff started an eighteen-hour day. He went to the backyard and pulled the tarpaulin from the wreck. The smell was overpowering and the dog went crazy. It was time to search the car, something he'd been dreading. The car was a mangled mess but Geoff did his best to look over the entire vehicle, collecting a number of personal items as he did so.

Back in the station, Geoff entered the property details into the miscellaneous property book before applying for permission to attend the funerals. It was denied, on the basis that funding was not available. He was devastated. He would now not have the closure that he had hoped the funerals would give him, and he was bitterly disappointed that he couldn't fulfil his promise to Antonino and the orphaned children. Next, he followed up on what was happening to the car, but was told it would have to stay put, for which he was given no explanation. Geoff argued that its presence was distressing to his wife and kids, and that the dog was still barking. This fell on deaf ears.

Over the next couple of months he attempted on a number of occasions to get permission to remove the car but still nothing was done. Then one evening he attended an Apex meeting during which the men present discussed the obvious distress the car was causing him and his family. They decided to help him get rid of it. Geoff knew that to wait for approval was pointless. Fuck it – it simply had to go.

On the agreed time and date, the Apex club members arrived at the police residence with a truck. The Valiant was loaded onto the tray and taken to the tip, where a hole was dug that was big enough to bury the vehicle. Geoff and the men said a prayer after they set it alight and watched as it slowly burned itself out; it was then covered with dirt and buried. All Geoff felt was relief. Within hours, though, he received an angry call from the divisional inspector demanding to know what he'd done with the car.

'I got rid of it,' Geoff said, then asked defiantly, 'What are you going to do about it?'

The commander threatened him with disciplinary action. Geoff was way past caring.

Some months later, the divisional inspector attended Urana to check the station books. He found a number of separate entries on the occurrence pad relating to property the Carrafa family owned. He called Geoff in and demanded an explanation. Geoff described the mangled state of the car and explained how difficult it was to retrieve the property entangled in the wreckage, both on the night of the accident and later in the holding yard. The commander wasn't satisfied with this explanation and accused Geoff of sloppy work. Geoff couldn't believe it; after everything he'd done – the long hours he'd worked, including identifying the bodies, and without so much as a single phone call from the commander to check on his welfare – he was incensed. He knew he'd done his best and was pissed off at being criticised for a minor property issue. The welfare of his staff didn't seem to Geoff to be the commander's first priority.

Fuck you, Geoff thought.

From then on, he lost all respect for the divisional inspector.

The week after the crash, Geoff drove to Wollongong to meet up with his family. His moods were erratic and he couldn't erase the details of the accident from his mind. He was exhausted yet couldn't sleep; he constantly woke in a lather of sweat with images of that sad time before his eyes. He had taken a couple of extra days off, but he knew he had to return to Urana and get on with things.

Over the next few months, he worked hard to prepare the coronial brief. Meanwhile, every Roads and Traffic Authority inspection day would dredge the incident up again, as the local townsfolk probed him about it when they had their cars examined for registration. He also had constant contact with the deceaseds' family, as they needed assistance and support. In order to prepare the coronial brief, he went reluctantly over every fine detail again and again until all the evidence was compiled. He began to have nightmares about the little boy's head squashed to a pulp and about the mass of human tissue inside the car.

After fending off questions all day at work, the last thing he wanted to do was talk to Annette about the accident at night, and he refused to discuss it with her, telling himelf that he was protecting her from unnecessary details. He started to drink more than before; a few beers would help him sleep, or so he believed.

Hell, I am a cop, I can handle this but my family doesn't have to, he thought.

Three years later, when he was the local Scientific officer, Geoff returned to 'No Man's Land', when on his way to examine a fatality on the Newell Highway. In a twist of fate, Linton Gooden, who had assisted all those years ago in the very spot at which the Carrafa family accident occurred, was killed when he pulled out of his driveway into the path of a truck.

As Geoff drove past the place the tragedy occurred, he pulled over and got out of the car. His thoughts went back to that night in 1984. Standing in reflection for several minutes, he recalled the smells, the sounds and the horrible things he saw. He kicked the dirt with his shoe and unearthed something. He bent down and picked the object up. It was a broken denture plate. Geoff threw it as hard and as far as he could – he knew where it came from.

4

BLOOD IN THE SAND

After the Carrafa family accident, Geoff felt different, although not in a way he could put his finger on. Annette noticed that he was drinking more than usual; he'd become withdrawn, increasingly wanting to spend time at the local bowling club with a beer and his thoughts. She was now on her own with the kids much more, but she also understood that he had work pressures and she didn't want to make things worse.

By 1986 Geoff was coming up for promotion to senior constable and he knew that it was time to move on. Although he loved country life, and the kids were settled at a local school, he'd outgrown Urana and was ready to pursue a career in scientific investigation. After making inquiries, he learned that a larger station, such as Wagga, would be the best option. Wagga, New South Wales's largest inland city with a population of 55 000, nestled on the banks of the Murrumbidgee River in the heart of the Riverina district, is only an hour's drive from Urana, so it was in the area that Geoff and his family had come to love. Geoff submitted a request for transfer and was glad when he was notified that his new position, on general duties, would take effect 1 July 1986.

Typically, the close-knit Urana community gave Geoff and Annette a wonderful sendoff to show their appreciation for everything they'd done for the town. Geoff knew he would miss Urana and all the friends he'd made through his community work, but at the same time he was excited about the prospects of a new job and looking forward to moving to Wagga. Annette was especially pleased that they would be living in a larger town now that the kids were older.

After a relatively smooth move, they found a lovely home, settled the kids into school, and began to build their life around community events. Geoff sought out the local footy side and connected with the team and its followers, although this time he preferred to stay in the background and take a breather from having an active role. One of the first people he met was Mark Ingram and his partner, Tracy, who owned the local service station. He'd see Mark regularly when he stopped at his garage to get fuel, and they quickly struck up a friendship based on their mutual love of football. Before long, Geoff also got to know John Yerbury, the local tow truck driver, who'd often attend motor vehicle accidents Geoff was called to when working general duties. He liked John. He was a great bloke who would help out at scenes without hesitation, as was the nature of towies in country towns. At home, Geoff spent most of his spare time renovating the new house, which he found relaxing and enjoyable. He also took great pride in the garden, and spent a lot of time working outside, encouraging the kids to potter about with him.

Geoff found it exciting to walk into the station at Wagga for the first time, and he was looking forward to meeting the local police and forming new friendships with them. From his very first day of duty, though, he couldn't believe the number of persons who died on his watch. He seemed to be on duty every time a death occurred, and he quickly became skilled at dealing with bereaved families, not only in an official capacity but on an emotional level.

If he was called to a cot death, he'd call into the local florist first and purchase flowers that he'd later place with the baby. While he thought this was only a small gesture, he noticed it seemed to ease the parents' pain during the final viewing of their child. As time went on, it became the usual practice for the shift supervisor to ask Geoff if he wouldn't mind attending incidents involving the death of a baby or small child. Geoff seemed to cope with the difficulties and emotional strain of dealing with bereaved families better than others at the station, and he didn't mind helping out in any way he could. It seemed the natural thing to do and gave him a sense of fulfilment.

As soon as Geoff started work at Wagga, he made it known he'd like a career in plain clothes. Not long afterwards, he was approached by the local detective inspector, who asked if he'd like a transfer to scientific investigation.

Quite chuffed, Geoff replied, 'Bloody oath!'

The next day, he bumped into the sergeant from Scientific, Dave Frost. Geoff mentioned joining the section and was shocked when Dave got upset.

'I don't know anything about that!' Dave exclaimed.

This didn't get the two of them off to a good start, but it seemed Geoff was destined for scientific work; it wasn't long before he was, in fact, transferred to work with Dave.

In February 1987, Geoff began 'relieve and assist' duties at the crime-scene unit, Wagga physical evidence section. (The old term 'scientific investigation' was made obsolete around this time, with headquarters preferring 'physical evidence'). Geoff was now working in the office, on loan from general duties and learning the ropes by attending crime scenes, at the same time as relieving Dave of the more mundane and minor jobs, such as photographing exhibits.

The crime-scene unit was housed away from the main police station, alongside the administration block and the highway patrol office, which, in effect, isolated those working there. The office itself was small and cramped but extremely well organised. The best room in the section was the photographic dark room, but it was the place Geoff could stand least. The chemical fixer used to process the film irritated his throat. He often worked in intolerable conditions and he was constantly coughing. (Later, though, he found the dark room a place of solace where he could work alone and undisturbed, processing and printing the black-and-white film he'd taken at crime scenes.) Despite his problems with the dark room, he quickly took to the work he did in it and found it, as well as the myriad new scientific disciplines he was learning, enjoyable.

There was much to learn: photography, scene preservation, collection of evidence, motor vehicle accident scene investigation, arson and fire scene investigation, break-and-enter scenes with tool-mark impressions, sexual assault scenes, scale-plan drawing for presentation in court, brief preparation, suspicious deaths, suicides, plane crashes, bombings and incendiary device investigation, fingerprinting, and so on. Dave was overworked and exhausted. He did his best to train Geoff but the workload kept mounting and there simply wasn't enough time for him to do so. Dave quickly realised that Geoff was not fazed by working unsupervised, as his job at Urana had set him up well for this. At Easter, Dave took much-needed annual leave, in effect, leaving the crime-scene unit unmanned.

By now Geoff had attained the rank of senior constable, and had returned to general duties while awaiting confirmation of a permanent transfer to crime scene duties. Over the Easter weekend he was working in the station when a local man who had been jogging along the banks of the Murrumbidgee River at Wiradjuri Reserve contacted the police to report drag marks in the sand that led towards the water's edge. He also mentioned that he thought he'd seen what looked like blood, or red stains, in the sand. The station sergeant, upon checking the roster, saw that Dave was on leave and then wasn't able to contact him. Realising that Geoff had for a short time done relieve-and-assist duties in the crime-scene unit, he asked if he could go out to the scene and have a look. At first Geoff protested that he wasn't sufficiently trained, but the sergeant persisted, saying that there was nobody else to do the job. Geoff reluctantly went to the crime-scene office and collected a camera before driving out to the scene.

When he got there, he thought, *This doesn't look good.* There were, indeed, scuff marks near a large tree, drag marks, and red stains in the sand that could have been blood leading down to the water's edge. Geoff made a request by radio for the local State Emergency Services (SES) to attend and perform a search of the river and surrounding areas. When they arrived, he pointed out the area where the drag marks led to the water's edge and made them aware of the possibility there was a body in the river. The men and women in orange overalls got to work, some walking along the river's edge in groups of two and others entering the water with poles to probe the sandy bottom. It wasn't long before the body of a young woman was located, face down, on the river bed about two metres below the surface and some fifteen metres from the bank. Geoff's heart sank.

I'm well and truly out of my depth; what to do, where to start; shit, I can't do this! he said to himself.

He walked to the water's edge and watched as the body was carefully pulled from the water and stretched out on the sand. Stepping closer, he peered at the fully clothed, pale and bloated body of a young woman.

Shit, got to get some help, he thought, as he stood, full of dread, by the body. 'Leave her here – don't pull her any further up the bank,' he said to the SES workers, as he stepped away and then strode towards the police car to collect his thoughts. He slid into the driver's seat and picked up the radio handset, this time to report the tragic news of the discovery of a young woman's body and to ask for assistance from the crime-scene unit in Albury.

'Sorry, Geoff, but the closest crime-scene examiner is nine hours away in the furthermost part of the state examining another scene. We've tried to call Dave again but he's not answering his phone. You're it, I'm afraid.'

Geoff reluctantly agreed that he would begin to process the crime scene, but first he returned to the crime-scene office to collect vital equipment. He couldn't believe he was in this situation; with no prior experience of examining a murder scene, he'd just have to use his commonsense.

Inside the crime-scene office, he grabbed handfuls of film, gloves, sketch paper, paper bags and a swab kit, before quickly returning to the car and driving back to the river. Back at the scene, he went to the young woman lying on her back on the sandy riverbank. After taking a couple of photographs, he snapped on a pair of rubber gloves and bent down to make a cursory examination of the body. He gently picked up her hand and examined the fingers, which were stiff with rigor mortis as a consequence of being in the icy water. He lifted her shoulder and looked at her underside, peering at the clothing that covered her cold and wet torso. He made a note describing her jeans, belt and shirt. His eyes fixed on the multiple holes around the neck, back and shoulders of the shirt, where something sharp had ripped through the fabric. Lowering her shoulder and resting her back on the sand, Geoff looked straight into her staring eyes. *God, I hope I can do this.*

Then, *Gotta call the pathologist,* he thought, as he rushed up the bank to make the call over the radio. The thought of Doc Lennon, the GMO with whom he'd previously worked on the multiple post-mortems of the Carrafa family, attending the scene eased his anxiety. Shortly after, the doctor arrived and Geoff hurried over to his car to brief him. The two men then walked the short distance along the sandy bank and stood by the young girl's body.

Doc Lennon firstly examined the fully clothed body and described its rigor mortis, then pulled the clothing up and pointed out the multiple stab marks around the girl's neck, back and shoulders. They discussed the stab wounds, possible time of death and the physical surrounds for a few minutes, until Doc Lennon was satisfied he'd seen enough. Thanking him, Geoff walked the doctor to his car and agreed to meet him at the morgue.

He returned to the scene and picked up his camera for the second time. He walked around the entire crime scene perimeter, taking photographs of the body on the riverbank in relation to the drag marks and blood. He returned to the tree and recorded the scuff marks around its base and the position of the woman's boots, which he later placed in a labelled paper bag. Next, he crouched on the sand and scooped up a number of blood-soaked sand samples and placed them into bags for transportation to a Sydney laboratory for analysis. Then he collected water samples.

Finally he stood back and took in the overall scene, drawing it on a sketch pad.

Throughout the examination he questioned himself constantly. *Am I doing this right? Have I missed something?* Ultimately, no doubt, the evidence he'd collected would bring closure for the victim's family, and he was desperate to do his best. Satisfied, yet a little nervous and still hoping he'd covered everything, he ordered the body to be removed.

A few minutes later, two men in suits arrived in a white van. Geoff described the location of the body as the men opened the rear hatch and pulled out a gurney and bag. This time Geoff stood back to watch as they got to work, throwing open a large black plastic sheet and smoothing it out alongside the girl. With gloved hands, they rolled her onto the plastic and wrapped her tightly, before carrying her to the waiting gurney.

Geoff followed the government contractor's van to the morgue. Once there, he took several photographs of the young woman's body before Doc Lennon announced he would perform the post-mortem immediately. Geoff wasn't prepared for this, as the investigator from Albury would not be there for several hours.

'Can't we wait until the crime scene man from Albury arrives?' he asked.

The doctor was firm. 'No, we must get started – the evidence is waiting.'

There was no use arguing further; the doctor was already dressed in a plastic apron and, with gloved hands, was busily lining up instruments along a steel bench. As the body was wheeled over to the autopsy area, Geoff resigned himself to getting on with it.

Her clothing was removed, a layer at a time, finally to reveal the naked form of the pale young woman whose life was cut short so senselessly. As each layer was removed, Geoff clicked frame after frame until he had shots of the entire corpse. When the girl's underpants were removed, they were surprised to find a second pair underneath. Both pairs were placed on a bench, where Geoff and the doctor examined them for any trace of bodily fluids. The inner pair were turned inside out and a prominent stain on the gusset was found. Geoff photographed the evidence while Doc Lennon explained how the second pair of underpants had inadvertently protected the inner pair while the young woman was immersed in the river, and, in effect, had protected vital evidence. The underpants were placed into separate labelled paper bags for later transportation to the laboratory for further analysis. Both men were excited at the prospect of the laboratory finding a blood grouping and possibly DNA evidence on this single item of clothing; it was their best chance of connecting an offender to the crime.

The doctor then examined the numerous stab wounds around the girl's neck, back and shoulders. The clothing was compared with the stab wounds, which showed that the girl had been stabbed while fully clothed. Each wound was methodically measured, photographed and drawn on an anatomical chart, with descriptions of each recorded, including the clear correlation between the wounds and the damage to the clothing fibre. At the same time, the doctor recorded his findings, including the size and location of all twenty-one wounds, into a Dictaphone. From the sheer number of injuries, it was obvious the girl had been subjected to a vicious and frenzied attack. With the smell of death hanging heavily over the room, the doctor removed her lungs and placed them in a jar; an examination of them would show whether the victim was still alive when she entered the water. Then other organs, and blood and urine, were collected and placed into jars for transportation and analysis at the laboratory.

Towards the end of the post-mortem, Ian, the crime-scene examiner from Albury, turned up and stood talking with Geoff and the doctor as the body cavity was sewn up and washed down. The body of the girl was wrapped in plastic, wheeled over to a refrigerated shelf and pushed into the darkened cavity. Clearly there was nothing more that Ian could do; he turned to Geoff and commented on what a fine job he'd done, before disappearing as swiftly as he'd arrived. It wasn't exactly the introduction to crime-scene work that Geoff had anticipated, but he felt a sense of achievement after completing the initial phase of his first murder investigation. Even though his adrenaline was still pumping, he also felt calm and detached. He had no idea how familiar this place would become to him; that before long, he'd be an old hand at photographing and examining such scenes as he'd worked at today. The morgue would become almost a home away from home.

By 4.30 p.m. that afternoon, detectives had identified the dead girl as eighteen-year-old Sally Ann Jones of Ashmont, a Wagga suburb. Her mother was contacted and given the terrible news. She tearfully told police she had dropped her daughter at a friend's house around 7.45 p.m. the night before. The girls had gone to a local nightclub and the last sighting of Sally had been at around 3 a.m. that morning. She was seen standing with a bleeding hand outside the club. A witness said Sally had had a fight with a friend and cut her hand on a smashed glass in the toilets. She was later seen walking towards the railway station. It was out of character for the intelligent and well-liked teenager to accept a lift from a stranger and her mother was at a loss as to what had happened. Believing Sally was staying with a friend that night, she had no idea that her daughter hadn't come home until one of her friends rang that morning asking after her. She immediately realised that something was wrong and contacted the police.

The local detectives, with the assistance of the homicide squad from Sydney, began their interviews and, over the next twenty-four hours, spoke to at least thirty witnesses. As days, and then weeks, passed after the murder there was no significant breakthrough, and the case remained unsolved until the inquest some six months later.

At the inquest, Geoff gave evidence describing the scene and where Sally's body had been found. Photographs were tendered showing the scuff marks near the tree, the drag marks down to the water's edge and the blood stains in the sand. The Coroner then viewed photographs of the victim at the scene and at the morgue, which showed the multiple stab wounds around her neck, back and shoulders. Then Kenneth Barry Cannon, the man who found the body, entered the witness box.

Cannon gave evidence that he'd been at home watching videos with friends on the night of the murder. He stated that around 9.30 a.m. the following day he went to the video store to return a film, and afterwards decided to go jogging along the riverbank at Wiradjuri reserve. As he ran past a large tree, he stumbled upon a pair of ladies boots. He then saw scuff and drag marks and what he thought was blood leading to the water's edge. The solicitor acting for Sally's family questioned him at length about why he was at the scene and if he'd ever gone jogging before. Evidence his ex-wife had given indicated that, in fact, he'd never been jogging. Also, the friends who had watched videos with him had stated they saw him leave in his car at the same time they left his house, at around 11.30 p.m. that night. Cannon himself said that he'd never met Sally Jones but had seen a picture of her in the newspaper a few months before she died.

It seemed that Kenneth Cannon was telling lies. After the inquest concluded, he became the prime suspect, and detectives interviewed

him again and double-checked his story. They were highly suspicious of Cannon but still didn't have enough evidence to charge
him. Geoff, too, had his suspicions of the man, telling the detectives the blood in the sand at first looked dark brown in colour and
was not obviously blood; he thought it unlikely that a member of
the public would presume it was blood unless they had first-hand
knowledge of what the substance actually was. But when Cannon
had reported the drag marks, he had appeared sure that the red
marks in the sand were blood.

Several years later, a sixteen-year-old girl was raped and then
frogmarched at knifepoint to the banks of the river in Wiradjuri
reserve, slightly upstream from where Sally Ann Jones had been
murdered. The girl was forced to kneel and perform oral sex while
the offender held a knife at her throat. He released her afterwards and
she went straight to the police. Geoff was notified, and he attended
the station to compile a Penry photofit picture of the wanted man.
During this interview with the victim, he began to see parallels with
the earlier murder of Sally Ann Jones. When the photofit picture
was completed, such was the likeness to the offender that the victim
became hysterical at the sight of the man's face.

Geoff then pieced together the possible link with this offence
and the way in which Sally had died. Was it the case that the second girl was released because she had complied with the offender's
request for oral sex? He wondered whether Sally had been abused in
a similar fashion. Perhaps she struggled and fought off her attacker.
Did she bite him on the penis and, if so, was this the catalyst for
his frenzied knife attack around her head, neck and shoulders? Her
injuries certainly indicated that the stab wounds were inflicted from
behind, suggesting that Sally was kneeling at the offender's groin
when she was murdered.

Once the photofit picture of the offender was completed, it was published in the local newspaper. Within a day or two, Cannon rang the police, admitting that the image in the newspaper looked like him and wanting to offer an alibi. What Cannon didn't realise was that the newspaper had accidentally published the wrong date on which the rape occurred and that the alibi he now offered was for this incorrect day. The detectives now linked Cannon to both crimes and brought him in for further questioning. During the interview, they asked Cannon for a blood sample. He was happy to oblige, stating that he had nothing to hide.

Geoff delivered the blood to the Division of Analytical Laboratories in Glebe, a suburb of Sydney. By this stage, the laboratory had found semen on the inner pair of Sally's underpants and were keen to compare DNA evidence from the stain with the suspect's; however, this technology was not yet available in New South Wales. Fortunately, the Coroner, Sev Hill, had the foresight to instruct that the samples be kept for future DNA analysis. The blood sample, along with the underpants, were sent to England for DNA analysis and comparison. Within days of the sample arriving at the lab, Geoff received news from England that it was a match.

Cannon was arrested and charged with the murder of Sally Ann Jones, and placed in the police cells. Bail was refused. A clear picture of this sexual predator then started to appear. In the cells that night, he masturbated in clear view of the other prisoners, obviously having little or no control over his sexual urges. As well, his former wife had revealed that Cannon would demand sex six to seven times a day.

In August 1991, Cannon appeared in the Griffith Supreme Court to answer the charge of murder. When giving evidence he changed his story, saying he had, in fact, met Sally Ann Jones on the night of the murder. He said she'd hailed him in Baylis Street, near the nightclub, thinking his car was a taxi. He said that he stopped and asked if she wanted a lift, and she accepted and then agreed to go to his house on the pretext he had given her of attending to the cut on her hand. He said that they'd had sex and afterwards he'd dropped her back near the nightclub, around 3 a.m. At the conclusion of a five-day trial, Cannon was found guilty of the murder of Sally Ann Jones and sentenced to life imprisonment. It was a landmark case, as this was the first time DNA evidence had been used in an Australian criminal proceeding.

Afterwards the investigators and legal staff returned to Wagga and adjourned to the pub for a quiet drink and debrief. It was less a celebration than it was a mark of respect for Sally and justice achieved via the successful outcome of the trial. Sally's mother, despite having chronic asthma and needing to avoid smoky places, entered the pub and approached Geoff. She sat down beside him and thanked him for everything he'd done during the investigation. Tearfully she explained that she was in ill health and feared her life was drawing to a close. She had wanted to tell Geoff how much it meant to her to have closure.

Several years later, Sally's mother indeed succumbed to chronic respiratory disease and died peacefully. On the day Geoff was told, his mind returned to the riverside and the events of that Easter long weekend. He reflected on Sally's life and on the impact her death had on her mother, and he thought that at least now they were both at peace.

5

IN THE PALM OF HER HAND

By early 1988, Geoff had been working at crime scenes for a year and he was mastering the work. He pulled his weight from the start, working twenty-four-hour call-out, seven days in a row every second week, unless Dave was on annual leave, when he'd continue being on call-out indefinitely. Technically, Geoff was on duty twenty-four hours a day and his life was no longer his own, with the chance of the phone ringing at any time of the day or night, usually with bad news. He also spent many hours in the car driving to outlying areas of the patrol to attend scenes. He often drove to Cootamundra, Junee, Young, Narrandera and Gundagai, and on average travelled around 800 kilometres a week and in some cases as much as 2000 kilometres a week.

Annette began to see less and less of Geoff, as he was constantly at work or on call-out. She was left alone to cope with the kids most of the time, and began to realise she could no longer depend on her husband as she once had. The constant demands of his job were unpredictable and inflexible. Geoff was more and more immersed in his work and always seemed preoccupied with the horrible details of the latest job he had attended; Annette constantly advised him to 'let it go'. He seemed to be filled with adrenaline when he was on call-out but then flat and emotionless on his days off, on which he would disappear to the pub. Geoff found it difficult to talk about his feelings, and even though he knew things weren't right at home, he couldn't work out what to do. He and Annette argued constantly about social occasions, with Geoff flatly refusing to go, instead preferring to stay close to home and isolate himself. At first, Annette stayed home too, but then she realised it was better if she went with the kids and without Geoff. She knew their marriage was in trouble, but tried her best to keep things together for the sake of the children.

That February, Geoff was pleased when he was given permission to travel to Sydney and attend the Crime Scene Examiners course. This was his first opportunity to have formal training, and he enjoyed the two-week course, which was on all facets of forensic investigation. Later, he attended the fingerprint section, located at Parramatta, to do the four-day fingerprint course, so by that time he was fairly knowledgeable and confident in going about his work.

From the start, he found the crime-scene office in Wagga to be understaffed. It seemed he ran from one major incident to the next, and never had a block of time to commit to paperwork, including the endless complex briefs of evidence for court. He was constantly working on his own or sitting alone in the office doing paperwork; while he missed the banter of a busy station, he had so much work to do that he really didn't have time for idle chatter. Geoff found himself working on average sixty-five hours per week. He was earning substantial overtime pay but it was his practice not to claim in every instance. It was easier to forgo it, due to the commander's scrutiny of such payments and the constant reminders he was given of the local budgetary restrictions. There were occasions where he was called out two and three times in a twenty-four-hour period and still had to work his eight-hour day shift. He found that when he was recalled any time after 4 a.m., it was easier to go straight to the office rather than get out of bed having had only an hour or two of sleep. Once there, he'd attend to the ever-growing pile of paperwork.

It was a relief when the office was finally assigned a full-time fingerprint expert, which meant fingerprint work was no longer the crime-scene unit's responsibility. While this lightened the load somewhat, it didn't alleviate the long days and nights driving through the 4824 square kilometres the division encompassed. At times, it could take up to six hours to drive to a scene if a job was located in the outer limits. Fatigue was ever present, especially on the long road trips during which Geoff battled to stay alert.

As in general duties, Geoff seemed to get all the 'dead'uns' on his shift: in a short period of time, he investigated a number of road fatalities, suicides and accidental deaths, and did so seemingly in his stride. The run of deaths continued, when, on 28 August 1989, a young man and two teenage boys died at a local sporting field. The trio had been sniffing petrol inside a small tent pitched alongside the Jubilee Park dam during heavy rain storms, when, it appeared, the tent slid down the wet embankment into the murky dam water, trapping all three inside. A local council worker found the partially submerged tent at around 7.45 a.m. On closer inspection, he saw one of the bodies and quickly reported his find to authorities. The local rescue squad soon arrived and found two further bodies trapped inside the partially submerged tent.

When Geoff arrived, he found the collapsed remains of an orange and blue tent at the water's edge, along the northern bank of a large earthen dam within the hockey playing fields. Beside a large tree were the remains of a makeshift campsite, including the remnants of a campfire, a water bottle, bedding, fishing lines, meat, vinyl bags and a kerosene tin containing petrol. The tent was secured by a length of rope attached to a tree branch, as well as a number of other lengths of rope and three kitchen forks. Approaching the tent for a closer look, Geoff lost his footing and slid down the muddy riverbank in the wet conditions. Steadying himself, finding solid ground at the waterline, he moved closer and saw one of the victim's legs protruding from the open zipper compartment. The young man was lying on his back, with his legs pointing towards the bank, and wearing a blue jumper, jeans and red and white socks. His pale contorted face was tilted to the side, clear of the water line. As Geoff bent closer, a shot of petrol fumes hit him in the face, and he gasped for fresh air as he turned away for a minute to catch his breath. Just beyond the dead boy were two containers, which he presumed were the source of the fumes, and the protruding legs of a second victim.

Doc Lennon arrived, and the two men stood talking for a few minutes by the waterline while Geoff filled him in on the details. Geoff then lifted the tent flap and they saw a third pair of legs jammed into the back of the tent. He also saw that the two containers inside the tent were missing their lids, and that one had a hole cut into its top; neither contained any liquid. The odour of petrol was even stronger now. Geoff and the doctor had seen enough and clambered back up the embankment.

After Geoff took a number of photographs of the entire scene as he had found it, the three bodies were brought up the embankment and laid out on plastic sheets. Doc Lennon examined each, before pronouncing life extinct. The first boy was fully clad but shoeless, the front of his jumper was damp, and beneath his clothing his skin was just warm. Rigor mortis was evident but not fully established, as his arms and legs flexed and extended fairly easily. The second body was also that of a teenage boy, fully clad with no shoes. His clothing was soaking wet, due to total submersion, and his skin cold to the touch. Rigor mortis was evident but, as with the first body, his limbs could still be moved easily. The third body was that of an adult male, fully clothed, in overalls, but shoelesss. His clothing was also soaking wet, and his skin was cold to the touch; as with the other bodies, rigor mortis was evident but the limbs could be moved. Doc Lennon found death to have occurred within six to ten hours prior to his examination. As the doctor did his job, Geoff took a number of further photographs, prepared a sketch plan and took notes. The bodies were then loaded into a van and the government contractors took them to Wagga Base Hospital.

Geoff and a number of rescue squad men took hold of the tent, dragging it up the muddy embankment to level ground. He examined it and found it to be a two-person nylon tent with a zip front and gauze screen. Several thin pieces of twine, together with coat hangers and a kitchen fork, were tied to the tent lugs. He concluded that the torrential downpour during the night had caused the tent to pull away from its moorings and slip down the hill into the murky water. Once the tent was submerged, the occupants were trapped, possibly drowning inside. It was an accident that could have been prevented if the victims had taken notice of the weather forecast, although later the Coroner's findings would indicate the possibility that all three were either unconscious or already dead before the tent was swept away, due to the fumes they ingested while sniffing petrol.

The boys were all well known to the local police and, while

investigating the scene, Geoff was horrified when he heard two of his colleagues talking.

'They got what they deserved,' one of them said.

'Yeah, that will teach them to sniff petrol,' the other commented.

Geoff couldn't believe their callous and ignorant attitude; it made him sick. He had to walk away, and try to calm down and ignore it, telling himself that it was their way of coping. But he was still upset by the way his colleagues judged the victims. He wondered why it was that such a senseless tragedy had occurred. *What the hell were they thinking when they pitched that tent on the riverbank in such foul weather?* Anger rose in him as he stood shivering in the cold. It was a bleak and unforgiving day, with dark and heavy clouds and short bursts of pelting rain; it was fitting weather for being at the scene of such a tragedy.

Geoff went straight to the morgue, where he met with Doc Lennon and continued his examination. The clothing was removed from each body one layer at a time, revealing angry red blistering covering all three victims' backs, consistent with exposure to petroleum product. It appeared the petrol had escaped from the tins and soaked the victims, burning their skin as it permeated their clothing. Geoff systematically photographed each body and made notes on anatomical charts, describing the burn marks and placing diagrams on the paperwork that indicated the appropriate body parts. Doc Lennon then proceeded to conduct all three post-mortems, with Geoff again shooting photographs and taking possession of blood and organs, which were conveyed to the government forensic laboratories for analysis.

As soon as word about the drownings got out, a huge media contingent descended on Wagga. There was national coverage and reports of a petrol-sniffing epidemic. The petrol-sniffing debate continued for at least a month, with talkback radio and other media outlets sparking public concern about whether measures were in place to fix the problem. It seemed as though every time Geoff turned on the radio or television there was talk of the incident. But then, as quickly as the debate started it ended, which incensed him, as the families were still left with their grief.

The vision of the three bodies trapped in the tent haunted Geoff. He felt a cold shiver down his spine each time he drove past the hockey field where the tragedy had occurred and unconsciously began to avoid the area. When his daughter played hockey on the field, he couldn't bring himself to go there and watch her play. The smell of petrol now reminded him of death, and he hated filling the car and exposing himself to the fumes. All the while, he kept his feelings to himself.

In September that year, Geoff received a call that affected him deeply. His colleague, Dave, had lost his six-month-old granddaughter to cot death. It was the first time Geoff had had professional involvement with the death of a relative of someone he knew and it took an enormous toll, especially as his own children were still quite young and his marriage was falling apart. After attending the scene and photographing the baby, he sat with Dave and talked him through the tragedy.

Geoff said gently, 'I know I haven't seen anything as bad as you've experienced in this job, and I can't possibly begin to understand how you feel, but I was thinking it would do you good to see the baby one last time and, if you want, I'll come with you.'

'I can't do it,' Dave said.

'We can do it together,' Geoff suggested.

Dave continued to be adamant that he couldn't cope with seeing the baby, but eventually he realised that Geoff was probably right, as it would at least give him a chance to say goodbye.

Geoff and Dave agreed to meet at the funeral home, but first Geoff visited the family to collect a couple of items of clothing that had been especially chosen for the baby to wear. Geoff then went straight to the funeral parlour, where he was told that the funeral director was ill and wasn't up to dressing the child. Expecting Dave to arrive at any moment, Geoff decided to dress the baby himself and gently placed the clothing on her body. He put her stiff little hand in the perfect shape to cup her grandfather's finger. Dave entered the room and tearfully placed his finger in the palm of her hand as he said his last goodbye. Afterwards, Geoff realised how important it was for families to view their loved ones one last time, and he was glad he'd made the effort to dress the baby for the viewing. In later cases involving the death of a child, he always took special care to have them dressed for the family's viewing if at all possible.

Geoff continued to take the death of Dave's granddaughter very hard. He found the post-mortem procedure distressing and he constantly compared the dead child with his own. He also felt he wasn't emotionally equipped to deal with his supervisor's distress, which changed the dynamics in the office, the work of which involved death every day. After Dave lost his granddaughter, he went to pieces. Unbeknown to Geoff, he had been undergoing treatment for stress for some time. In those days it was part of the police culture that emotional distress was kept quiet, for fear of ridicule or transfer to a desk job.

After twenty years' service mostly spent on crime scene duties, Dave finally cracked and was pensioned out of the force, hurt on duty. On his last day, he confided in Geoff that he was the only man he'd ever been able to trust and work with comfortably. Even though the pair had got off to rather a rough start, they enjoyed working together and Geoff respected Dave's way of doing things. He was a stickler for routine and was particularly sensitive about the physical-evidence-section car space. One day, he and Geoff returned from a job to find a gleaming new BMW motorbike sitting in it. Dave simply backed into the bike with the crime-scene wagon, pushing it out of the way. If Dave didn't like the way things were done, he would say so, and he demanded that other police didn't interfere with his equipment or routine. For this reason, Dave had been misunderstood by many of his colleagues over the years. He came across as a hard man who didn't suffer fools, but Geoff knew another side of him and he also understood how difficult it was to cope after suffering a death in the family when you were faced with working with death every day. It was no wonder Dave seemed like a hard man; turning his emotions off for all those years was the only way he could continue working as hard as he did, year in, year out, on tragedy after tragedy, with no support or opportunity to debrief. Geoff was sad to see Dave go but, at the same time, knew it was for the best, as he was already learning that one could only take so much. Geoff kept in contact with Dave after he left the force and still speaks to him regularly.

With Dave gone, Geoff quickly became accustomed to working completely alone and to the sense of responsibility that accompanied dealing with major incidents daily. Also, he wanted to prove himself, in order to get the sergeant's job when the time came for promotion. He was on a mission, refusing to acknowledge his stress levels and instead feeling bulletproof as he rushed from one job to the next.

On an August morning in 1989, Geoff was called to a disused quarry near Tarcutta, where the bodies of two people had been discovered in a four-wheel drive, apparently the result of a murder-suicide. When the car was found, its engine was still running and a black rubber hose was connected to the exhaust pipe and inserted through a rear window. Geoff peered in through the front passenger door. Inside at the back, he found a young woman's body with a gunshot wound to the head, and, nearby, a pillow with a gunshot hole in it. It appeared the pillow had been held against her forehead and a .22 calibre weapon used in the killing. Next to her was the body of a man in his fifties, with a gunshot wound to his head and a sawn-off .22 calibre weapon between his legs. His right hand had frozen on the trigger, in a classic cadaver spasm. Cigarette butts, beer bottles, a will and a note apologising for everything were found inside the vehicle.

On further inquiry Geoff discovered the man had been charged with sexual assault-related matters involving the couple's two children, aged nine and six. The children were with carers in Griffith and a message was sent informing them of the tragedy. After photographing the scene, examining the bodies and collecting evidence, Geoff went straight to the morgue, where he was told by the grief counsellor that the children were on their way to view the bodies. After the GMO had completed his preliminary examinations, Geoff placed patches over the head wounds. He then bought a bouquet of flowers and placed them beside the dead mother. He wasn't sure if the children would want to view the father, given the pending assault charges, but the grief counsellor insisted they should view both parents.

Upon arrival, the two children were taken, in the company of a welfare worker, to the viewing area so they could say their goodbyes. As the curtain was drawn back and the children saw the body of their mother, they seemed to be totally bewildered. Geoff watched from a distance and noticed them both looking at the flowers. The little girl was quite taken with them, so Geoff leaned across and gave a flower to each of the children. He also noticed that both children were very apprehensive when it came time to view their father. They seemed almost relieved when they had done so. Afterwards, the welfare worker mentioned that Geoff probably didn't realise how much it meant to the children each to be given a flower from their mother's side.

A month later, Geoff received a letter from the dead woman's grandmother, thanking him for helping the kids during such a difficult time.

Dear Geoff,

We would have liked to have seen you to convey our sincere thanks for your kindness and the help you gave our children on the sudden death of our grandaughter. Your being there, your caring and thoughtfulness has meant a lot to us. Once again thank you and god bless you.

Geoff also received a letter from the district commander, conveying his commendation both to Geoff and to the detective involved for their caring attitude and attention to the bereaved. This was in response to a letter of thanks he had received from the district manager of Family and Community Services.

I would like to take this opportunity on behalf of members of my staff at this centre to express my gratitude to two officers involved in a recent distressing case. Late on the afternoon of 17 August I was contacted by Det. Sgt Barry Hardwick concerning a murder-suicide. The two children, aged six and nine, were in the care of this centre. As you will appreciate it was a traumatic time having to inform the children of the death and in making arrangements for their future placements.

I liaised with Det. Sgt Hardwick by phone on a number of occasions and can only say that he was most helpful in his dealings. Through a combined effort the children's maternal great-grandmother was located and subsequently arrangements were made for her to have the children in her care.

With [the] assistance of Sister Weeks, arrangements were also made for the children to be taken to Wagga so that they could say 'goodbye' to their parents. On that trip Mr Raveanne, District Officer, Sister Weeks, the children and the maternal grandmother were met by Det. Sgt Hardwick and Det. Sgt Geoff Bernasconi who had arranged for the bodies to be seen. Det. Sgt Geoff Bernasconi had provided, I believe from his own funds, a bouquet of flowers to be placed next to the bodies. One of the comments made by Sister Weeks was that this assisted the children greatly because both of them noticed these flowers. The care taken by your two officers greatly assisted the relatives in this difficult task.

It is pleasing to see that it is still possible for various units and departments to work in harmony towards ensuring a better future for these young children. I would appreciate it if you could pass on my gratitude to the two officers involved.

Alan J Smart

District Manager

Griffith District Centre

Geoff was pleased to receive the letter but, more than anything, he was satisfied he'd done his best in assisting the children to deal with saying goodbye to their parents. It seemed his crime-scene work had put him in the position of caring for relatives at the scenes and afterwards at the morgue. He was quickly learning there was a whole different side to policing and, especially after his experience with Dave when he lost his granddaughter, Geoff was starting to understand a great deal about grief.

6

ONE OUT

Over the next twelve months, Geoff was the only member of staff at the Wagga crime-scene unit, which meant he was on twenty-four-hour call-out, seven days a week. During this difficult time, he repeatedly asked for assistance in the hope that a 'relieve and assist' position could be filled. Even if a second person performed only the more minor and mundane tasks, they still would have lessened Geoff's load. To his disappointment, though, the division was reluctant to let staff go from other areas to fill the position.

Geoff also felt isolated due to the minimal contact he had with the physical evidence section in Sydney; they seemed to be aware of his plight but unable to do anything about it. He had total trust in the section leader but this man was unable to make a decision on new staff until Dave had officially retired, as Dave was on sick leave but still officially attached to the section.

To make matters worse, the constant restructuring of the physical evidence section meant that capital equipment was scarce and inadequate. It seemed the country sections were the last to get supplies and, while inner-suburban sections had the latest technology such as pagers, Geoff was forced to stay home while he was 'on call' so that the station could locate him easily if there were a major incident. In particular, office furniture and equipment were seriously lacking, which meant Geoff had to beg, borrow or steal what he needed.

When he discovered a storage area full of cast-offs, he realised that the main station and administration block were regularly receiving new furniture. He asked if he could have a couple of items but his request was firmly denied and, furthermore, he was told that it was unlikely anything would be coming his way in the near future. After that, Geoff would sniff around in an attempt to find out what flash new piece of furniture was on its way to one of the other sections in the building. Once he found out where the equipment that had been replaced was kept, he'd sneak in there at night and help himself to anything – from telephones, storage and filing cabinets, to desks, chairs or whatever he could get his hands on. As Geoff hurriedly struggled with the stolen property to get it secured before anyone caught him, he'd chuckle to himself. *Two can play at this game*, he'd think. He would sigh with relief once he closed the door of the crime-scene office behind him. The presence of biohazards in the office – thanks to the exhibits and bloodstained clothing hanging out to dry – meant that the furniture, or whatever else he'd scavenged, was now officially contaminated. The removal of it would be a breach of occupational health and safety!

The same went for the crime-scene wagon – its smelly state deterred other police from borrowing it, which suited Geoff just fine. It was not uncommon for the car to be used to transport body organs and samples to laboratories in Sydney, and on one occasion Geoff sped down the highway from the city with a severed head in a styrofoam esky to get it to the undertakers in time for the person's funeral. As he rushed through the door with his parcel, he was surprised to see the funeral director screwing down the coffin lid.

'Have you forgotten something?' Geoff asked with a laugh.

The casket was quickly opened, and the head popped inside just in time for the funeral service.

Another concern Geoff had with equipment in the office was in relation to the fume and drying cabinet; he asked constantly for a properly vented fume cabinet instead of the one he had. It was often used to dry blood-soaked clothing, to examine items covered in body fluids or contaminated materials, to ink or dust fingers to enhance their prints, or to mix chemicals. The existing cabinet consisted of a stainless-steel box, minus the sliding isolation door that would normally seal a unit like this, so that when it was turned on, it would fill the office with foul-smelling fumes. Those fumes that made it into the exhaust duct only went as far as the ceiling cavity, where they'd circulate throughout the roof rather than being vented outside the building. Geoff was often doubled over in coughing fits as toxic substances wafted around the office, and afterwards he would have a sore throat, but still nothing was done.

Geoff and the fingerprint expert's repeated requests for the outdated equipment to be upgraded fell on deaf ears, until one evening when everything went horribly wrong. Earlier that day, Geoff had been called to a suicide gassing out on a dirt track in the state forest near Temora. In the back of a station wagon, he found a man's highly decomposed body; it appeared he had died at least four to five months before. His whole body had virtually turned to honeycomb, with sinew on bone all that was left. As Geoff rolled the corpse over, he found a hand that, as the torso had protected it, was still intact and perfect for taking fingerprints.

At the post-mortem, the pathologist detached one of the dead man's fingers and handed it over to Geoff so he could pass it on to the fingerprint expert, Mark Sykes, who would ink or dust the digit. It was normal practice to do this back in the crime-scene office, where the finger would be placed in the fuming cabinet. Geoff put the decomposing digit in a glass jar and took it to the office, where he handed it to Mark. It was then washed and placed in the fuming cabinet to dry and left overnight.

The minute Geoff stepped into the office the following morning, he knew he had a problem. It appeared the finger's stench had contaminated the whole building. The foul odour had been vented up into the ceiling cavity, from where it had spread throughout the building and administration block. Within a few minutes of his arrival, the station superintendent, accompanied by the office cleaner, came rushing in.

'What the hell's going on?' he yelled.

Geoff burst out laughing and could hardly speak.

'I told you we needed a properly vented fuming cabinet,' he said.

'What's in the cabinet that's making this stench?'

'A finger, sir,' was all Geoff could say.

The superintendent wasn't impressed and stormed out, muttering something about the office girls vomiting upstairs. The building was promptly evacuated. Geoff ran around spraying air freshener but this did little to quell the revolting smell.

A week after the incident with the finger, a brand-new fume cabinet with isolation door arrived, along with a technician, who installed it correctly including the ventilation. Geoff and Mark agreed that they should have put a decomposing finger in the cabinet years before. It was incidents like this that kept Geoff going; some black humour lifted the often sombre mood in the office.

With the introduction of occupational health and safety standards, hands and fingers are no longer detached and placed in office fume cabinets. Understandably, all inking and dusting is now done at the morgue.

While it continued to be the case that some days would pass with very little communication with anyone outside the office, Geoff found it less and less desirable to talk to others. At home, he was withdrawn and found it difficult to talk about his emotions with Annette. His marriage kept weakening under the strain – he was no longer as close to his wife as he had been. He continued to believe that he needed to protect Annette from his work, but, in fact, he wasn't paying anywhere near enough attention to her, nor was he interested in anything she was interested in. When she told him she wanted to learn ballroom dancing, he scoffed. He realised later what a mistake this was but at the time he couldn't see the importance of doing anything with Annette; all he could think about was work and his own concerns.

Finally, towards the end of 1988, Annette made up her mind that the marriage was over and, soon after, Geoff moved into a small flat above a Wagga car yard and began life as a single man. He began to sink further mentally, but went less to the pub and instead committed himself even more to work, which was busier than ever.

Geoff's friend John Yerbury, the tow-truck driver, lived just up the road, and knew that he was struggling due to his separation from Annette. One day, he and Geoff met at a job, and John asked him if he was all right, saying that he was worried about him. Geoff confided in him and, from that time on, John took Geoff under his wing and kept an eye on him. Later, Geoff would sing at John's wedding and come to know his wife. He was also invited to his friend Mark Ingram's place for dinner on several occasions, which got him out of the house and helped cheer him up.

On his birthday the following year, Geoff woke and thought of the Carrafa family, wondering how they were coping with the loss of their six family members, as he had every year since the accident. This instantly put him in a dark mood and he couldn't shift his sense of unease. He was on call but had been invited to a friend's house for a birthday lunch.

He'd only just arrived and sat down with a drink when his friend answered a knock at the door. Geoff could see the familiar blue of the police uniform through the doorway. *Shit*, he thought. Sure enough, they were looking for him. They'd driven around most of Wagga looking for his car to get him to attend a serious accident. *Yep, that'd be right. My birthday wouldn't be the same without a bloody accident.* Geoff apologised as he left his friends to celebrate his birthday without him. He drove straight to the office to collect the work vehicle to make the short drive out to the scene. This would be the first of three fatal accidents he attended that day.

By nightfall, Geoff was back in his lonely flat, contemplating the carnage that seemed to dominate his birthday every year. Why would all these terrible accidents happen on the one day he was supposed to celebrate? He struggled to make sense of it, all the time feeling a sense of foreboding that something weird was happening.

Later, he talked it over with the family, and his sister commented that, perhaps, instead of celebrating his birthday on the 14th of May, he should do so on the 15th. This would normally seem a bizarre solution, but she was deadly serious and he thought it was a real option. Over the years, he would be called to the scene of several more road-accident fatalities on his birthday and, as a result, now stays at home, and certainly never drives anywhere, on the 14th of May. To this day, Geoff feels dread at the very mention of his birthday.

Considering the reasons why his marriage collapsed, it was ironic that Geoff would meet his new partner, Jocelyn, at the funeral home at which he spent so much time. The two had first met when Geoff went to the parlour with Dave Frost's family. Geoff was also called out to a double motorbike fatality involving two young men while he was there and later returned to the parlour. Geoff and Jocelyn were instantly attracted to each other and, given their common ground, fell easily into a friendship. They were both thrilled when things between them became serious, and eventually they were engaged and started looking for their first home.

Not long after he'd met Jocelyn, Geoff was called to a horrific murder-suicide in a Wagga house. When he arrived, the first thing he noticed was the mass of blowflies trapped inside the front window. Upon entering the house, he was struck by the putrid odour of rotting bodies, which were located inside a bedroom. The air was so thick he could hardly breathe, and he stood for a minute at the doorway, taking in his surroundings, before moving closer to the source of the smell.

It took him some time to gain entry into the main bedroom, which was barricaded from the inside. As the door finally flung open, a hot jet of fetid air shot out, along with a burst of blowflies making their escape. Geoff turned away in disgust for an instant before collecting himself and entering the room, where he saw the decomposing bodies of a young woman and child. The house had been locked from the inside, sealing the bodies in and literally cooking them in the searing November heat for at least a week.

Geoff went back to the car, and pulled out the camera box, the planto kit containing bags, jars, swabs, gloves and tools, and a folder. He put a white body suit on over his clothes and returned to the house, setting down the gear outside the bedroom. He then took a number of photographs depicting the method the woman had used to barricade the door shut from the inside. It appeared she had done this before fatally stabbing her six-year-old son and then stabbing herself once through the heart. The bodies were bloated and their skin stretched to the brink of bursting. Geoff struggled to breathe as he took his photographs and made notes on the evidence at the scene. His distress increased as he examined the little boy, all the time wondering how and why this could happen. In the kitchen, he found a book on anatomy, opened at a page showing the heart's location. It was obvious the woman had planned the murder-suicide carefully, making sure she knew exactly where the heart was.

Geoff later went over it all again at the morgue, as he photographed the bodies during the post-mortem examinations. The child's father requested a viewing, not being able to understand why he couldn't see his little boy. Geoff met with him at the funeral home, where he'd earlier placed flowers on the coffin. He spent about half an hour with the father, gently explaining what he'd seen at the house and trying to piece the whole tragedy together for him to at least give him some closure. As they stood by the little white casket, the father's head buried in Geoff's shoulder, Geoff explained the advanced state of decomposition of the little boy's body and the need to place it in a medically sealed bag. The father nodded, now comprehending why a viewing would not be possible. He took a few moments to say goodbye, while Geoff silently held him as he wept. It had been especially difficult for Geoff to communicate with the man, because he'd spent time in jail for manslaughter and wasn't one to listen to or respect police. Afterwards, though, over coffee he told Geoff that he appreciated the time he had taken to explain things and that it meant a great deal to him.

Later, Geoff met with the dead woman's father and explained to him, too, what he had found at the scene. Over the next few months he met him several more times, and struck up a friendship that lasted for years. The father would often do odd jobs around Geoff's house, and at one stage used the garage as a workshop to do lead-lighting in. This was Geoff's way of helping him out, but this link to his work would constantly remind Geoff of this particular case and, without him realising it, trapped him in that moment.

The following January, Geoff was called to investigate an apparent suicide in Junee; when he arrived at the scene, though, he found something very different. The general duties officers quickly ushered him to the garage, where he found a young man hanging from a rope attached to the rafters. The dead man's legs were bent at the knees and his feet were touching the ground. His jeans were undone and hanging around his ankles, and, as Geoff moved closer, he could see the dead man's penis protruding through an opening in his underpants. On the floor around the dead man were a number of pornographic books and other sexual paraphernalia.

While recording the scene, Geoff examined the rope around the man's neck as well as the point where it was attached to the rafters. As the man's legs touched the ground, it was obvious he had intended only to lean on the ligature rather than hang and could have stood up at any time. It was typical of an autoerotic death, in which the victim gets carried away with the sexual act and partially asphyxiates themselves while masturbating. This man had been masturbating and had placed a ligature around his neck to constrict the oxygen flow; as he climaxed, he tightened the ligature to enhance his orgasm. Before the man realised he was in trouble, the air had been cut off to such a degree that he was asphyxiated. Inside the house, Geoff discovered more hardcore pornographic magazines and dildos, which also supported the view that the man had not intended to take his own life. From the evidence in the garage and house and the manner in which the man died, Geoff declared it an autoerotic death.

The next day he was at the morgue, assisting with a post-mortem and taking photographs of a deceased person from another case, when he got a call from the station. The young man's family had gathered there and were asking questions. This incident was so out of the normal sphere of general police work that Geoff, having examined the scene, was the only person who could explain the circumstances of the death to them.

As Geoff entered the station conference room, he was surprised to see at least ten family members waiting for an explanation. They shot a volley of questions at him, further catching him off balance. After calming the family down, he quietly described, as best he could, the scene in the garage. Stunned silence engulfed the room as he struggled with the confronting and complex details. They looked increasingly shocked and horrifed but he continued to try to reassure them.

'Just because he experimented sexually and had this tendency doesn't mean he wasn't a good person. He didn't hurt anybody.

Perhaps he was just lonely and this was the way he got his sexual gratification,' Geoff explained.

The looks of shock were replaced by ones of relief, as now they at least understood what had happened; that their loved one hadn't meant to take his own life. Afterwards, though, Geoff was exhausted. His only release was a few quiet beers, which he had because he wanted to clear his mind before he went home to Jocelyn.

Over the coming weeks, Geoff attended a number of scenes where young men had either been drinking or affected by drugs, and died because they had tripped on the train track into the path of fast-moving freight trains or because they had been playing chicken on the track. Each one of these was as bad as the last and Geoff dreaded the sight of the mutilated bodies laying on the railway tracks. The bodies were invariably ripped to pieces; dismembered parts were scattered about as the young men were dragged along the railway line ballast when the carriages ran over them. More time was spent picking up the pieces than in processing the scene.

Geoff found night scenes were particularly unnerving, especially when he was working in the dark and hearing the humming sound of a locomotive idling nearby. He found it eerie and it made him jumpy and anxious. At each scene, Geoff took photographs, measurements and notes relating to the place, time and topography of the accident. Afterwards, he would pick up the pieces and place them in bags to be ferried to the morgue.

The next day, during the post-mortem examination, Geoff would be faced with putting the dismembered body parts back in place. The sight of them was like viewing a horror movie at close range, as he peered through the camera lens and recorded each part as the body was put back together. Later, when Geoff was living near a railway line, he suffered flashbacks when trains rumbled past.

Dealing with death on a daily basis was now part of Geoff's life, just like his drinking and mood swings. He was riding a wave of depression that would take over as quickly as it would subside.

7

EVIL NEXT DOOR

In early 1990, Geoff and Jocelyn were eagerly inspecting houses together. They found a lovely property behind Calvary Hospital and Geoff planned to make an offer on it the following day. He didn't know that, coincidentally, Annette was also inspecting the same property. The next morning he received a call to attend a horrific murder scene in a house outside Wagga. Annette secured the purchase of the house before Geoff had a chance to contact the agent. He was bitterly disappointed when he heard he'd missed out.

While Annette was celebrating her new purchase, Geoff was attending the scene of a brutal murder of a young mother on a property in the rural township of The Rock, some thirty-one kilometres south-west of Wagga. When he arrived, he saw a large contingent of police standing in groups at the front. Within the hour, journalists and film crews were arriving.

Inside the small weatherboard house, Geoff found the body of thirty-six-year-old Irene Julie Glanville lying on the kitchen floor, covered in blood. There'd been a violent struggle, during which the dead woman had been stabbed with a knife more than twenty times.

It appeared she had first encountered her attacker in the front entry to the house, as there were obvious signs of a struggle in the hall. In the kitchen, chairs were upturned and papers littered the floor; the victim had clearly fought for her life. Blood-splash patterns covered the walls because the knife had been drawn back again and again after the infliction of each puncture wound. The blood was then splashed in an upward trajectory along the walls as the offender repeatedly stabbed the young mother. There were also blood smears covering the floor where the struggle had taken place.

But the scene and the overpowering smell of blood horrified Geoff less than what he was told about her young children, who'd witnessed the violent attack. The victim had obviously been preparing lunch when the attack occurred, as there was a half-made sandwich on the kitchen bench. Two of her children, aged four and two, were sitting at the bench and witnessed the murder; they were so paralysed with fear throughout the attack that they couldn't move. The older child was found still sitting at the kitchen bench, with the youngest child strapped in his high chair, when the woman's husband and their two eldest children entered the house, having come from school, at 3.15 p.m. that afternoon.

The four-year-old told his father, 'Mummy is sleeping,' and pointed to her dead body on the floor. Later, he would give police a clear description of his mother's attacker and of the events that led up to her murder.

In the kitchen, Geoff took a number of photographs before moving towards the woman's body, which was lying on its side with the head up against a wall. She was dressed in a T-shirt and terry-towelling shorts. Geoff focused on the blood-soaked clothing, which indicated where she'd been stabbed. She had numerous wounds on the chest, stomach and waist, which were all soaked in blood. He picked up her hands one at a time, and held them in his palm as he studied the multiple defensive wounds where she'd desperately thrust up her hands to protect herself. The knife had sliced through her fingers as it pierced the skin repeatedly.

Suddenly, Geoff was sickened by the smell of her blood; it had been building steadily as he worked by the body, invading his senses until he could almost taste it. Moving outside for some fresh air, he decided to call Fingerprints and wait until they arrived before continuing his examination. It was imperative they work together in order to collect all physical evidence in the correct sequence. The radio operator informed him that the fingerprint examiner was at least an hour away. Geoff elected to wait.

A short time later, the detective in charge approached Geoff and, after a short discussion, demanded that he get straight to work. It was unusual for Geoff to disagree with the detective, as he generally enjoyed a good working relationship with the local office, but in this instance a heated argument followed. Geoff stood his ground and insisted the scene should not be compromised.

'I can't wait around here all day, mate – you need to get started,' the detective demanded.

'This scene can't be compromised and I need Fingerprints to be here before I start touching things; you'll just have to wait,' Geoff responded.

'You'll get started now.'

'The hell I will.'

I'll do it my way and the right way, Geoff thought as they reached a stand-off. He felt it was obvious the detective regarded him with contempt and thought that he was carrying on like a spoilt child throwing a tantrum when he didn't get his own way. Geoff stood firm and was relieved when the fingerprint expert finally arrived.

Together they walked through the scene, jointly assessing the order in which they would process the evidence. Then Geoff got to work, taking more photographs, making sketches, interpreting the blood-splash patterns and collecting evidence. The telephone in the kitchen was off the hook; did the victim desperately try to call 000? During the search for trace evidence, a note was found on the kitchen floor near the deceased. After photographing the piece of paper in position, Geoff read its contents. It was addressed to the owners of the neighbouring property and referred to their sheep wandering onto the Glanville property. Geoff later discovered that the victim wrote it shortly before she was murdered; establishing why and how it came to be lying on the floor near her body would be an important part of the investigation.

Geoff worked at the murder scene most of the night. When he eventually went home, he slept fitfully, his mind going over and over the bloodstained scene at the house and the two young children frozen to the spot. He just wanted to get the smell of blood off him and find some peace.

The phone rang at 6.30 a.m. the following morning. Two businessmen who were well-known in the local area had been killed after being struck by a semitrailer while on a bike ride on the Mangoplah Road, about twenty-five kilometres from Wagga. Geoff dragged himself from bed and prepared for another day of carnage. He drove the short distance to the scene and got straight to work, photographing the roadway and determining the point of impact. He examined the damaged front area of the semitrailer, and photographed the marks along the roadway where one of the bikes had been dragged 200 metres jammed beneath the rig. Walking along the roadway with his measuring wheel, Geoff took measurements of gauge and scuff marks, and plotted the position where the bikes had finally come to rest in relation to the point of impact. These measurements would be used to draw a scale plan to be presented at the inquest.

The truck driver explained how shocked he was when he realised he'd hit something. He couldn't remember seeing either of the cyclists in the darkness, and it wasn't until impact that he heard a scraping sound and realised he'd hit something. After stopping the rig, the driver saw the crumpled remains of one of the bikes wedged beneath the truck. When he walked along the road to see what had happened, he saw another bike and then the bodies of two men. He realised at this point that he must have inadvertently hit both cyclists from behind. The driver denied having seen the tail-lights of the bikes riding along the side of the road and repeatedly accused the cyclists of being at fault.

Geoff walked over to the crumpled remains of the bikes and knelt down beside them for a better look. He was particularly interested in the tail-lights and in whether they were operating at the time of the collision. Next, he photographed and examined the remains of both bodies, which had sustained horrific injuries. Just as he was finalising his notes, he received a radio message from the station. He now had another death to attend – the suicide of one of Jocelyn's friends.

This was yet another blow to Geoff's already fatigued mind; there seemed no end to the senseless carnage he faced on a daily basis. He was yet to finalise the paperwork and attend the post-mortem for the Glanville murder. Everything seemed to be piling up, one job after another, and a wave of anxiety swept through his body as he contemplated his mounting workload.

Got to get this job done and get to the next one, he thought. He jumped into the car and took off for the next scene.

The next day at the morgue, Geoff greeted Doc Lennon, who was preparing to conduct the post-mortem on Irene Glanville's body. During the autopsy, photographs were taken of more than twenty stab wounds around the young mother's stomach and chest area. Again, the overpowering smell of blood sickened Geoff; it now seemed a darker and thicker odour that almost hung in the air like a veil. But still he assisted while the pathologist measured and described each injury, writing descriptions on an anatomical chart. Afterwards, Geoff took the clothing, blood and a number of organs for later transportation to Sydney for analysis. Next, Geoff took photographs and assisted while Doc Lennon performed autopsies on both bodies from the accident on Mangoplah Road.

At the inquest into the Mangoplah Road accident, the Coroner was satisfied that both the bicycles' rear tail-lights were operating and that the semitrailer's headlights would have illuminated the roadway sufficiently to alert the driver to the cyclists' presence. In the absence of further evidence or witnesses, though, the driver was merely issued with a summons for negligent driving. *Two innocent family men wiped out for no reason*, Geoff would reflect.

The day after the post-mortems, he woke feeling tired, but dragged himself out of bed and headed for the office. He rang the detectives for an update on the Glanville murder and was pleased to hear there'd been a breakthrough. The detectives had begun canvassing the area, and interviewing family and friends known to the deceased. They approached the neighbouring property and asked the family to read the note found at the scene. Darryl John Phillips, aged nineteen, was the son of the owners. During the conversation, it became clear that the man was psychologically unstable, and he became agitated and anxious. The detectives asked him to accompany them back to the station for questioning.

During the interview, the young man suddenly admitted killing Mrs Glanville in what he described as a psychotic episode. As well, statements from the parents gave a picture of a very disturbed young man. As a boy, he had been diagnosed with behavioural problems. His parents couldn't cope with him and had repeatedly sought assistance from several government departments to contain his violent outbursts, during which he would punch holes in walls and generally inflict damage on the house. Afterwards, he would collapse and cry uncontrollably, and this would be followed by a wave of exhaustion. Later, he would claim to have forgotten the details of his outburst. As it seemed there was no health facility that could help, his parents were forced to deal with their son's behaviour on a day-to-day basis, never imagining that it could lead to such horror.

In court, much was made of the offender's psychiatric condition. The defence called several psychiatrists to give evidence of the man's mental state in an attempt to exonerate him. It had also been discovered that Phillips had watched a number of violent movies immediately prior to committing the murder, and this may have contributed to his psychotic outburst. To everyone's relief, the jury convicted Darryl Phillips of murder.

Now that it was all over, Geoff had to contact the victim's husband and give him the court's findings, as Mr Glanville was now living in Canberra with his children and had been unable to attend the day the verdict was handed down. Leaving the darkened courtroom, Geoff stopped and spoke to the officer in charge, explaining that he'd call Mr Glanville. The detective was relieved, as he was rushing back to Sydney to attend yet another murder. Walking towards Wollongong police station, a block away in a temporary building, brought back memories to Geoff of the time he worked in the area. Then his mind turned to how and what he would say to this poor man.

Inside the police station, Geoff found a quiet room, where he dialled Mr Glanville's number. After introducing himself, he said, 'I know this won't bring your darling wife back, but he's been found guilty of murder and is going to be sentenced in the coming weeks.'

'Thank God that's over,' Mr Glanville replied.

'All I can say is that I wish you and your kids a happier life in the years to come,' Geoff told him.

Mr Glanville then asked a number of questions relating to the sentencing and when it would occur, which Geoff answered as best he could. Mr Glanville also talked about how he and the children were coping; one child was receiving counselling and finding things very difficult. Geoff's heart went out to the family.

Over the following years, Geoff would play over and over in his mind the whole dreadful scenario of the terrified children watching their mother being stabbed to death. It would flash into his sub-conscious without warning. He felt a sadness for Mrs Glanville's husband and children, but it was the sight of the house that sick-ened him most and he would do anything to avoid driving past the small fibro cottage set back from the road.

Over the Easter weekend following the Glanville murder, Geoff and Jocelyn found a quaint two-bedroom weatherboard cottage on a large block in a lovely street in Turvey Park. Coincidentally, it was owned by a local ambulance officer who Geoff knew from Urana, and the house had a familiar feel. Although it was partially reno-vated, Geoff knew he could put his own stamp on the place, so they decided to buy it.

Geoff moved in straightaway rather than waiting until he and Jocelyn were married, so that he could immediately start work on the house and garden. He also explored the local area. He offered his services in a social capacity to the Turvey Park Football Club, but, due to the possibility of his work commitments making him unreliable, turned down an offer of working on the committee. That year, the club sponsored him for 'Crop a Cop', which involved him having his head shaved to raise awareness for cancer research, and with their support he raised much-needed funds. Following this, Geoff felt part of the club and got to know most of the members.

After the footy one weekend, he was drinking with mates at the Turvey Tavern when he was introduced to Merv Alchin, a local plasterer. Geoff was looking for someone to help out with the renovations and asked if he'd come over and quote. Merv promptly accepted the job, and turned up regularly at the house to complete the gyprocking work Geoff had asked him to do. The two men got on well and, over the next few years, Geoff got to know Merv's partner, who was his son's schoolteacher, as well as Merv's two brothers. He would also bump into Merv at the footy club, where he was the strapper and team masseuse. Geoff loved being part of the club and getting to know the locals, and it seemed that life was taking a new and exciting direction, in his personal life at least.

On 2 May 1992, Geoff and Jocelyn finally married and she moved into their new Turvey Park home. Jocelyn was blissfully happy but, from the very start of their marriage, she realised Geoff's work would take precedence over everything else. They had planned to spend their honeymoon in Port Douglas but, at the last minute, Geoff was directed to attend District Court and their holiday plans were cancelled. Instead, they drove the short distance from Wagga to the south coast and enjoyed a short break touring Eden, Bermagui, Merimbula and Narooma.

The early days of their marriage were a happy time for both of them, but, at the same time, Geoff felt he was burning the candle at both ends. It was difficult juggling work and home commitments and, with the added pressure of financially starting anew, he struggled to make ends meet; but he was deeply in love and determined to make a go of things.

From the very beginning, he vowed to talk with Jocelyn about work issues. He showed her through his office and explained his crime-scene duties. He also asked for permission to show her through the Sydney district crime-scene unit and to take her on a tour of the city morgue in Glebe. As Jocelyn worked in the funeral industry, she was intrigued to see the city morgue first hand. As she stepped into the main refrigerated area, she was a bit taken aback at the sight of the many shrouded corpses inside clear body bags lined up on rows and rows of steel shelves. In Wagga, they used white bags so that the bodies were hidden. She walked closely beside Geoff as he guided her through the facility, taking everything in with fascination.

Next on the list was a visit to Rookwood cemetery. Jocelyn found it amazing and was in awe of the size of the vaults in the Italian section. She and Geoff shared an interest in cemeteries, and they enjoyed walking among the crypts and reading the headstones. Jocelyn was glad they'd had this time together; it made her feel closer to Geoff and, later, when he was working in Sydney, she could envision exactly where he was.

In July 1990, Geoff had been promoted to sergeant and, after nearly two years of working alone as the only crime-scene examiner in the Wagga district, he was joined by a junior constable. In effect, this initially meant more work for Geoff, as he had responsibility for training the new officer, but Geoff was still pleased. After the introduction he had had to crime-scene work himself, Geoff was determined that Joe Lavin, the new constable, would be fully trained before he was assigned 'on call' duties. Within a couple of months, Joe was able to take over the more mundane inquiries and jobs that came in each day.

However, Geoff's life still carried on the same way, with him being on call twenty-four hours a day without a break. Even his days off were often disturbed, due to the mounting number of major crime scenes that required the collection of physical evidence. With his ever-increasing workload, he became more and more intolerant of incompetence, or what he perceived to be incompetence, and his concentration levels fluctuated as his mind drifted to thoughts of what the next job would be while he was still investigating the one before it. He was careful not to be aggressive, though, because he'd seen this in other people and he didn't like it.

What really angered him was being asked to attend scenes of jobs some time after the event, so that he could take a few 'happy snaps'; this attitude that his work only entailed taking a couple of quick photographs trivialised it. Each time this happened, Geoff would feel rage in the pit of his stomach but appear calm on the outside. This was just another example of how he hid his true feelings, appearing to take each incident in his stride. Also, Geoff came to hate the sound of the phone ringing, especially when he was in the office, because it would often be a detective chasing a statement, and Geoff's time was so stretched that he'd have to give excuses and string the task out just so that he could keep up with the work he already had.

Another issue was that Geoff would have to sort through photographs of crime scenes when they came back from the printers and compile the brief of evidence. This meant he had to relive the scene for a second, or even a third, time and then he'd have to go over everything again in court. The most shocking scenes he attended haunted him and he would have a gnawing, aching feeling in his stomach when dealing with work related to them.

To lighten things up, Geoff often turned up at the office wearing his signature 'Mr Happy' tie, which Jocelyn had given him because of his constant complaints about work. His colleagues came to expect the tie and its funny cartoon character; his wearing it had become part of Geoff's persona. On a bad day, if he didn't laugh, he'd probably cry.

8

THE YOUNG PLANE DISASTER

On a wet winter's evening at the start of the Queen's Birthday weekend in 1993, a light plane carrying seven passengers made an approach to land at Young Airport in central-west New South Wales. The driving rain and wind gusts reduced the pilot's visibility significantly and he struggled to get his bearings when attempting to guide the plane towards the airstrip. At the last minute, he aborted the landing and instead circled the airport before trying to land a second time.

Inside the *Piper Chieftain*, three schoolgirls, all boarders from Pymble Ladies College in Sydney, were looking forward to getting home for a mid-term break. There was an excited mood as Jane Gay, Alanda Clark and Prue Papworth chatted and giggled among themselves. Also on the plane were Sydney barrister Bill Caldwell and Cootamundra grazier and president of the NSW Shires Association Stephen Ward. Wayne Gorham was at the controls with his co-pilot, Brynley Baker.

What the passengers and their families didn't know was that Monarch Airlines, the owner and operator of the ill-fated plane,

was technically bankrupt. The airline had resorted to unortho-
dox methods to obtain spare parts and fuel; at times, pilots were
paying for fuel on their personal credit cards. Over the preceding
twelve months, there had been systematic abuse of airline safety
regulations, and complaints to the Civil Aviation Authority (CAA)
as well as to the New South Wales Air Transport Council that had
been overlooked. But worse still was the removal in May 1993 of
vital autopilot equipment after it had been reported as inoperable
in March. On this flight, the co-pilot was only there to negate the
absence of the autopilot equipment. The presence of an extra pilot
technically allowed Monarch to fly the flawed plane, but, apparently,
didn't give the passengers the right to know what was happening.

Approximately two kilometres south-south-east of Young Airport, in searing wind and rain, the *Piper Chieftain* made its second
attempt to land. Suddenly, the plane clipped the top of some trees
on a private property at the highest point on the approach to the
runway. The plane careered out of control, shearing through the
dense canopy and bursting into flames. It broke up and finally came
to rest in a ball of fire deep within a rock-filled grotto. Six of the
people on the plane were incinerated on impact, while the seventh,
Prue Papworth, was flung from the fuselage, still strapped to her
seat, and landed close by. So fierce were the flames that Prue's body
suffered serious radiating-heat burns, as well as multiple fractures.

Rescue efforts got underway immediately as distraught relatives,
who could see the flames from the nearby airport, looked on helplessly. At the time of the collision, two light planes were due to land
at the airport simultaneously, and as news came in confirming that
one of the planes had crashed, relatives frantically sought information about whether it was the plane their loved ones were on.
Minutes after the accident, ambulance and rescue operators were

directed to the plane's wreckage by a local property owner, who'd witnessed the sickening sound of the initial impact. On arrival, the intensity of the flames, with the fuselage still well alight, forced them back. Prue was quickly attended to and ferried by ambulance to a waiting helicopter to take her to the burns unit at Concord Hospital in Sydney. Her impact injuries, although severe, were thought to be non-life threatening; her greatest battle would be to overcome the severe burns she'd sustained.

Shortly after the crash, Geoff received a call to attend the crash site at Young. His thoughts initially were of the victims' families and the tragic loss of life, but once the extent of the disaster sunk in, his mind turned to the dismal weather conditions. He knew from past experience that he'd be out in the elements, and he wasn't looking forward to working in the freezing conditions. He pushed this thought from his mind and quickly made his way to the scene.

After driving 170 kilometres to Young, Geoff arrived around 9 p.m. In total darkness, he met with the local inspector, Jock Rogerson, from Young.

'I need you to take a few photographs so we can get the bodies out,' the inspector said.

'With respect, sir, this job's a little more than taking a few photographs. I know it's hard on the families and I can understand the need to get the bodies out, but my priority is the identification of those deceased and to ascertain why this plane crashed. I won't be doing anything until I've contacted the CAA and the Coroner.'

The inspector was clearly taken aback but Geoff quickly returned to his vehicle, where he intended making a number of calls. His first task was to telephone the CAA and the Coroner, who confirmed his earlier direction that all bodies were to remain in situ until such time as a full and thorough examination by all governing bodies had taken place. Geoff then rang the physical evidence section in Sydney and asked for assistance from the crime scene, video and photogrammetry units.

The conditions were even worse than Geoff had expected; as he and the inspector stood talking, the howling wind and driving rain whipped about their bodies making it almost impossible to hear each other. Wearing only police-issue blue overalls, a parker and boots, Geoff realised he was insufficiently dressed for the elements. He ordered that gloves and balaclavas be brought to the scene in a bid to ward off the minus-twelve-degrees chill factor; he quickly realised that this would be impossible until the following day, though. Shivering, Geoff set about roping off the scene and putting a guard in place until the next day, when all necessary personnel would be able to reach the aircrash site.

Geoff's first impression of the scene, upon cursory examination that night, was the number of trees whose tops had been sheared off as the plane crashed to the ground. Further down, on the side of a hill in a grotto lay the main fuselage, and strewn about were the remains of the plane. Within the wreckage lay six bodies, the two pilots and four of the passengers, that were burned beyond recognition. Geoff took a minute to digest the sight: the charred remains oozed with body fluids and each body was in a pugilistic pose, clearly in response to the intensity of the flames. The smell of burned flesh confronted him in bursts as the wind whipped about taking the odour with it.

My God, this is even worse than I expected. Where do I start and how the hell am I going to get them all out in one piece?

His thoughts were interrupted by the local inspector, who, for a second time, demanded the bodies be removed immediately.

'I need these bodies removed,' he said.

'No, they stay put until the Coroner gets here,' Geoff replied firmly.

'There's absolutely no need to leave them out here in this weather. We'll get them out now and the families can go home,' the inspector argued.

'To hell with that; they stay put and that's all there is to it. You'll have to explain to the families that we're waiting on the Coroner, and you can talk to him when he arrives,' Geoff answered. 'It's going to be a hell of a job identifying these bodies, and it's got to be done by the book. It's disaster victim identification or nothing. I'm sorry for the families, but I can't do it any other way. You'll just have to explain it; I'm sorry.'

The intense discussion continued, during which Geoff set out the correct sequence of a full and proper investigation and emphasised the importance of correctly identifying the deceased. He realised, more than ever, that he couldn't do this alone and was glad that assistance from the physical evidence section in Sydney was on its way.

By 1 a.m., Geoff was satisfied that the scene was correctly secured, and he left the site to go and meet the crime scene examiners from Sydney, Detective Sergeant Pieter Strik and Constable Geoff Hampshire, at the hotel in Young. After discussing the facts as they were known so far, the trio retired to catch a couple of hours' sleep, agreeing to rise at daybreak. By 5 a.m., Geoff and the other two men were on their way to the scene.

Geoff was sad that the victims' families had to endure another day with their loved ones' bodies still at the crash site; it was all the more reason to get started as soon as possible. The weather conditions were even worse but soon the balaclavas and gloves arrived, which made things a little more bearable.

Later that morning, a video operator and photogrammetry expert arrived from Sydney and got to work, initially capturing the crash site on video and then with a photogrammetry camera, which used glass plates to record the scene three-dimensionally. Geoff assisted as cones were placed at one-metre intervals before a sequence of stereo photographs were taken onto the glass plates. The photographic plates would later be developed in Sydney and then placed in a plotting machine so that a scale plan for presentation at the inquest could be drawn. Meanwhile, Constable Hampshire found a vantage point high above the wreckage where he perched on a rock and painstakingly sketched the entire scene. When Geoff received the finished plan, he was most impressed and grateful to his workmate for the tremendous job he had done.

While Constable Hampshire was working, Geoff approached him and asked to see the sketch; the two men shivered as they stood close to each other, discussing the scene and comparing it with the plan. Geoff took in the view of the site from above. His devastation deepened as he absorbed the sight of the plane and its contents against the beautiful backdrop of the Australian bush, but he was quickly jolted back to the stark reality of the investigation. He got to work again, calling the men together to form a DVI team, with the addition of Constable Phil Malligan as property officer. In the small area where the six bodies were confined, they pegged stakes to the ground to form a grid pattern of small sections. Once all the team was satisfied with the grid pattern, they were ready to commence their examination.

Geoff was then met by CASA and BASI representatives, who commenced their independent investigation. Geoff spent considerable time examining the scene with them, and it was during this part of the investigation when it was ascertained that the plane's engines still had power as it sheared the tree tops off on approach to the site.

Next, Derrick Hand, the State Coroner, arrived and again Geoff walked an official through the scene, explaining what was known so far. As they stopped to view the dead, they spoke about a number of issues.

'It's up to the dead to tell their story and, in fact, knowing the very spot in which the passengers were sitting could help reveal the cause of the crash,' the Coroner remarked.

'I'm wondering if you wouldn't mind speaking to the local inspector about that?' Geoff asked. 'It's been a point of disagreement between us since I arrived. I'm having trouble convincing him that the bodies need to stay put until our examinations are completed. I'm sure having it come from you would make all the difference.'

Derrick Hand nodded. 'I'll do it right away,' he said as he walked off.

Around this time, Geoff was glad to see a Salvation Army chaplain arrive. The chaplain spoke briefly to him about the families. 'The relatives are becoming anxious and want to see the scene. They're also clearly upset at the delay and want to know what's going on.'

'There's still much to be done and I can assure you that I'm doing my best to finish my work here as quickly as possible,' Geoff explained

Next, an ABC helicopter, the perfect vehicle to take aerial photographs, landed nearby. The pilot was happy to assist and soon took off with a photographer on board.

With all the preliminary work out of the way, it was time for the DVI team to concentrate on the recording of all deceased persons. Each body was systematically tagged and photographed, and all identifiable items that were on them or nearby were recorded both visually and in writing. Each body was plotted and sketched in place, using the string line that the team had erected earlier when they constructed the grid.

Next, the three forensic police made preparations to remove the first body from the burned remains of the fuselage. They discovered the head was deeply charred and broke away from the body when it was moved. After a short discussion during which the best possible way of keeping the body intact was determined, Geoff ordered that neck braces be delivered to the scene. He also ordered special glue to help hold teeth in place. A short time later, the braces and glue arrived from the local hospital, allowing the men to turn their attention back to the first body. They set about gluing the teeth in place to stop the jaw and its contents from collapsing and teeth being lost. It was imperative that the jaw and teeth be preserved, as dental identification was the most likely means of making positive individual matches. It was a distasteful task, especially due to the odour of burnt flesh, which filled the air and was impossible to escape.

With Sergeant Strik holding the victim's head and neck, Constable Hampshire placed the neck brace over the charred remains while Geoff attended to gluing the brittle, heat-affected teeth to the jaw. He struggled with the intricate job, as his hands were frozen and the gloves slippery. All but one of the deceased persons had had their scalps burned off, which meant that facial identification would be out of the question. Therefore, Geoff was determined to maintain the integrity of every one of the deceased's dental work, if at all possible. Each body was painstakingly prepared in exactly the same manner in readiness for transportation by refrigerated truck to the morgue at Glebe in Sydney.

By now, quite some time had elapsed since the tragedy had occurred, and the families were still standing by, waiting to attend the scene. Geoff understood that viewing the scene would give them closure, but he still had a job to do. He was constantly interrupted and pressured to finish quickly so that the families could enter the crash site; he stood firm in denying access until the job was complete. It was impossible for the relatives to understand what was taking so long, but later at the inquest, when all the evidence was presented, they would acknowledge the importance of the investigation.

Geoff took a breather, and then focused on the six white body bags laid out in a neat line beside the remains of the crashed plane. The stark whiteness of the bags as they fluttered in the wind that gusted in bursts throughout the dismal day made the tragedy seem all the more unbelievable. The anxiety was rising in Geoff's chest, and he knew that this hell on earth would only become more unbearable the longer he had to endure it.

One by one, the team of three men lifted from the wreck the charred remains of each body and placed it into the body bag. They were then put into the truck to go to the morgue; however, the driver had been up most of the night and told Geoff he would be heading home for a rest before driving the van and its human cargo to Sydney. Geoff emphasised the need to keep the truck refrigerated and, shortly after sealing the doors, watched as the van slowly negotiated the rock-filled paddocks that led back to the main road.

Now that the bodies were gone, BASI and CAA were comfortable with giving permission for the family members to attend the crash site. They were ushered into a safe area a short distance from the remains of the plane. There they stood solemnly in the late afternoon, bound together by their grief. Geoff quietly requested they be sure not to move or touch anything, and explained that their loved ones' bodies would be transported to the mortuary in Glebe for forensic examination. He then kept his distance, as he couldn't begin to answer their questions; the full examination results from both air investigative bodies were to come and he knew it would be quite some time before even the interim results were released. It would be a long and emotional wait for the families; he hoped that, in time, they would get the answers they deserved and fully understand what had happened to their family members.

At 6 p.m., Geoff finally left the scene. Thirteen hours had passed since he'd arrived that morning and he'd spent some twenty hours in total there. He now made preparations to escort the bodies to Sydney. He informed the truck driver and told him he was ready to go. Shortly afterwards, a convoy of vehicles rumbled over the rocky ground, leaving behind the shattered remains of the plane's fuselage looking like a monument constructed from burned and twisted metal. Once on the open road, Geoff turned the heating to high, and he slowly came back to earth as he settled into the five-hour journey straight to the Division of Forensic Medicine in Glebe.

The forensic odontologist at Glebe had informed the staff of the impending arrival of the crash victims' bodies. Preparations were underway for full-scale DVI. Meanwhile, back at Young, the local police had made inquiries with the victims' families and compiled a list of the seven passengers on the ill-fated flight. They requested dental records that, once sourced, would be sent straight to Sydney to assist with identification.

Arriving in Glebe at 11 p.m., Geoff entered the morgue and spoke to the staff. The truck was still on its way, so he went to the meal room and, after making coffee, tried to get comfortable in a cane chair. Completely exhausted, he finally drifted off for a couple of hours.

Around 3 a.m. he was summoned to the delivery dock, where he broke the seal on the truck doors and then watched as the six white body bags were brought into the main receiving area. Each bag was placed on a separate trolley, unzipped, checked, photographed, weighed and tagged. Geoff was mindful of not disturbing the victims' jaw and teeth area, and explained to the staff that it was vital the neck braces stayed in place to support the entire head region. Once the bodies were in the large refrigerated storeroom, he went out to the police vehicle and set off to find something to eat.

He was drinking coffee in the morgue tearoom when he received a phone call from John Merrick, the morgue's grief counsellor. John told him that the family of one of the pilots was on their way after having requested a viewing. At the accident scene, Geoff had spent around half an hour explaining to the pilot's family that he was the only deceased who could possibly be identified visually, as his facial injuries weren't as severe as the others'.

Geoff returned to the refrigerated area of the morgue and assisted with the preparation of the body. The small area of the face that was identifiable was cleaned and the burnt areas covered to save the family further distress. The neck collar had been slipped down to expose the intact facial features and a sheet had been pulled over the burned area. As Geoff stood by the body, a morgue attendant approached him.

'We've just received word from Concord burns unit that the young girl from the plane crash has died.' Geoff stood in silent shock. 'She's on her way,' the attendant added as he headed back into the office.

There would now be seven post-mortems to deal with the following day. Geoff dreaded this, as he knew only too well what would have to be done. For a split second his mind drifted back to the Carrafa family, but he pushed the thought from his mind; it was something he could not afford to dwell on.

Around 9 a.m., John Merrick arrived with the pilot's brother and his son. Geoff spoke briefly to John about the crash and its victims, before meeting the relatives and accompanying them into the viewing room. The trolley was positioned at the viewing window, and John and Geoff stood with the family to give them support.

'Because of the injuries, I've concealed some of the body from view, because I feel you would be distressed further by seeing it,' Geoff told them.

They nodded as they prepared for the worst. The curtain was drawn back, and the family tearfully looked through the window at their loved one. It wasn't long before Geoff was given the signal that the viewing was over and the body could be taken away.

Geoff then headed into the Sydney Police Centre, a short ten-minute drive to Surry Hills close to the heart of the city, where he went straight to the fifth level and the crime-scene unit. There he spent the rest of the day completing paperwork, and receiving and making numerous calls in a bid to chase up all seven victims' dental records, which were required prior to the commencement of the post-mortem examinations. Late in the afternoon, he realised that the autopsies would not take place until the following day, which was the Monday of the long weekend. The fact it was a long weekend had made it all the more difficult to obtain records, or even to get hold of dentists, who were away for the holiday break. Geoff's frustration grew as his exhaustion sank in and, having had little rest or food, he was starting to feel the strain.

In the afternoon, he walked to the Macquarie Hotel, a short five-minute stroll down a lane from the Sydney Police Centre. As he walked in the shadows of the cityscape, he rubbed his hands together against the cold. Instantly, he was taken back to the chilly and intense scene at Young. Geoff felt a world away from it now.

Glancing up at the blue sky, he saw a plane in the distance and wondered who was in it and if they knew how fragile their existence really was. He stepped into the warmth of the hotel, a popular police haunt in which he'd stayed before. Geoff somehow felt safe within the smoky atmosphere of the pub, away from the isolation of the cold city street. Later, he sat at the downstairs bar and sipped on a beer as a constant stream of smoke wafted from a smouldering cigarette at his side. He had done a marathon forty-eight hours of nonstop forensic work. The day had slipped by in a blur of exhaustion, emotional fatigue and adrenaline. Only alcohol could stop the hyped-up feelings he'd had over the past two days. He just wanted his mind to stop.

After only a little sleep that night, Geoff pulled on his dirty overalls the following morning and set off for the morgue. It was 7 a.m. and the team was assembling in the admission area to commence the post-mortems and identifications of all seven crash victims. Geoff pulled on a white gown over his overalls and covered his shoes with cotton boots. Again, he was met by Detective Sergeant Pieter Strik, who'd assisted at the crash site, and who was helping now, along with Detective Sergeant John Goldie of the Goulburn crime-scene unit. Also in attendance was a video operator, who would record the identification and post-mortem examinations of each victim.

Geoff entered the main autopsy area, where he saw six of the deceased passengers laid out on stainless-steel tables, three each along parallel walls. To his left, he saw the body of Prue Papworth on a gurney against the far corridor. Each table was connected to a common bench that ran the length of the room. In readiness for the day's work, knives, scalpels, cutters and scales, all gleaming under the harsh lights, sat neatly alongside stone cutting boards. The air was full of the stench of burnt flesh. Each body lay contorted, burnt beyond recognition, a mass of charred remains permeated with bright red where the skin had exploded and allowed bloodied fluid to seep through. Geoff quickly focused on the body closest to where he stood, in an effort to block out the multiple images.

Suddenly, a stream of white-coated forensic dentists filled the room, and stood side by side in readiness to begin. An X-ray machine was rolled in, along with all the dental equipment required for the jaw extraction process. Dr Joe Deflou, chief forensic pathologist, and the chief odontologist joined the group and handed a wad of paperwork to Geoff, including dental records for all the deceased. Geoff was grateful for the tireless efforts of the Young police; if it hadn't been for their total commitment to retrieving the necessary dental information, the post-mortem examinations would have been postponed for yet another day.

With pathologists, dentists, morgue assistants and police all working together, the examinations began with the two pilots' bodies, followed by the two male victims, the two young girls and, finally, the girl who'd died the day after the crash. A production line was established, with each body X-rayed, photographed and searched. Meanwhile, DVI forms were completed as all items of charred clothing, property and jewellery were removed, described, recorded, collected and bagged. As Geoff worked, the room began to fill with the strong smell of aviation fuel, mixing with the odour of the charred bodies. Added to this was the sight of seeping body fluids oozing through the sinus of cracked skin, and the difficulty of handling the victims, as their arms and legs were frozen together in twisted positions sealed by the heat from the crash.

The odontologist got to work, using bone cutters to excise the upper and lower jaws from the skull, and laying them out on the table to commence his examination. The dental profile was carefully compared with the existing records supplied by each victim's dentist. Geoff was witness to each dental profile as notes and photographs were taken. He hoped it wouldn't be necessary to remove the entire jaw of the young girl who had died in the burns unit at Concord, so that, at least, her family could have a last chance to see her.

By mid-afternoon the post-mortems were still underway, with the dentists working hard to match teeth to charts. There were also the usual post-mortem examinations to be conducted, including opening the body cavity and examining and weighing organs, the taking of blood and urine samples, and the opening of the skull and examination of the brain. Each injury, whether external or internal, was noted, examined and photographed. Those organs required for pathology were dissected on a stone cutting board, before being bottled and labelled and lined up beside each body on a stainless-steel table in readiness for packaging and transportation to the appropriate laboratory.

Finally, the last body was wheeled over and placed gently on the examination table. Her lifeless form was covered in monitors and bandages, the legacy of the hospital staff who'd tried frantically to save her life. Her eyes were wide and bulging, transfixed by her last moment. As Geoff's eyes met hers, he felt such sadness that he could hardly bear to stay focused. Just then, a coldness came over him again; it took him back to the accident scene and pierced every part of his body in a chill he could barely control. The odontologist stood to his left and prepared to get to work, picking up the bone cutters in readiness to excise the upper and lower jaw.

'Is there any need for this?' Geoff asked bluntly.

The odontologist was taken back. 'This is a fantastic opportunity to test the training of our staff,' he replied.

'Do we really have to do this!' Geoff yelled. 'You're ruining any chance of the family having a viewing before the funeral. I can't see why you should subject her to this – she's already been identified'.

'I have a whole team of dentists here today; this is a good exercise,' the odontologist spat.

Geoff couldn't believe what he was hearing. *This poor girl. What the fuck's wrong with him?*

The odontologist continued saying what an opportunity this was, as all the dentists were here together, for them to perform the entire dental identification. Geoff reluctantly resigned himself to the fact that the procedure would go ahead.

Up to this point, Geoff had felt he was coping and, even though the day had been absolute hell, he'd remained almost entirely focused and clinical. Now, though, he could feel his emotions taking over, and, mentally and physically drained, he was almost at breaking point. His anger became resentment as he stood beside the dentist, seething in silence at being forced to witness the young girl being subjected to the jaw-extraction process. It took all his strength not to express his anger. Much later, Geoff would be plagued by this anger consuming him without warning – a simmering resentment that kept him stuck in that hellish moment.

Still, once the post-mortems were over, Geoff felt a sense of accomplishment; all the victims had been positively identified, which meant they could be returned to their families for burial or cremation. He was relieved that the relatives could now make the necessary arrangements, and at least move forward in the grieving process.

Geoff took possession of several paper bags containing the victims' property, which he would later return to the families in Young. He was relieved finally to walk out onto the street, get into the car and leave the smell of death behind. He went straight to the crime-scene unit at the Sydney Police Centre, as there was still paperwork to be completed and phone calls to make. Afterwards, he went to the Macquarie Hotel, where he met up with two of the dentists he had worked with that day at the morgue.

The next morning Geoff woke early, threw on his overalls and made the five-hour trip back to Young. Around midday, he arrived at the police station and got straight to work entering details into the property book. As he was doing so, the station constable told him the families were anxious to receive their loved ones' property as soon as possible. Geoff decided to take the property straight to the relatives, to save them any further distress.

It was now Tuesday afternoon, the fourth day after the tragedy, and Geoff still hadn't been home or taken a break. He was unshaven, pale and exhausted, but the adrenaline kept pumping. He quickly pushed away the need for rest and drove south towards Wagga. He would be stopping first at Old Nubber station, which Alanda Clark's family owned.

When Geoff arrived, he quickly realised from the number of cars present that a large group had gathered there, for which he was completely unprepared. Alanda's father met him at the door.

'Are you all right?' he asked Geoff.

'I'm okay, just a bit tired,' Geoff replied.

'We'll get you some hot soup,' said the man, as he gestured for Geoff to follow him inside. He was led into a room full of people, who all focused on him as he entered. All three sets of parents and relatives of the girls killed were present. Before Geoff could take a seat, or even get his bearings, questions flew at him in quick succession.

'Did our daughter suffer?'

'What went wrong? Was it pilot error?'

'How did they die?'

Geoff tried his best to answer, but as soon as he'd finished responding to one question, another would be fired at him, forcing him to relive the accident scene and the post-mortems. It was difficult to remain professional and not allow his emotions to interfere with him giving the clinical details.

Geoff explained that his role was different from that of the CAA, and that there would be a full investigation by the appropriate aviation body. He also explained the Coroner's role and how all the details of the accident would be examined during the inquest. He told them about the inclement weather, and the fact that there was another plane taxiing on the runway at the same time that the ill-fated plane was due to land. He described the pilot having aborted the first attempt to touch down and circling to try to land a second time, then coming in too low and hitting the tree tops on approach to the runway, and, of course, the crash itself. Geoff explained that all the girls had been positively identified, briefly covering the procedure of the dental records and charts being matched to each victim. He also explained that the bodies could now be released and so the families could start making funeral arrangements.

As Geoff gave them the news that the girls had now been positively identified, the scene became all the more distressing, as the families came to realise that the deaths were now official and their loved ones were never coming home. As the focal point, Geoff felt their grief as though he'd been punched in the chest. At least at the crash site and at the morgue he had been able to maintain some distance, but now he felt part of the tragedy, forever linked to these people in a way he would never forget.

Geoff turned the conversation to the clothing and jewellery he'd brought to return to the family, telling them of a watch he thought belonged to the Clark family. He held it out to Alanda's father, and suddenly the mother of one of the other victims snatched it out of his hand. The watch wasn't the Clarks' at all. In that moment, he realised the significance of the watch – it represented a mother's last chance to hold something her precious daughter had worn. It tore at his heart to see her pain and suffering as she clutched the item and sobbed uncontrollably. Now the others demanded something – anything – of their loved ones'; just one last reminder of their daughters to hold.

'Was one of the girls wearing riding boots?' Geoff asked.

'Yes, we gave them to our daughter for her birthday. Can we have them back?' one of the fathers asked.

'The boots are burned,' Geoff warned him.

'We don't care. Can we have them?' the father pleaded. 'We just want to hold them.'

Geoff went to the car and returned with the boots in a paper bag, and handed them over solemnly. The father broke down when he opened the bag.

'Yes, they are my girl's,' he said as he held the boots.

Finally, it was all too much for Geoff as the shock started to set in. He was totally shattered, and thought that nothing could be worse than what he was faced with in this room. He felt paralysed, that there was nothing more he could do.

After the property was all distributed and signed for, Alanda's family offered Geoff a bowl of hot soup once again. As he drank it, they all sat and talked in hushed tones; the atmosphere of urgency had passed. Afterwards, they all held hands and said a prayer.

Geoff found it difficult to leave but it was time to go. He set off home, where Jocelyn had been waiting patiently. She was pregnant with their first child and was to enter hospital the next day to have a stitch inserted in her cervix. The previous month she'd had a cervical tumour removed, and this surgery was to prevent her losing the baby. She needed Geoff more than ever, and had had a difficult four days, with no word, not even a single phone call, from him. Jocelyn was terrified of losing their child and hoped Geoff would give her support, although she was aware of what he would have been through at the morgue. Having worked at a funeral home herself, she knew better than most people what dealing with the dead was like. It was Jocelyn's wish that Geoff would be able to focus on their personal needs and put the past week behind him. She didn't know, though, the profound effect this case had had on her husband.

Instead of going home, Geoff went straight to the pub, where he called Jocelyn and asked her to meet him for dinner. By the time she arrived, he was already drunk, slurring his words and acting strangely. Over dinner, Geoff continually found fault with Jocelyn until they had a fully blown argument. Distraught and unable to cope with Geoff's mood, Jocelyn left, rushing home to pack a bag before fleeing to her parents' house. She couldn't believe his lack of concern about her operation and felt that all she could do was to leave him alone to calm down. But she felt totally alone and needed her husband by her side. *What's happening to us?* Jocelyn asked herself. Geoff says that that evening he simply wanted to drink himself into oblivion; his mind had far too much to process and had become numb. He couldn't deal with Jocelyn's fear of losing the baby; it was too much on top of everything else he'd had to deal with over the past four days.

The following morning, Geoff woke up alone and wondered where Jocelyn was. He rushed to the hospital and caught her moments before she went into surgery. He asked her where she'd been, admitting that he had no memory of the night before or that she had left the pub alone and spent the night at her parents'. Geoff was shocked when Jocelyn told him about the argument they'd had the previous night; he had no recollection of being aggressive and abusive. But suddenly he told Jocelyn that he had to get back to work to attend to an urgent job.

Jocelyn couldn't believe it. She thought Geoff had finally come to his senses, and was now filled with frustration and resentment that, yet again, work took precedence for him. She had hoped he would spend the day at the hospital with her. Nothing she said could change his mind, though, and he rushed out as quickly as he'd rushed in. Later, Jocelyn would hear that in fact he'd spent the afternoon at the pub.

After one day off, Geoff was back at work, attending a debrief at Young police station; he hoped it would help get him back on track and put the crash behind him. He was disappointed when he realised there wasn't a psychologist present – only a room full of people who had attended the scene. It became merely a pat on the back for those who already thought they'd done a good job. Geoff sat in silence, feeling apart from it all. Once again, he felt his anger rising. *Why isn't there a proper debrief? I've just spent four days with seven dead bodies; how the hell am I supposed to put this in perspective without help? Surely there's a budget to cover this sort of thing?* He felt almost invisible.

Geoff wrote a letter to the Salvation Army and to the SES, thanking them for the great work they did in assisting at the Young plane crash scene and later helping with the families. He didn't know what he would have done without them. He knew that those in the Salvos and in the SES were often volunteers, and that all they did just got taken for granted. Geoff wanted to make sure they knew how much he appreciated their support and help; it wasn't the first time they'd helped him and he knew it wouldn't be the last.

In the days and weeks after the crash, Geoff slowly retreated within himself. He didn't want to talk, and his once happy disposition had been replaced with a deep-seated anger that he just couldn't get rid of. He felt incredibly sad and stayed away from home, preferring to sit alone at the pub. During this time, he drank as he never had before.

Geoff found some solace when he heard the families of the plane crash had built a monument on Old Nubber station. At least he could go there and pay his respects – or so he thought. On the day of the memorial service at which the monument was unveiled, he was directed not to attend it. The police hierarchy felt that his work commitments should take precedence. Once again, Geoff felt the anger rise; instead of talking about it, he harboured it silently.

Later, in his own time, Geoff went out to the monument and stood in front of the monolith that had been placed alongside seven beautiful trees planted in honour of the victims. He read out each name on the plaque before him and quietly reflected on those who had lost their lives and on his own pain, before wondering how the families were coping.

He still visits the memorial from time to time, and over the years he's watched the trees grow; each one reminds him of the beauty of life but also the sorrow of loss. The last time he went to the memorial was in 2003. He was amazed at the size of the trees; it was obvious that the site had been lovingly cared for. As Geoff looked up at the trees, he realised that he had grown too. In coming to terms with his grief, he now knew that it would never pass.

In the months after the crash, Geoff sat down and, during the long preparation of the Coroner's brief, went over every technical detail again and again. This sorting and evaluating of photographs and evidence brought back strong memories not only of the day of the incident, but of the post-mortem examinations and the families' grief afterwards. During this time, he developed a fear of light aircraft, which has developed into a general phobia of flying, in particular of flying in dangerous weather.

On 6 June 1996 in Sydney, some three long years after the Young plane disaster, Coroner John Gould handed down his findings into the tragic circumstances surrounding the crash. His report was highly critical of Monarch Airlines, the CAA and the Air Transport Council.

He found that there were several reasons why the disaster had occurred. The deregulation of the Australian airline industry in the 1980s set the scene for a reduction in standards of small commercial airlines. Commercial considerations, such as the fostering of competition, flights to more specific destinations and lower fares, were placed above safety. Safety budgets were slashed, allowing unfinancial operators to operate unsafe fleets. The other glaring hole the new guidelines left was the Australian Transport Council not considering an operator's financial fitness when it was applying for a commercial flying licence. Between 1991 and 1997, safety regulatory staff were cut by a massive 191 personnel, meaning the individual airlines had more responsibility to make inspections and generally maintain safety standards.

The CAA inquiry into the accident reported that Monarch Airlines was in breach of several regulations and that the *Piper*

Chieftain was inadequately maintained. Some of the instruments that were inoperable on the day of the accident were the compass, the horizontal indicator, the altimeter and the autopilot; however, the CAA had given permission for the carrier to fly as long as it had two functioning controls operated by two pilots. Pilots desperate to accumulate flying hours were willing to work without pay for Monarch as co-pilots, further jeopardising passenger safety. With inoperable equipment, bad weather and having to fly into darkness, the attempt to make a pilot-controlled flight into terrain landing spelled disaster. Pilot error and equipment failure were at the core of the disaster, but stricter regulations would have prevented it.

Insurance also became an issue. The victims' families found themselves without cover when the company that insured the airline stated that because Monarch had not maintained adequate safety standards, they voided their cover. Legislation has now been implemented to stop insurance companies avoiding their responsibilities. Finally, as a direct result of the Monarch Airlines disaster, the Commonwealth government established a new airline safety regulatory body, the Civil Aviation Safety Council, which would replace the old CAA.

9

LOST IN THOUGHT

Jocelyn observed that Geoff didn't return to normal for some time after the Young plane crash; he was distant and often lost in his thoughts. It was during this time that she realised he had stopped talking to her about his work, but she didn't attach a great deal of importance to it. It was a busy time for her, as she was preoccupied with their baby daughter, Emily, who was born on 3 December 1993. Still, having worked in the funeral industry Jocelyn was well aware of the bereaveds' grief and trauma. She felt equipped not only to listen but to understand Geoff's role as a crime-scene examiner. Jocelyn also appreciated the need for whatever he told her to remain strictly confidential. She'd always made herself available to discuss any of Geoff's concerns or thoughts about his work but, since Emily had come along, she simply didn't get around to inquiring why Geoff no longer talked to her about his job.

Jocelyn did notice, more than ever before, Geoff's absence from home. He seemed to go from one job to the next, and she became accustomed to doing things on her own. She also knew that Geoff was spending even more time at the pub; it got to the stage that she didn't know where he was, if he was at work or not. Her concern grew when she realised that Geoff was taking on even more job-related responsibility.

In early 1994, the NSW Police Association, in a combined initiative with the police welfare section, introduced a peer support scheme. Geoff decided to volunteer to become a police peer support officer (PSO). He had realised that support networks within the service were all but nonexistent and that this was his opportunity to make a difference. He knew that he was well versed to help others; he'd had plenty of experience in dealing with trauma and could understand how fellow officers in need were feeling. However, taking on this role would only burden him further when he was in great need of support himself.

Even before Geoff officially became a peer support officer he had been performing the role for years. His colleagues would often go to him for advice and emotional support after facing traumatic incidents. He had also been a police association branch delegate for a few years, having initially been elected to the state executive in 1989. Geoff's working-class background helped give him a broad understanding of the many issues his workmates faced, and he became a strong and worthy advocate. He had a straightforward sense of justice and always treated others the way he wanted to be treated himself.

A prime example of Geoff's commitment to helping others occurred when he attended Junee Gaol to investigate the murder of a twenty-year-old prisoner who'd been stabbed to death while in custody. The prisoner in question was doing time for armed robbery, drugs and serious assault matters, and was tattooed with the words 'I hate cops'. He also had Hepatitis B, which, obviously, put Geoff at risk while handling the body.

After thoroughly examining the stabbing scene at the gaol, and without taking a break, Geoff set off for the five-hour journey to Sydney to accompany the body to the morgue. (All post-mortems involving a death in custody are performed in Sydney, rather than the smaller mortuaries, such as the one at Junee.) Once he was at Glebe, the officer in charge of the case, as well as the senior psychologist and grief counsellor in the forensic medicine division, asked Geoff if he could meet the man's family and assist them during the viewing of the body.

When the relatives arrived, the parents asked a number of questions and, during this time, their teenage son stood glaring at Geoff with all the hatred for police his older brother had had. Geoff explained to them why they were not permitted to have a contact viewing with their son, whose body was now being held pending the murder investigation; until all evidence had been collected, it was necessary to avoid close contact. The family understood and accepted the situation. When the time came for the viewing, though, the boy was obviously distressed. Without hesitation, Geoff went to him and slid his arm around his shoulders, holding him while he said goodbye to his dead brother.

During the killer's trial, Geoff got to know the family well, and the deceased's mother offered him her sincere thanks for the way he had helped her younger son when they were at the morgue. She told him how much it had meant to her to have compassion shown to her family, even though her dead son had obviously hated police and been in a lot of trouble with the law. She told him that his gesture had an enormous impact on her younger son. It was times like this that Geoff realised why he had joined the police force in the first place.

Training for the original group of PSOs consisted of a three-day course conducted at the Goulburn Police Academy. It was developed and run by the police psychologist of the welfare section, David Mutton, and focused on teaching the participants how to look for and identify specific psychological issues and about the impact of trauma on their colleagues. In a nutshell, the key role PSOs were trained to perform was to listen, assess and refer for internal counselling.

The peer support scheme was very well received, and Geoff believed it was an important step in assisting police to cope with workplace stress; however, he would soon realise that it was under-resourced and understaffed. He had been told that there would be follow-up from the welfare section psychologists, who would monitor his role as a PSO and give assistance where required. He was also told there would be more courses for the PSOs. The backup, monitoring, assistance and future courses never eventuated, though. It was obvious to Geoff that funding simply wasn't adequate to run the initiative properly.

Former British police officer Commissioner Peter Ryan was then at the helm of the NSW Police and didn't appear to be committed to the peer support scheme. He commented at a graduation ceremony for new probationary constables at the Goulburn Police Academy that he just wanted the new constables to give him five years' service. The peer support scheme, on the other hand, aimed to assist police better to manage their mental health, therefore encouraging long and healthy careers.

When Geoff was working with the police association state executive he was disappointed at the force's upper echelon's obvious lack of commitment to supporting PSOs, and he almost walked away from the idea of working in peer support. After much consideration, and discussion with other members of the executive, he chose to battle on, believing that if he gave up he would be just as bad as those higher up who didn't back the initiative. As well, Geoff was acutely aware of the needs of those working on the front line, and, ultimately, didn't want to let his workmates down, even if he had to be involved in peer support in his own time and on his own initiative. He continued his work as a PSO even though he was resigned to the fact that support wouldn't be available to him if he needed it. He can only remember one or two calls from the police welfare section to see how he was going as a PSO. Over time, Geoff came to expect no more from the welfare section and just got on with the job.

As well, as part of Geoff's police association work, his colleagues would come to him for advice on industrial issues. Their discussion of these concerns would often flow over into their fears and worries. Geoff realised that internal welfare services were often inadequate so, as he had been taught in the PSO course, he would refer his colleagues to external psychological assistance. He would also do follow-up with these officers, checking on their welfare at regular intervals. Geoff advised female police officers, too, giving them guidance and advice about women's issues and unfair treatment. He kept all conversations completely confidential. The fear of what they said being reported was one of the reasons many police did not seek help; however, they knew that anything they said to Geoff would stay strictly between them.

It was dedicated people such as Geoff who helped peer support develop into the lifeline it is today. Now, there are a thousand officers performing the role of PSO statewide. Their training is much more intensive, with a specific focus on coping with the effects of critical incident stress; communication and listening skills; problem solving; cognitive aspects of managing stress; suicide awareness;

addictive behaviours; respiratory training and relaxation; ongoing training; and regular reviews and development. This means PSOs are trained to be both proactive and reactive in assisting colleagues to deal with stress and seek early intervention in a crisis. Their role includes offering information about internal health services, such as the healthy lifestyle branch, the psychology branch and the chaplaincy, as well as external services such as the employee assistance branch. PSOs also have twenty-four-hour backup, with consultation, referral and other resources available to them, and they undergo consultations with the PSO coordinator and psychologists when required. To stay on the program, PSOs must now attend monthly meetings, take part in six-monthly training days or participate in an annual PSO conference.

There are now many highly trained and committed officers working as PSOs to assist their colleagues when stressful situations have placed them under enormous physical and emotional strain. This work is done without additional payment or incentives, showing the dedication of those who commit to doing it purely to help others. This reflects a big change from the 1980s and early 1990s, when officers were expected to cope with workplace stress by drinking and adopting the 'stiff upper lip' approach. As Police Commissioner Ken Moroney would say in 2007, 'It's okay for police to cry.' This highlighted the realisation that police are not robots or superhumans, but real people who react to real situations.

As 1994 continued, Joe Lavin left the crime-scene unit to pursue a career at the Coroner's office in Sydney and was replaced by Constable Scott Coleman. Geoff was glad to have Scott on staff, as he was already a trained and competent crime-scene examiner. He and

Scott got along well and shared the load by attending call-outs one week on, one week off. Geoff was able to leave Scott in charge and continue his work with the police association as well as fulfil his commitments with the physical evidence section. He often attended the monthly PES supervisors meetings by flying to Sydney for the day in his own time. At other times, he drove to Sydney and stayed for two days in order to attend the bimonthly association executive meeting, or to attend and adjudicate on appeals at the Government and Related Employees Appeals Tribunal (GREAT). There were particular issues facing country police, particularly isolation and lack of resources, and Geoff enjoyed his work as advocate for his colleagues in Wagga. He also sat on internal committees, took part in focus groups and helped coordinate work with the Salvation Army. He assisted during the periodical reviews into the physical evidence section's management, which meant sitting on a committee that examined such issues as changing forensic police from plainclothes to uniformed officers, and other general practices. Geoff later instigated the Forensic Services Focus Group, along with Terry O'Connell, which was headed by Detective Inspector Mark Edwards.

As a result of the Gibson Review into the running of the scientific investigation section in Sydney, many changes were made to how each crime-scene unit operated around the state and to whom they were responsible. The review's ninety-two recommendations were handed down in a 1990 report that covered such areas as proposed structural changes, equipment, training, staff wellbeing, and facility upgrades. Specifically the physical evidence section took on some of the scientific investigation section's responsibilities, but the suburban and country crime scene units were accountable at a local level. This meant the Wagga crime-scene unit was responsible to the major crime squad, south-west. Geoff was now answerable to three different supervisors: the superintendent in charge of the major crime squad, south-west; the commander in charge of the physical evidence section in Sydney; and the commander in charge of Wagga. Geoff also took on the role of zone supervisor, which meant supervising all the crime scene examiners attached to Wagga, Griffith and Broken Hill.

Due to funding issues, the Wagga crime-scene unit was known as a 'State Scarce Resource', which meant payment for equipment and training was centrally funded but overtime and travelling allowances were funded from the district budget. On average, Geoff was working sixty-five hours per week and typically working on about twenty jobs at any given time. He was earning a lot of overtime pay, which he often wouldn't claim in order to avoid conflicts with management. Even though Geoff didn't claim all his overtime, he was the highest paid officer in the district between 1988 and 1990, showing the sheer volume of hours he worked. He was typically called out more than once in a twenty-four-hour period, meaning that he missed out on an eight-hour break and, at times, survived on just a couple of hours sleep.

It was also time for Geoff to think about promotion and further study. Policing had changed dramatically since the mid 1980s, when the old positional promotion system became obsolete and was replaced with a merit-based system. Geoff knew if he wanted to move through the ranks he'd have to think about gaining tertiary qualifications. First, he enrolled in a Diploma in Professional Leadership and Management at TAFE, which meant studying via distance learning for three semesters and then attending a face-to-face residential component at Strathfield. He also enrolled, as part of the inaugural group of thirty forensic police, for the Diploma of

Applied Science in Forensic Investigation (NSW Police). This was a four-year course undertaken through distance learning, with a residential block of two weeks' face-to-face study in Canberra twice a year.

If Geoff had thought he was stretched for time before he undertook the diploma, he found out quickly that this added workload would take things to a whole new level; he was working harder than he'd ever done before. For several weeks in mid-1995 he also took on the role of relieving staff officer, operations/intelligence, at the rank of inspector. All this meant that Geoff was left with virtually no time to spend with his family. Any nights or days off he had he now spent studying or completing assignments. He also began to bring work home, often asking Jocelyn to help him prepare statements for court.

Geoff had come to realise that police work was cyclical. When there was a full moon, serious jobs would flow as they did at no other time. Just as the moon cycle would influence the general public's behaviour, so, too, would it affect police – Geoff referred to this syndrome as the 'Coppers' Full Moon'. At this time, he would be at his lowest. He would fixate on horrific crime scenes, which would play over and over in his mind as he suffered in silence. Added to this was the time and distance he spent on the road. During a full moon, he would spend hours driving, with a head full of ideas about how and why these tragic incidents had occured. The further he had to drive, the more his mind would play tricks on him, to the brink of insanity. Often his thoughts would drift to the deaths of children; sometimes he would lay blame on their parents or other family members, only to realise later how wrong he had been.

Geoff was only just holding his head above water. He found drinking to be his one and only escape from the constant demands of work and study; he could simply sit in silence and clear his mind while he downed a few beers. The problem was that the one or two drinks he had once had were escalating to five or six. With a baby at home, full-time crime-scene work, and twenty-four-hour call-out every second week combined with tertiary study, Geoff was clearly working above and beyond the call of duty. Yet he always thought about the horrors he'd seen and maintained the attitude, 'There but for the grace of God go I.'

10

THE COOLAMON AIR CRASH

At 9 p.m on 28 July 1995, Geoff was called to yet another plane crash. This time the accident occurred in a paddock some sixty kilometres from Wagga and about fifteen kilometres north-east of Coolamon, when a Cessna 310 was attempting to land at Wagga Airport. Just as was the case with the Young air crash two years before, the weather was dismal, with freezing conditions, driving rain and a howling wind.

Geoff made his way to the scene immediately. When he arrived, he was shocked to discover the plane's wreckage stretched over a huge area of about 500 square metres. Initially, it looked as if it had disintegrated in midair, resulting in four distinct crash sites. The main fuselage had landed in one area, with the pilot entangled in the wreckage. The other three sites contained the partial bodies of each of the three passengers. Such was the impact that each body had made a crater in the ground, and arms and legs had been torn away. As Geoff peered into the fuselage, he was struck by the strong odour of aviation fuel combined with the distinct smell of blood, a mixture that instantly took him back to the air disaster at Young.

A cold chill ran over his body as he stood contemplating by the light of his torch the awful sight of what appeared to be a large section of torso and a severed piece of a moustached lip. He realised quickly that nothing more could be done until first light, and that it was pointless struggling with the wet and dark conditions. He began organising a guard to attend and secure the site until daylight. As the initial group of police stood by the crash site, a number of foxes began to dart about the open paddock, obviously moving towards the bodies. The guard used a spotlight to stun and ward off the pack until the following day, when Geoff and BASI could begin their investigation. Geoff also began organising assistance from Sydney, asking for the photogrammetry and video units to attend the following day. He arranged to meet the BASI representative at the site in the morning, too.

News of the accident spread quickly and the pilot's and passengers' names were established from the outset. Geoff was saddened to learn that he knew all four passengers, in particular, Dallas Gooden, forty-two, a stock buyer from Wagga, whom he'd befriended while doing community work. The other two victims were locals Bruce Campbell, fifty-four, a stock and station agent; and his son-in-law, David Larwood, thirty-three, a bricklayer. The man who had flown the plane, Don Knight, sixty-four, was a well-respected local pilot with an impeccable flying record. His wife, Morna, had spoken to him via mobile shortly before the accident. During the conversation, Don had mentioned he was having problems with the plane's electrical circulatory system and that he'd lost the artificial horizon on his navigational system.

At daybreak, Geoff returned to the scene and initially walked the length of the entire crash site, scanning the pockets of twisted metal and checking that the bodies were still intact. Satisfied, he returned to the wagon, pulled out a full protective suit and slipped it over his overalls. He then sectioned off the entire area containing evidence, by smashing small stakes into the ground and attaching to them a string line, which divided each area into a well-formed grid pattern. Pulling on industrial-strength rubber gloves, he placed DVI numbers over each victim's wrist or ankle. Tags were attached separately to severed body parts until all persons were identified by sequential numbers.

By now the video and photogrammetry personnel had arrived and got to work recording the scene, first on videotape and then using a large tripod to position the photogrammetry camera, with measured cones positioned at one- and ten-metre intervals. Geoff walked alongside the photogrammetry operator, helping to carry the tripod after each three-dimensional photograph was taken and then repositioning the camera for the next series of photographs.

As the photogrammetry operator packed his equipment away, Geoff returned to the car and retrieved the camera kit, opening it and connecting the flash to the camera body before filling it with fresh film. He fumbled over the film, making several attempts to load it with his frozen hands that wouldn't do what his mind wanted them to do. He returned to the scene and took photographs over the entire sectioned area, focusing in and out as he caught all the evidence on film. Unlike Young, where resources were scarce, this scene had plenty of personnel and equipment; Geoff moved through each phase of the investigation quickly and easily. Something he hadn't dealt with before, however, was having a personal attachment to each of the victims. He constantly pushed such thoughts aside, preferring not to connect a name with the remains he was working with.

Finally, when Geoff had collected all the evidence, it was time to remove the bodies. He gently picked up each dismembered part, as well as flesh and bone, trying his best to collect as much of each body as was physically possible and placing everything into the appropriate body bag. Recovering the pilot's body was particularly difficult; each of the recovery crew carefully lifted a segment and, in unison, extricated it from the fuselage. Afterwards, Geoff returned his focus to the remnants, which had shredded into mincemeat. He bent and picked up clumps by hand in an effort to make sure the body was complete. By late afternoon, all deceased persons were loaded into a refrigerated van in readiness for transportation to Sydney, where the post-mortems would be conducted at the city morgue the following day.

Geoff got an early start the next morning and, with fingerprint expert Senior Constable Mark Sykes, set off for the five-hour journey to Glebe. On arrival, they entered the large refrigerated holding area, where they saw the four body bags lined up on trolleys against the wall.

The same forensic odontologist with whom Geoff had clashed during the Young plane-crash victims' post-mortem examinations was in charge. He was about to begin the dental identification of all four bodies and, no doubt, cut the jaws from each. When he greeted Geoff, a vision of the young girl who'd died from horrific burns the day after the Young plane disaster flashed before Geoff's eyes. The deep-seated anger he had harboured after the odontologist's insistence that the child's jaw be excised in order to perform dental identification rose from the pit of his stomach. His mood changed: suddenly, he was cold, tired and pissed off. *Fuck this*, he thought. *I'm sick of this shit; it's just all total shit, fucking bullshit.* He turned away to hide his reaction and, with his head down, moved aside to let the man pass.

Geoff stared at the odontologist's back as he prepared the first body. As the body bag was opened, the odontologist announced it contained the body of Mr Larwood. Geoff looked at the remains and knew instinctively that it was not David Larwood, but Dallas Gooden.

'No it's not,' he said.

Mark interjected, 'No, it's not Mr Larwood, it's Dallas Gooden; that's Mr Larwood over there.' He pointed to one of the bodies on the other side of the room.

The ordontologist argued. 'That is Mr Larwood!'

'I'm fucking telling you, that is Dallas Gooden; he only had about this much of his face left. Dallas Gooden was a mate of mine – we've identified him from his fingerprints!' Geoff yelled.

The odontologist glared at Geoff, apparently recalling their previous disagreement as he realised Geoff was right. 'Oh, I must have made a mistake from the dental records. Never mind,' he replied, doing his best to play down his error.

Geoff couldn't hide his contempt and glared at the doctor; this wasn't about the job any more – it was about a mate. He was fucked if he was going to let this man treat his friend with such disregard. He wanted to yell, 'Make him wake up and open his eyes. They've got it wrong!' His dark mood sank to a new low, and he still had four post-mortems ahead of him.

Throughout the day, Geoff picked up the camera again and again, focusing on the bloodied remains and recording each phase of the multiple post-mortems. He spoke in hushed tones as the pathologist questioned him about what body parts had come from where and about how he'd located each piece at the scene in relation to each body. Geoff was relieved when the last body was returned to the refrigerated storage area and he was free to go.

Packing up his equipment, he walked from the main autopsy area to the change rooms, where he ripped off his gown and the booties covering his shoes. He stood at the basin scrubbing his hands and throwing cold water on his face to erase the stench of the morgue. Mark then entered, and the two men chatted for a moment before leaving. Meanwhile, back in Wagga, a debrief was underway for all police who had attended the tragedy; that is, of course, everyone except for Geoff and Mark, who were labouring over the shattered remains of their friends.

That evening, Geoff and Mark drove the short distance to Mark's parents' house in the inner western Sydney suburb of Canterbury, as they planned to stay the night before driving back to Wagga in the morning. Geoff suggested a drink at the local RSL, so they headed there for a beer. Once there, Mark realised he didn't have any money, as he'd rushed straight from home to the accident scene and hadn't had time to get his wallet. As luck had it, Geoff had grabbed a $50 note before leaving home and had shoved it into his overalls pocket. He dug deep and found the note, but quickly realised it was soiled with body fluids, and God knows what else, from the scene and from the morgue. It was far too dirty to use.

'We can't use this!' Geoff exclaimed. 'We'll have to wash it. It's filthy.'

Mark peered at the dirty note as the two men discussed what to do. They then walked the short distance to the men's toilet, where Geoff placed the note in soapy water in the hand basin and scrubbed it clean. Afterwards, they held it under the hand drier until it was dry. Each time someone entered, they'd turn their backs and hide the note from view, and got more than a few funny looks in the process. Once it was dry, Geoff commented that the note was a 'stiff fifty'. They couldn't help but laugh as they realised the irony of the situation. The previous twenty-four hours had been hell on earth; all they wanted was a beer and even that seemed an arduous task.

At the bar, Geoff placed the $50 note on the bench and ordered two beers. While they waited to be served, the note curled around the edges into a stiffened form unlike anything they'd seen before. As the barman picked up the note, he gave Geoff a weird look but didn't say a word.

On his return to Wagga, Geoff went straight to the station, where, he was told, the relatives were waiting to attend the crash scene. He drove to the site and stood waiting in the cold until the relatives arrived. After answering a number of questions, he solemnly escorted the grieving group to the crashed plane. While standing there, he caught sight of particles of body tissue and blood scattered about; the remnants of those who had been killed were clearly visible. He quickly steered a nearby woman away in a bid to protect her. His chest ached at the prospect of those present seeing the legacy of the accident; he just wanted to get them out of there but had to allow them time to work through their feelings. He struggled to maintain his composure, but his anxiety was ballooning. Grief was rising from the pit of his stomach and shock was setting in.

When he eventually arrived home, Geoff disappeared to sit on the back step and drink a six pack of beer alone. As Jocelyn watched Geoff staring off into space, her heart sank. He clearly didn't want to discuss this latest tragedy and she didn't know what to do. Jocelyn had known Bruce Campbell well, as he had been friends with her boss, and she had been involved with the funeral arrangements. She had her own distress to deal with but was worried about Geoff – he was grieving for a friend but wasn't permitted to feel the way any normal person would after losing a mate. Instead, he had to function as the local policeman and get on with things.

Over the ensuing weeks, Geoff struggled to deal with the families' grief, which challenged his usual professional distance. At the end of each day, he would grab a six pack, take it outside, and drink in peace while just staring blankly. Finally, Jocelyn spoke to him about his drinking and obvious inability to talk about what was troubling him, saying, 'Geoff, you've got to do something about this.'

These simple words played on Geoff's mind, but he was struggling to get a decent night's sleep and would often wake in a lather of sweat that drenched the bedsheets. As well, he was often called out the minute he had slumped into bed. He was so exhausted, he couldn't summon the strength even to think about how he might be able to help himself.

Two months later, he got a call to say the police psychologist wanted to speak with him about the Coolamon plane crash. He also received a call from the psychology unit, where a debrief was set up that would include Mark Sykes, as well as the other crime-scene examiner working in the Wagga office, Scott Coleman, and a psychologist, Senior Sergeant Jennifer Lette from the welfare branch. The debrief went for approximately ten minutes and at its conclusion each of the police officers present was given a relaxation tape. Geoff presumed this was the debrief he'd missed out on when he was at the post-mortems; it seemed to be a little late, but who was he to question something he had little experience or knowledge of, he thought.

Next, Geoff tackled the complex brief of evidence. He'd had to do this for the Young plane crash two years earlier, and here he was again dealing with distressing details of how four innocent people lost their lives. He had to go over all the photographs time and time again while typing his statement and collating the evidence as he'd found it at the scene. Raw and vivid memories of the Young plane crash came flooding back.

The smell of aviation fuel invaded Geoff's mind and seemed to became almost real. To him, flying was becoming less a mode of transport than a dark and dangerous activity that involved him in a personal and distressing way.

11

LOSING FRIENDS

Between 1989 and 1995, Geoff worked in a number of relieving positions that strengthened his prospects for promotion to a commissioned rank. Amongst them were staff officer (operations/intelligence), staff officer (personnel), patrol tactician and duty officer, all at the rank of inspector. In early 1996, he applied for the position of inspector (staff officer, personnel) and shortly afterwards became an incremental sergeant. He also graduated with a Diploma of Applied Science in Forensic Investigation (NSW Police). On 13 April 1997, Thomas, his and Jocelyn's second child, was born, and Geoff's life went on as before, work taking precedence over everything else.

During the mid to late nineties, he was called to a number of serious incidents that involved close personal friends. It would have been preferable for him to have handed these jobs over but locally there wasn't another suitably trained crime scene officer who didn't know the victims or their families and who could attend. Staffing was at a critical low. Geoff found the emotional burden of investigating such crimes overwhelming and, with no real coping strategies, struggled to maintain his sanity.

One wet November evening in 1995, Geoff received a call to attend a suicide involving a male on a property just outside town. The address was in an industrial area where a couple of houses were peppered among the various industry sheds and businesses. Mark Ingram popped into Geoff's mind, as he remembered he lived out that way. Just as he rounded the bend close to the house, he realised the victim had to be Mark. Again, though, he thought to himself, *Don't be ridiculous – it must be someone else.* As he entered the driveway he recognised Mark's car. Then he also saw the tow truck of his friend and colleague John Yerbery parked in the driveway. As Geoff walked to the front door, John came out and said, 'I can't believe it, Geoff.'

The general duties officer ushered him inside, where he saw Mark's girlfriend, Tracy, pacing the floor, frantic and incoherent. Nearby was her sister, who had been having dinner with them that evening. Geoff asked Tracy what happened and, through bouts of uncontrollable sobbing, she explained the horrible details of how Mark had taken his own life.

During the meal, the three had consumed alcohol. As the night wore on, an argument developed. Tracy explained that Mark had suffered from depression and that once the disagreement flared, he had become agitated, eventually threatening to kill himself. He said that he had a gun in the house and warned them he would use it. Shortly afterwards, he disappeared and returned holding a rifle.

The two woman began to panic. Tracy told Geoff that she had frantically tried to talk to Mark, asking him to give up the gun, but he refused and, before she knew it, he had vanished out through the back door. The two women had followed, calling to him to calm down and come back inside. As Mark got to the pool gate, he had turned, looked at Tracy, placed the rifle to his head and pulled the trigger, blowing the whole side of his face off.

Tracy was now sobbing, slumped on the lounge holding her head in her hands. Geoff went to her but, with the shock cutting him deeply, struggled to speak. After a few minutes, he explained that he would have to go and look at what Mark had done.

Geoff walked to the back pool area, where two ambulance officers were waiting who showed him where Mark's body was. As he approached, he saw the body lying face up against the pool fence. By Mark's side was the high-calibre rifle he'd used to end his life. It was a dismal and wet night, the drizzling rain soaking Mark's body as he lay in the elements. Dread rose in Geoff but there was no time to process what had happened; he just had to collect the evidence and record the scene as though it were any other suicide. For a minute, though, he stood staring in a daze, as it dawned on him that it was so easy to cross the line from policeman to friend.

Geoff told the ambulance officers that they could go, and that he would call the government contractors, who would take the body to the morgue once he'd completed his examination. Geoff then went back to the car and collected the camera kit and a folder to take notes. Standing beside the body he began with such details as the time and date of the incident, the position of the body and calibre of the weapon. On autopilot, he prepared the camera and walked around snapping shots of the overall scene, and then close-ups showing the details.

Donning rubber gloves, he crouched over the body and closely examined the head injuries, checking for consistency with the weapon's position. He then rolled the body over, and looked for other injuries or signs of trauma. He found nothing except the catastrophic blow to the head where the projectile had torn Mark's face apart. On the concrete path nearby were globules of brain matter, which Geoff scraped into a paper bag to save anyone else seeing them. (Later, he also went into the house to get cleaning materials with which he thoroughly washed the outside area once the body had been removed.) He rendered the weapon safe and placed it in a large paper bag, to be forwarded to the ballistics section in Sydney. The government contractors arrived and hovered about until Geoff gave them the order to take the body away. As he packed his equipment up he saw them placing a large plastic sheet on the ground and lifting the body onto the sheet. Mark was wrapped and placed on the waiting trolley, wheeled to their van and taken inside, in readiness to be transported to the hospital for life to be pronounced extinct.

Once the body was gone, Geoff re-entered the house and sat beside Tracy on the lounge. He explained that Mark had been taken to the hospital, where a doctor would confirm he was dead, and that he would then be transported to the morgue, after which, in a day or two, there'd be a post-mortem examination to establish the exact cause of death. She could make funeral arrangements in the interim but would have to wait until the Coroner released the body before setting a date. Tracy asked if she could see Mark one last time to kiss him goodbye. Geoff gently explained the severity of Mark's facial injuries in a bid to dissuade her; however, she pleaded to have one last moment with him. Geoff promised he'd do his best, and agreed to meet her at the hospital once a doctor had pronounced life extinct. Geoff then asked John if he could take Tracy and her sister to the hospital.

Once at the hospital, the resident grief counsellor approached Geoff and asked if he could assist the family with the viewing of the body. He argued that he knew the family and would prefer to keep some distance but she insisted that he was the only person who could help. The discussion became heated, until finally Geoff agreed to assist. He was mindful that the grief counsellor's own partner had committed suicide a few years before and that this was obviously still very raw for her.

He reluctantly followed the body to the morgue, where it lay on a steel trolley as the paperwork was prepared. Geoff put on a gown and rubber gloves before signing the body register. The morgue attendant unzipped the bag and Geoff searched the body for personal effects. He then set about cleaning and preparing the deceased for viewing. Geoff had hoped to cover the damaged side of Mark's face in an effort to allow Tracy the opportunity to give him one final kiss on the cheek. He pulled the skin up over the wound so the other side of the face was less distorted, pulling and stretching until he was satisfied with the result. Geoff assisted Tracy to the viewing space; she was still hysterical and tearful, and he felt his own distress rising as he struggled to give comfort and prepare her for what she was about to see. *Hold it together*, he thought. He held Tracy as they approached the dead man. She slumped forward, and Geoff drew back the sheet and held onto her tightly as she bent and kissed him goodbye. He led her, sobbing, back into the waiting room, where she collapsed into a chair. That night as Geoff lay awake going over and over the scene at the morgue, he couldn't get the picture of the crying woman out of his mind as his own tears flowed.

After Mark's death, the service station closed and was eventually bulldozed. It saddened Geoff to see the vacant lot in disrepair, with the piles of rubbish and overgrown grass a constant reminder of Mark's death. In life, he had kept everything in pristine order. A prime block of land had gone to waste, as had Mark's life. Geoff still drives past the site several times a week and each time he does, he can't help but think of Mark and what might have been.

In March 1998, Geoff was called to the scene of the murder of the local football strapper and masseuse, his friend Merv Alchin.

Merv had agreed to allow a talented young footballer from Darling Point in Melbourne to live in his house while he played for the local club. The house was right in central Wagga and Merv would often go home from his plastering job for lunch. On this occasion, he went home for lunch and the young boarder confronted him in the laundry, taking him by surprise. In a frenzied assault, he stabbed Merv with a knife multiple times. Merv was disembowelled and left to bleed to death on the floor. The next-door neighbour rang the police after hearing a ruckus from inside the house and identified his neighbour's voice when he heard him screaming out for help.

Geoff was relieving as the local patrol tactician and immediately set off to supervise the scene. He arrived at the premises within minutes of the original call and was led straight to the laundry. He saw the body of his friend Merv, who had obviously bled to death after the offender had fled. Geoff was in shock and didn't know what to do; he just kept shaking his head and trying to take it all in. After a minute or so, he stepped further inside the small laundry, where Merv's body lay in a pool of blood. He scanned the blood-soaked walls and the scuff marks in thick patches of blood on the floor. The sickening smell caused him to step back to get some clean air.

As the relieving inspector, Geoff was spared the task of investigating the scene and quickly called in his junior forensic colleague, Scott Coleman, as well as local fingerprint man Mark Sykes. Both investigators also knew Merv and when they arrived, Geoff tried to prepare them by giving them the details before they entered the scene. Scott thoroughly examined the scene, collecting evidence and making notes. Geoff checked on him from time to time, aware that working in such close confines with the body in the small laundry would be difficult; the worst aspect of this was that as the clots of blood dried they gave off a pungent odour.

While still at the scene, Geoff heard a call over the police radio requesting a car crew attend a serious motor vehicle accident nearby. A car matching the description of Merv's vehicle had collided head on with a tree and the sole occupant was seriously injured. Geoff answered the call, stating that he was on his way. With lights and sirens blazing he sped to the accident, and instantly recognised the smashed car as Merv's utility. He read out the number plate details over the police radio and the car was confirmed as Merv's, having obviously been stolen from his house a short time earlier. The driver was already en route to the local hospital by ambulance.

Geoff walked around the crashed car, inspecting the damage and looking for possible evidence. After assessing the scene, he went back to the police vehicle and radioed a message for Scott to attend as soon as possible. The area was now a secondary crime scene and vital to the investigation. Geoff called for a local car and a guard to be put in place before he left to drive to the hospital to speak with the offender.

Geoff went straight to Emergency and inquired after him, and was directed to a nearby bed. He approached the injured man, who was in his early twenties. After introducing himself and reading the official police caution, he asked, 'Did you kill Merv Alchin?'

The man's eyes glazed over and then almost bulged out of his head, sending a chill down Geoff's spine. He looked straight through Geoff and uttered in a slow steady voice, 'The Devil made me do it.'

He then described how he'd stabbed Merv more than eighteen times; a chilling account that made Geoff feel physically sick. The offender admitted having stolen Merv's ute with the intention of driving it into a tree in order to commit suicide. Later Geoff would learn that the young man had a lengthy history of mental illness; it was a pity Merv hadn't been warned of the mentally unstable timebomb in the shape of a strapping young footballer that he'd allowed to live in his home. Merv's generosity and love of football had ultimately led to him losing his life. Afterwards, Geoff radioed the station and asked the detectives to meet him at the hospital. Once they arrived they took over, after Geoff had given them the details and told them of the offender's confession. Geoff needed to keep moving, as he wanted to go straight to the school where Merv's partner worked.

Once at the school, the principal was summoned and quickly fetched Merv's partner from the classroom. She smiled when she saw Geoff but her expression changed quickly when she saw the solemn look on his face. Quietly, he gave her the terrible news; it was a shocking message to have to deliver but he felt it would be best if it came from someone she knew.

At the murder trial, the court heard that the attack on Merv was unprovoked. The offender subsequently pleaded guilty and was committed to a mental institution for life.

The day after Merv's death, Geoff made an appointment with his local GP, Dr Lennon. He felt numb but also preoccupied with the details of what he'd seen at the house that day and the sight of the offender's bulging eyes. His hands shook constantly and he was frightened that he was about to go right off the rails. He'd finally realised he needed help. Dr Lennon referred Geoff to Dr McGrath of St John of God Hospital in Burwood. He suggested that Geoff consider undergoing the live-in alcohol treatment program. Jocelyn had warned Geoff that the marriage was over unless he did something about getting help. Although he'd cut down on his drinking, he was still relying on alcohol to calm his nerves and help him sleep. Also, he had started sleeping in the office due to his problems at home. This made things worse, as he was now literally at work twenty-four hours a day.

Jocelyn could see Geoff was falling apart after Mark's suicide and Merv's murder. He was still consumed by work and falling deeper into what appeared to be a state of depression. Jocelyn had little knowledge of how to deal with this condition and didn't yet realise that Geoff was actually very ill. She couldn't reach him on an emotional level at all, and feared that he was close to physical and emotional collapse. She put this down to his years of sleep deprivation and that he appeared to cope with his never-ending work commitments without assistance from other sections. She also found Geoff's reaction to blowflies disturbing. He'd started to shake when he saw them and couldn't stand one to touch him. He'd yell, 'Rotten fucking flyblown bodies,' as he'd swat the blowflies away, snarling and gritting his teeth. Jocelyn was greatly relieved when Geoff sought help from Dr Lennon and was pleased he had been encouraged to attend the alcohol-treatment course at St John of God.

Although Geoff had finally reached out for help, he didn't really think his job was to blame. He was convinced that the way he was feeling was just a normal response to crime-scene work. He remembered Dave Frost's experiences and he'd spoken to colleagues who said they thought his response was normal. Geoff focused more on his marital problems, blaming his home life for how he was feeling; although he knew he felt some distress about work issues, he still didn't understand how that could make him depressed or feel unable to cope.

He would come to realise that perhaps his passion for and loyalty to police work was stopping him from thinking clearly about the type of pressure he was under. Unconsciously he pushed from his mind any connection between his work and his mental state, for fear of being judged or the threat of transfer. According to the police culture, cops didn't complain, because it was a sign of weakness. He didn't examine the underlying reasons for the gradual increase in his alcohol consumption. At this stage, Geoff couldn't see himself as anything other than a police officer and, after all the hard work of the past fifteen or so years, he didn't want to lose his opportunity for promotion. He was sure that if he could just get his marriage back on track, everything else would fall into place, so he was willing to do anything to patch things up with his wife.

A few weeks later, Geoff was admitted to the drug and alcohol unit at St John of God Hospital. He had decided to take annual leave and pay for the treatment himself, through his private medical fund. Geoff did this because of the police culture's unsympathetic attitude to stress leave. He still wanted to be a respected member of the force. Although Geoff's commander knew about his hospitalisation, nothing further was said, and nor was Geoff contacted or his welfare checked on.

When Geoff began the alcohol treatment program, the first thing that struck him was the state of some of the other participants, as he saw people experiencing the full effects of detoxification. He, on the other hand, felt a little unwell for a day or two, and after that coped physically very well. The program covered such areas as motivation for change; identifying the physical effects of alcohol and drugs; stress and its effects; refusal skills; urges and cravings; self-esteem; relapse prevention, and education of friends and family; and conflict management and listening. Participants were also introduced to Alcoholics Anonymous and encouraged to attend regular meetings.

Shortly after Geoff's admission, his treating doctor realised that he had a full-blown depressive disorder, and he was therefore treated with the antidepressant Luvox, or fluvoxamine. Geoff responded well to this medication and felt a degree of relief. If he had been placed in a depression or anxiety treatment group, he'd surely have been diagnosed with post-traumatic stress disorder (PTSD). Although the alcohol treatment program assisted him with his drinking, it didn't delve deeply enough into why he was drinking; it would have been helpful for him to have been placed in the PTSD program at Richmond after completing the program.

On 1 May, Geoff discharged himself from the program a week early and returned home to Jocelyn. He cut right back on his drinking and things gradually improved at home; by August, though, he realised that things were going downhill again. He began going to marital guidance alone in an attempt to resolve things with Jocelyn. During these sessions he mentioned a few work-related things to the counsellor and they discussed strategies for dealing with the emotional side of Geoff's job. This mainly concerned his inability to let go after having attended scenes at which people had died and trying to find ways for him to deal with these deaths. He and the counsellor also discussed the incidents involving his friends, and, again, talked about ways he could learn to cope and move on.

On 25 September Geoff was called to attend yet another incident where he knew the family involved. A four-year-old boy in the same preschool class as his daughter Emily had fallen from a tree and sustained life-threatening injuries. The child was swiftly taken via ambulance to Wagga Base Hospital, where the staff tried in vain to save his life.

When Geoff arrived at the scene and realised who the child was, he immediately felt the same dread he'd experienced attending those of the deaths of Mark Ingram and Merv Alchin. Still, he photographed the scene and made notes before driving to the hospital to examine the little boy.

When he arrived, he was sent to a private room, where he found the mother cradling the dead child in her arms. A grief counsellor was present and Geoff said to him that he thought he should do his examination as soon as possible. The grief counsellor wanted the mother to have more time with the child, which Geoff understood, but as time went on he became a little agitated. It wasn't only that he needed to examine the little boy to see what injuries he'd sustained; the mother's distress was tearing Geoff apart. After what seemed like an eternity, Geoff realised he'd have to try to get her to hand the child over.

He approached her and knelt down to make eye contact as she gripped the boy in her arms. Geoff quietly explained what he had to do and what would happen during the investigation. He also explained the process of the post-mortem and how long it would take. After he'd explained to her that they needed to do certain things in order to find out why her little boy had died, he asked if she'd like to say goodbye to her son now. As she handed him over, Geoff promised they'd have the little boy back to her in a couple of days, after they'd worked out exactly what had happened, so she could organise the funeral. He gently reached across and took the child from her, carried the body over to a stretcher, and covered him up before leaving to make his way to the morgue.

At the morgue, he checked the little boy in and commenced his examination, firstly unwrapping the hospital sheets and closely checking the body for injuries. The little body lay cold on the table as if he were sleeping on ice; Geoff's heart ached and he took the necessary photographs almost in a daze. Lastly, he made notes, concentrating on what was needed and trying not to think about his own, similarly aged child, before wrapping the little boy tightly and leaving him in the hands of the morgue attendant.

He then returned to the room in which the mother was still waiting with the grief counsellor. She told Geoff that she was in desperate trouble, as her husband was away on business in New Zealand and she couldn't get hold of him. A number of further phone calls were made and finally the child's father was located and given the terrible news. Shortly after, Geoff arrived at the family's house, where he was introduced to the child's grandfather, who had rushed to his daughter's side. There, Geoff made a number of inquiries to airlines regarding bookings on compassionate grounds for family members to fly directly to Wagga.

That evening at home, both Geoff and Jocelyn struggled with their grief; neither could help the other, as they were both consumed with sadness. Jocelyn was particularly affected as she met the little boy's mother through her work assisting with the funeral arrangements. Geoff grabbed a six pack and sat out on the back step alone, staring off into space. Later, he tucked his daughter into bed and hoped to God that nothing would happen to her. He couldn't help comparing the sight of his own beautiful child sleeping soundly with that of the awful scene with mother and child at the hospital earlier that day; the ache in his heart was so bad, he thought he might die. Suddenly, Geoff began to shake, and the tremor took hold of his entire body, lasting for only a few minutes but seeming like an eternity. In shocked disbelief, he wondered what was happening to him.

On the day of the accident, the child's body had been flown to the Glebe morgue and an autopsy performed. It was discovered that the little boy had died of a brain aneurysm that he had had at the very time he was climbing the tree. The fall was not the cause of death but secondary to the brain aneurysm. There was nothing anyone could have done to avoid the tragedy.

Geoff took the time to go to the family's house, and sat with them as he carefully explained the results of the post-mortem, which, at least, let them understand why they'd lost their son. He had earlier made arrangements to have the child's body flown back to Wagga as soon as the post-mortem was complete and, through sheer persistence, was able to organise its return by 9 p.m. of the night after the accident. Geoff also constantly checked on the family until the father arrived home from New Zealand.

A few days later, Geoff attended the funeral, which was held in Wagga's town centre. He wore his police uniform – something he hadn't done for years. It was a mark of respect, his way of honouring the little boy. Throughout the service he stood at the back of the church and, at its conclusion, as the tiny coffin made its way to the hearse in readiness for its final journey, he held close to his chest his own grief. As the family gathered around the funeral car, he walked to the next intersection and waited solemnly for the funeral procession to pass. As the hearse moved along the street, he stood on point duty and saluted the tiny casket, standing to attention until the hearse had disappeared from view.

That evening at home, Geoff, consumed with sadness, cradled his little daughter in his arms. He was on the brink of losing it but managed to keep it together somehow. *Have to be strong, I'm a cop. Shit, what's wrong with me? I shouldn't be feeling like this.*

Jocelyn had her own way of coping, which was to throw herself into supporting the little boy's mother. The two women became very close as together they worked through the ebb and flow of their grief.

Two days later, tragedy was to strike Jocelyn and Geoff yet again.

During 1998, Jocelyn had met Father Phil Price, an Anglican priest who often attended the funeral home where she worked. Whenever he called in, they always took the time to catch up. In September of that year, Father Phil invited Jocelyn's boss, along with Jocelyn and Geoff, to his home for dinner. Geoff felt a little uneasy at the beginning of the evening, but once Father Phil realised Geoff was a police crime-scene examiner they began talking about Geoff's work, and the priest was obviously fascinated.

Father Phil also talked of his love of light aircraft and, specifically, his ultralight airplane. Passionate about flying and loving anything to do with planes, he spent most of his leisure time working on and flying in his plane. Naturally, the conversation turned to the Young air disaster, and Father Phil asked Geoff a number of questions. Geoff explained what his role had been at the scene, and talked about his work both at the Young and the Coolamon air crashes.

Geoff asked Father Phil if he was interested in becoming involved with the spiritual care of police who'd been traumatised through their work. The priest was, and the two men swapped phone numbers and agreed to discuss it in the near future. After dinner, Father Phil gave Geoff a guided tour of the house, stopping to point out photographs of interest. In each of them the father was wearing his signature 'Biggles' hat and posing with an assortment of light aircraft. Father Phil asked if he could have a tour of the crime-scene office where Geoff worked. The two men made a date to do this, and Geoff hoped that he'd be seeing more of Father Phil; he admired his work and had enjoyed his company. A few weeks later, as arranged, Geoff showed Father Phil around the office, and they discussed again the possibility of him committing to providing pastoral care for the local police.

A week or so after this, Geoff was called to an ultralight aircraft crash at Lockhart. He was told that a local farmer had seen the crash and had raced to the scene. He had pulled the pilot clear of the wreckage just as the plane caught fire, but the pilot had died in the farmer's arms. When Geoff arrived at the scene, the local police told him the dead man was Father Phil Price. It had only been a week or two since they last spoke, and here he was, standing next to his new friend's body and the crumpled plane he'd so obviously cherished.

Suddenly, Geoff was struck with an overpowering sense of dread. How could he break the news to Father Phil's wife and family? It was an unbearable prospect. As he prepared his equipment, he felt physically sick, and as he looked at his hands, he saw they were trembling. It wasn't the scene itself that distressed him as much as the victim being a mate. He sat at the back of the wagon and took a minute to gather his thoughts, but knew there was no use prolonging things. He returned to the plane and took a number of photographs and measurements, and contacted the appropriate aviation authorities. Afterwards, he watched sadly as Father Phil's remains were sealed in a body bag and loaded into the government contractor's van.

Geoff later attended the morgue, where he met with Father Phil's wife and daughter. There were lots of tears and hugs, and he did his best to console them. He also helped prepare the body prior to the viewing and stood with the family for support while they said their goodbyes. Father Phil had been wearing his favourite 'Biggles' hat when he was killed. Geoff took it home and carefully washed it in soapy water so that he could return it to the relatives. The next day, he went to the family's home and handed them the hat. They passed it around until it reached Father Phil's daughter, who promptly put it on her head. It was a special moment. Later that day, though, Geoff attended the post-mortem examination, and witnessing the autopsy was pure hell for him. That same sense of dread rose from the pit of his stomach. He struggled to contain it; feeling like this seemed a world away from the dinner he'd enjoyed a couple of weeks before.

Over the next few weeks, Geoff and Jocelyn tried to cope with their sorrow. Jocelyn, in particular, was shattered by Father Phil's death, especially given the recent death of Emily's classmate. Geoff had an additional worry: Scott, his young colleague, was struggling with the news that his wife had been diagnosed with a malignant brain tumour. They had two small children, which made the whole situation even harder, and she had to travel to Sydney for treatment. Geoff was as supportive as possible but the workload was still heavy. As much as he would have liked to take Scott off call-out duties, there simply wasn't anyone else to do the work. Even with the two of them and the fingerprint expert, Mark Sykes, in the office, they were struggling to keep up.

Geoff was now, more than ever, troubled by insomnia. It was

difficult for him to get to sleep and, when he did finally drift off, he would only sleep for short bursts before waking up or having a nightmare. As well, he had lost his appetite and was eating very little. He would often drive many kilometres to attend jobs, and would only have water and cigarettes, forgoing food altogether. On such occasions, he'd have a sleep in the car before the long drive back into town.

As Geoff sat behind the wheel, mesmerised by the grey bitumen, he'd think about how he could simply run off the road and be dead in an instant. His constant morbid thoughts exhausted him, and he was looking dishevelled and was often unshaven. Jocelyn was distraught, but not one of his work superiors took the time to inquire how he was travelling. It seemed that as long as Geoff was getting the work done, nobody cared.

12

OPERATION MELBECK

As the spring of 1998 continued, Geoff was, at least, enjoying the warmer weather and having time out in his beloved garden on his days off; it was a welcome distraction from work, as he found that he could switch off and clear his head. One Sunday evening, his peace was disturbed by a call from police radio requesting he attend a small block of flats in Jack Avenue in order to investigate an elderly man's unusual death.

The premises were next to a school and consisted of four small 1960s-style housing-commission bedsit apartments in a red-brick complex. Geoff parked the crime-scene wagon behind the ambulance and walked the short distance to the front of the flat. The detectives were waiting at the door, and explained that the deceased's sister had a short time earlier discovered her brother dead inside the flat. Geoff could see the woman, who was standing, agitated and distressed, near the body. She was talking to the ambulance officers, who were trying to help her. Geoff immediately introduced himself, and explained why he was there and what he was about to do. He then guided her away from the body in an attempt to remove her from the scene, as he knew that having a relative there would only make the situation even more stressful, but she insisted on staying and remained in the background while the investigation took place.

Geoff saw the body of Peter Wennerbon, aged sixty-two, lying face up on the floor. His eyes immediately fixed on the man's trousers, which were down slightly. Did that mean someone else was involved in the death? Or had the deceased been drunk? His complexion was ruddy, and it appeared he had been a social drinker. Geoff thought that the scene was suspicious and he decided to call Doc Lennon to examine the body. However, the radio operator explained that the doctor was on leave. *Oh well,* Geoff thought, *I've done plenty of deaths without him.*

Geoff started by taking notes describing the neat and sparsely furnished room, and the absence of any indication of disturbance or of a struggle. There was no blood or signs of forced entry. After making a sketch and completing the notes, Geoff walked through the tiny apartment, recording the position and state of the body and photographing the room and contents. He put gloves on, and then bent beside the body and closely inspected it for signs of injury.

From the stiffness of the limbs it was obvious that rigor mortis had set in, and Geoff estimated that death had occurred within the past twenty-four hours. As he scanned the neck area, he saw a slight discolouration of the skin. Unsure what it was, he made a note of it and took a number of photographs. He picked up the man's hand, and closely examined the fingers and then the wrist area, where again he saw slight reddish discolouration. While this wasn't an indication of major trauma, he felt it was significant. After taking photographs of the marks, he rolled the body over and inspected the back area, pulling up the clothing and checking the skin. Lividity was present on the back, buttocks and lower limbs, indicating that the man had died in the position in which he'd been found.

Although Geoff didn't feel he'd seen anything significant, he thought it necessary to explain to the detectives what he'd found. The government contractor then removed the body and took it to Wagga Base Hospital, where the duty doctor would pronounce life extinct. Geoff sent a message for the doctor with the contractors, asking them to wait until he arrived so that he could point out the markings he'd located on the neck and wrist.

After packing up the equipment and loading the car, Geoff returned to the flat and spoke again with the deceased's sister, explaining to her as tactfully as possible both what he'd found and what would now happen with her brother's body. He told her that, as Dr Lennon was away, the post-mortem would be conducted in Sydney and that the body would be taken there as soon as transport was arranged. She seemed to calm down slightly after Geoff had explained things to her, and he was glad that she now understood the procedure regarding the post-mortem and, later, the report to the Coroner. Outside, Geoff told the detectives that he was finished with the scene and was heading to the hospital. He promised to call them as soon as he'd spoken to the duty doctor about the marks he'd seen on the dead man's neck and wrists. In the meantime, the detectives had begun canvassing the local area, interviewing neighbours and asking if anyone had heard a disturbance or seen anything suspicious.

At the hospital, Geoff spoke with the duty doctor, who went with him to examine the dead man. Geoff pointed out the marks he'd found on the body and then stood back while the doctor made her examination. She looked over the man's body, and then shone a small torch into each eye in search of pertechial haemorrhage. This would indicate possible strangulation; however, there were no signs of it at all. She concluded that she didn't think the marks on the neck and wrist were significant, pronounced life extinct and signed the appropriate paperwork. There was nothing more to be done and the body was transported to the hospital mortuary to await transportation to Sydney the following day.

A few days later, Geoff was in the office when the phone rang. It was the pathologist from Sydney calling about the post-mortem results. They indicated no definitive cause of death but there were signs of heart disease, which was described as a contributing factor. Therefore, the death was presumed non-suspicious. Geoff opened the file and marked it accordingly but something just didn't seem right. He wondered if the scene had been cleaned up, as his instincts told him all wasn't quite as it seemed.

About a week later, Scott Coleman was on call when he received a request to attend a small housing-commission flat in Phillip Avenue, Mount Austin, where the body of a thirty-three-year-old woman had been found in the bath. When at the scene, he was told that the victim suffered from epilepsy and was also slightly developmentally delayed. On first impressions, it was presumed she'd drowned in the bath after suffering an epileptic fit. Scott was guided to the bathroom, where he saw a woman's naked body submerged in the tub. Based on the last sighting of the deceased the evening before, it appeared she had been dead for less than twenty-four hours. He toyed with the idea that she had drowned due to having had a fit, but he wasn't convinced that was the case.

Scott systematically examined the unit for signs of a struggle, ransacking or forced entry, but found nothing to indicate a second person had been in there. He then recorded the scene photographically before starting his physical examination of the body. After doing the kitchenette, living and bedroom areas, he returned to the bathroom and focused on the deceased woman, shooting a number of photographs from different angles to show the body's position in relation to the bath and its surrounds.

A short time later, two men arrived from the government undertakers to assist with the removal of the body. After a short conversation regarding the scene, Scott asked the two men to remove the deceased from the bath and place her on the bathroom floor so that he could examine her closely. He then took another series of photographs before putting gloves on and closely examining the body for signs of trauma or injury; however, he found nothing significant. Once Scott had completed his examination, he indicated to the contractors they could remove the woman from the scene and take her to Wagga Base Hospital.

A few days later, Scott received the post-mortem results. They indicated that drowning was not the cause of death and, further, that no definitive cause of death was established. He discussed the case with Geoff and they both thought it unusual, but without further evidence of how the woman had died, the file would have to be marked inconclusive.

In late November, a man was walking his dogs when he stumbled across a man's severely decomposed body in a table drain alongside Churches Plain Road, Uranquinty. Scott was at home when, at 7 a.m., he received the call to attend the isolated area.

When he arrived, detectives met him and immediately advised him of their concerns; from what they'd seen so far, this was not an accidental death but something far more sinister. Scott immediately put on a protective suit and gathered his equipment from the back of the four-wheel drive, before following one of the detectives to a table drain located approximately one metre from the roadway, and surrounded by thick grass and wild oats. As he stepped closer, he smelt the familiar stench of rotting flesh and his eyes focused on the masses of blowflies swarming around the bulging figure in the grass. It was already humid and his working conditions would only get worse as the sun rose further.

Taking note of the the body's position, and making reference to the conditions and topography, Scott concentrated on making comprehensive notes, including a sketch plan, before assembling his camera equipment and taking a series of photographs. He then closely examined the area for evidence that might assist in reconstructing the crime but, from what he saw, the man had been killed elsewhere and, some weeks before, his body dumped at this lonely spot hidden from the road.

Finally, Scott turned back to the rotting body lying in the drain and, after putting on two pairs of rubber gloves, commenced his examination. The body was bloated and severely maggot infested, which almost made it look as though it were writhing. The most exposed areas of skin were blackened from post-mortem putrefaction and any movement of the body could result in the skin bursting and expelling bodily fluids. Scott rolled the man over, stood back as far as he could in order to get some fresh air, and then moved closer and heaved the great weight over onto its side. He took a further series of photographs before deciding there was more to be gained by examining the body back at the local morgue.

The government contractors rolled the body into a plastic body bag, zipped it up and placed it in a steel trunk, and then drove away to the morgue. Arrangements would later be made to take the body to Sydney for a post-mortem. Once the government contractors had gone, Scott organised a ground search, and he and the detectives scoured the thick grass for further clues. The lack of evidence they found confirmed the theory that the man had been killed elsewhere and dumped in the table drain in a bid to conceal the body.

As Scott was examining the scene in Wagga, Geoff and Jocelyn were enjoying a short break in Sydney while Geoff was on 'rest days' between shifts. They had been looking forward to getting away and to attending the police association Christmas party to be held at the Marriott Hotel that evening.

At the party, they were enjoying catching up with people when Geoff's mobile phone rang. He heard Scott's agitated voice on the other end, saying that he'd been investigating the dumping of a body in a table drain and that they were treating it as murder. The alleged offender, who'd been picked up in Sydney that afternoon, had confessed to murdering two other people, one of whom was the young woman in the bath and the other, Peter Wennerbon, the death of whom Geoff had investigated.

Geoff was astounded and said, 'You've got to be kidding.'

'No, I'm not. Senior Sergeant Chris Smart is here and wants to talk to you; we can't find the notes from the Wennerbon job.'

Chris Smart was the zone supervisor and wanted a verbal briefing on the Wennerbon crime scene that Geoff had investigated in October. Geoff gave him a clear description of the scene, and an explanation of what he'd done and found during his examination. Geoff also told him that the pathology report had found no definitive cause of death. The supervisor was obviously agitated, complaining that he couldn't find the notes and that things were tense in Wagga, with the detectives wanting answers. There was a clear inference that evidence at the scene had been missed.

'I'll organise the notes when I get back at midday tomorrow,' Geoff said.

'No, I need to see the notes now. Where are they?' the supervisor demanded.

'They should be in the file, but what can I do about it now?'

'Just draw me a sketch plan and fax it to me right away. At least it will help until you get back. Basically, the shit's hit the fan, Geoff, and I need to sort this out NOW.'

After hanging up, Geoff went to the front desk and asked where the business centre was, explaining that he needed to use the fax machine urgently. He was guided to a quiet room, where he spent the next half an hour sketching the scene by memory. He then faxed the document directly to Chris Smart.

Back at the party, Jocelyn was wondering what the hell had happened, as Geoff had been gone for nearly an hour. He finally appeared, looking stressed. He explained that the zone supervisor had rung in relation to an unexplained death that Geoff had investigated and that now a man had confessed to murder. Jocelyn couldn't believe it, nor could she believe that their evening had been ruined. With his mobile constantly ringing, Geoff now had no desire to celebrate, and just wanted to go back to their hotel, where he could speak to the detectives in peace and try his utmost to convince them he'd done everything right during the original investigation. As the night wore on, he became more and more distressed due to the pressure of the looming investigation and the allegations of neglect of duty. He was so keen to get back to Wagga and sort this mess out that he managed to change his and Jocelyn's flights so that they could return to Wagga first thing in the morning.

The following day, Geoff went straight to the station, where he met with detectives and sat in on a number of briefings. He was told that the thirty-year-old offender had been picked up in Sydney after a tip-off resulting from the discovery of the man's body in the table drain outside Wagga. He had confessed to killing Ron Galvin, Yvonne Ford and Peter Wennerbon, all of whom were known to him, either through relatives or because of his job as a community bus driver. As the deaths of Yvonne Ford, who was found dead in the bath, and Peter Wennerbon had not previously been resolved, the task force considered the possibility of other deaths in the area being connected with this offender.

Geoff was shocked at the allegations of neglect of duty, and told the detectives that the the two unexplained deaths had been marked as inconclusive and were, in fact, still open cases. He denied that evidence had been missed and told them that each investigation had been thoroughly dealt with according to the correct procedures. In the absence of a cause of death, there had been nothing further that could have been done at the time. Geoff located the Wennerbon file and handed over the notes to the newly formed task force – 'Operation Melbeck'. A team of fifteen detectives was now assigned to the full investigation of the deaths of Yvonne Ford and Peter Wennerbon. Geoff was informed that he would have to undergo an interview with internal affairs in relation to the open finding of the Wennerbon death. It now appeared that Geoff's integrity as a forensic investigator was being questioned. He was devastated.

Over the next four weeks, the crime-scene office was filled with detectives hunting through files and demanding answers. Geoff printed out a summary of all jobs attended over the preceding twelve months, which the task force used to identify all deaths of interest. They would then be examined individually, including interviewing the crime-scene examiner, to ascertain if the job had been completed correctly. As well, the task force was going over every unexplained case on their files and checking for similarities. In all, there were around sixty crime-scene files to be looked at over the next month, as well as extra information relating to the Ford and Wennerbon cases to be collected and collated.

Every investigation was ripped apart and challenged. This made constant demands on Geoff's time and energy, as well as making him go over the details of every old job again. For most of the deaths, Doc Lennon had conducted the post-mortems locally, so Geoff had to call him frequently to discuss aspects of each case. The highly qualified doctor's assistance gave Geoff some relief. Still, the presence of the task-force members changed the dynamics of the office: people came and went constantly, files were piled up in heaps, and questions were constantly asked, giving rise to paranoia. Geoff felt that the men were checking up on him and his staff and looking for the slightest mistake so that they could discredit them. He struggled to continue with the demands of crime-scene work with a team of detectives looking over his shoulder.

As time went on, the atmosphere in the office became intolerable and Geoff could barely function. He thought about how he'd given his heart and soul to his job; he could completely understand why the task force had to be rigorous in their investigations, and he cooperated fully, but having the office under scrutiny made him start to wonder if it was all worth it. He retreated into his shell, not talking to Jocelyn about the investigation; he just couldn't believe it was happening. On one hand, he was positive that he and Scott had investigated all their cases correctly but, on the other, he began to question himself: *If only I'd found something to link the offender with Yvonne Ford, perhaps Ron Galvin would still be alive.* As well, he developed a severe distrust of others; he'd convinced himself that anyone would do anything to get their own way and had become suspicious of the motives of those close to him. He also believed that nobody understood how he felt and this only fuelled his distrust of those he worked with.

Geoff began to realise that he'd never have his credibility back and that it was time to get away from crime-scene work; his heart wasn't in it any more. He'd enjoyed his short periods as a relieving inspector. It seemed time to apply for transfer and put all this behind him.

Finally, after three months the task force completed their inquiry and internal affairs released the findings, which cleared both Geoff and Scott of any wrongdoing. This was no consolation to Geoff, though; the damage had already been done. Thinking to himself that he had to get out, he angrily filled in an application for promotion to duty inspector.

That same year, something happened that would shock the local station staff to the core. Geoff was acting as area supervisor when he received a call to attend a shooting in Temora, a small rural township eighty kilometres north-west of Wagga. The nine-months-pregnant wife of one of the local policemen had shot herself in the head with her husband's service firearm. Geoff immediately put together a shooting task force and called in Constable Ray Birchall from Griffith to examine the crime scene.

On the day of the incident, the victim's husband had driven to the shops and upon his return, and just prior to entering the house, heard the fatal shot. When he raced inside, he saw his wife bleeding from a gunshot wound to the head. An ambulance was called and, after realising the woman was dead, the officers got to work to save the baby, which was delivered and transferred to Canberra Hospital, where the father maintained a bedside vigil.

Meanwhile, back at the house, a contingent of police arrived to investigate. The fact that a police-issue service weapon had been used meant there would have to be an internal investigation into all facets of the event to discover how and why this terrible death had occurred. Geoff soon realised that those investigating the incident were leaning towards charging the young constable with neglect of duty for not having secured his firearm. While he understood that the incident had to be investigated fully, Geoff couldn't agree with this course of action, as the officer had already suffered the loss of his wife and would possibly lose his child.

The day after the tragedy, the local paper published a front-page story about the shooting along with a photograph of an obviously dead baby in a humidicrib. Geoff was sickened, and appalled at the amount of resources being thrown at an investigation that, to his mind, was nothing more than a witch hunt. This was especially so when compared with the inadequate resources allocated to the crime-scene unit. Geoff contacted the police association and requested assistance for the young officer involved. He also checked on the welfare of the police at the station, who were all affected by the death, and followed this up with support. As well, he spoke to the young constable after he learned the baby had died, and later assisted with negotiating a transfer so that he could start afresh.

During this time, Geoff was still undergoing marriage counselling and sought his psychologist's assistance immediately after the shooting. He realised that this type of 'debrief' would be most helpful in working through the myriad emotions he was feeling. But things were still difficult at home. Geoff felt old in comparison with Jocelyn, who was ten years younger than him. She wanted to go to the gym and stay fit, while he didn't care about looking after his appearance or staying healthy. He threw himself into cleaning and otherwise taking care of things at the house but avoided doing anything with Jocelyn. The slightest pressure at home would send him into a rage, as he simply couldn't deal with everyday problems the way he once had. Minor issues now seemed like insurmountable hurdles and he was frustrated at his inability to cope. Jocelyn was slowly slipping away from him; she was trying to get on with life but Geoff was stuck in his own emotional hell.

13

THE GROTH TWINS
FROM THIS MOMENT ON

Christmas was fast approaching and the likelihood of tragedy strik-
ing at that time of the year played on Geoff's mind. He was back at
work after a much-needed break. Typically, it was his turn to cover
the area and he was on call throughout the Christmas and New Year
break. The pressure the task-force investigation had put him under
had left him feeling flat and he struggled to motivate himself. He
felt he was slowly getting into the clutches of depression.

On the evening of 16 December 1998 at around 7 p.m., Geoff
got a call at home from the police radio requesting he go to Temora
about a drowning. Shortly after the first call, he received another
message to say that two children had been involved and he was to go
to Temora Hospital. He hurriedly left home with his usual words:
'Don't know what time I'll get home.'

On the drive over, he kept thinking, *How in hell could two kids
drown?* His mind turned to the high unemployment and struggling families Temora was known for, and he wondered if drugs
or alcohol were involved. He had never felt such rage, and he felt
powerless to stop it. He'd categorised the parents as no-hopers and

negligent. Were they pissed? On dope? His mind was racing as his anxiety rose.

He drove into the Temora Hospital car park, and the first person he saw was Greg Cox from the Temora Parachute School talking to Scott Haynes from the Temora police. He felt sick to the stomach. He had met Greg twice, both times regarding deaths of people at the school. He was a lovely man – genuine and caring. His wife, Elaine, was the same. The couple had always done their utmost to assist with investigations, explaining how the equipment worked and helping out with information. Geoff didn't think that Greg and Elaine had two children, and hoped it was a coincidence that Greg was at the hospital. Still, Greg and Scott's body language told him that Greg was in some way involved in yet another tragedy. Geoff greeted him warmly and Greg said, 'Oh, Geoff, why do we seem to always meet like this?'

Geoff didn't know what to say; he had no idea what was going on. He asked, 'How's Elaine?'

'She's fine; she's with Larry and Leah [the boys' parents],' Greg replied.

That told Geoff that Greg was somehow on the periphery. Scott took Geoff into the hospital and told him the story thus far. Two children, twin boys, had drowned in a pool just out of town. Scott hadn't yet been to the house, so they were both flying blind. It was time for Greg to go, but before he did so, he told Geoff he was going to get Elaine and go home.

Scott told Geoff the parents had identified the bodies and returned home to await his arrival. Geoff and Scott went to the small morgue at the side of the hospital. Geoff had visited this place many times over the years. His eyes immediately fixed on the large stainless-steel body cabinet in the corner and the examination table in the centre of the room. He walked over to the cabinet and pulled the door open; on the second shelf was a smallish parcel wrapped in hospital sheets. Placing both hands around the tiny bundle, he felt two little bodies through the sheets as he gently placed it on the cold examination table. It was unusual that they were wrapped together, and incorrect procedurally because of the possible evidentiary cross-contamination, but he could appreciate why it had happened. He focused on the sticking plaster securing the package and read the names written on it in texta: 'GROTH, Stewart and Jayden'. Removing the plaster, Geoff unwrapped the package and found two separate bundles, each wrapped in a further sheet. His mind was racing and his anxiety rose as he unwrapped each layer; he just wanted to get to the bodies, do the job and get the hell out of there. The same thought went over and over in his mind: *How could this happen?*

Finally, he unwrapped both bundles in unison and exposed the bodies. They were almost identical, with Stewart the bigger of the two. They were both well nourished, with the typical build of two-year-olds. He studied the two children, with their wet blond tousled hair, sky-blue glassy eyes and white milk teeth; both were uncircumcised and very fair skinned. They had resuscitation patches on their chests and intravenous lines in their left hands. They looked like dead angels but somehow also had an air of mischief about them, as boys often do, much like his own similarly aged son. Suddenly he had an urge to flee, forget this whole nightmare and go home, where he could hold his kids and shower them with kisses. A jolt of guilt brought him back to reality: *This isn't about me; going home isn't an option. What the fuck am I thinking?*

Composing himself, he turned his back on the bodies and pulled his camera equipment from its case. He photographed the two little boys, both together and individually. He then made notes in an effort to establish how, where and why the tragedy had occurred. Finally, it was time for his detailed examination of each child. He saw that both had aspirated cereal-type matter, together with a reddish liquid that was stuck to the sides of their mouths. He smelled the substance, which resembled Weet-Bix and watermelon. He checked all over their little bodies for bruising or other visible injuries, and found nothing except for a small abrasion on Stewart's forehead. They were both cold, yet pliable, the lividity only just starting to show on their shoulders, backs, buttocks and the backs of their legs. He took a further series of photographs and documented the examination on pre-printed forms. Once the examination was over, Geoff placed both boys together, secured an identification band on each ankle and rewrapped the delicate parcel in the same way it had been wrapped previously. He carried it to the cabinet and placed it on the shelf.

In the morgue office, Geoff made a few calls to Glebe, speaking to the duty pathologist and the long-distance contractor to arrange transport of the bodies to Sydney for post-mortem examinations. Walking out into the car park, he felt weighed down. He feared the worst was yet to come. He dreaded meeting the boys' parents, and his own unavoidable grief was barely contained. Memories of Old Nubber station after the Young plane crash flooded his mind. Geoff sat behind the wheel of the car for a moment gathering his thoughts. First, he had to drive to the station and make contact with the local Coroner, Adrian Kain, to explain the situation and also brief the local police before making his way to the Groths'. Once at the station, Geoff had a meeting with Scott, Detective Phil Malligan and Ken Finch, the duty officer. They agreed it was time to go to the house, which was about thirty-five kilometres west of the Temora township.

They travelled there in convoy, like police going to a sting, but it was Geoff's heart, rather than his adrenaline, that was racing. There was a couple of vehicles parked in the driveway of the house, which looked in need of a lick of paint and a good clean-up. The front door was closed and the lights were visible through the glass door panel. It was deadly quiet, except for the drone of an airconditioning unit and the chirp of crickets. The air was still and heavy; as Geoff stepped out of the car, he wiped perspiration from his brow. The front door opened as he reached the steps.

Scott entered first. As they filed into the room, all were silent with downcast eyes. Geoff saw Leah and Larry sitting on the lounge comforting each other, surrounded by their other four children. There was a Christmas tree in the corner, and although the place was modest, it was very cosy and reasonably clean and tidy. Geoff crouched down to the Groths' eye level. He began his explanation and it wasn't long before he sensed he had their full attention. The next half hour was taken up with explaining the roles of the police and forensics and answering their many questions about what was going to happen to the boys. Leah was a very attractive young woman with an aura of strength. She explained to them what had happened that day and night. Larry was more reserved, and continually wiped his eyes. While they were talking, Geoff was aware of the other children, who were aged between five and eleven. At various times, he talked to all four of them. Scott's daughter went to school with the oldest boy, who was visibly distressed. Geoff couldn't help but feel guilty about having pre-judged this lovely family. They were down-to-earth people who were struggling with the enormity of their collective loss.

Leah described the boys having their baths, and then watching television while they had their last meal of Weet-Bix and watermelon. She had wanted them to go to bed early, as they were tired from Christmas shopping in Wagga earlier that day. Geoff thought that he might have walked straight past them, as he'd spent time in the marketplace himself. The other kids had been swimming in the pool all afternoon and Larry prepared their tea while the twins ate. When the older kids came into the house by the back door, the pool gate lock didn't engage. A strap that normally secured the rear sliding door wasn't used and lay limp against the frame. After they ate, the twins made their escape to the backyard and got into the pool area, resulting in a parent's worst nightmare.

Leah said that Stewart had been the leader and Jayden followed him everywhere. They had been born prematurely and fought for their lives for six weeks, but afterwards had had no major health problems. They were typical fun-loving, mischievous two-year-olds. The boys loved it when Shania Twain's 'From this Moment On' would come on the television. They would dance around their mother, humming the tune mixed with a few words. As her words sunk in, Geoff felt a lump in his throat and his heart ached; his feeling of dread returned with a vengeance.

Larry took Geoff and the other investigators outside and showed them the pool area. The pool was surrounded by what appeared to be the regulation fencing and gate. It was an inground fibreglass pool and was surprisingly large; the water was crystal clear and still. Larry showed Geoff where each boy was found, floating face down in the water. Stewart was on the far side and Jayden on the side nearest the house. Larry was visibly shaken, so Geoff took him back inside, his arm draped around his shoulders. Geoff again crouched down with him and Leah, and extended a hand to each of them. Larry and Leah held each other and cried for what seemed an eternity, while Geoff quietly stayed with them. Eventually, they told him about the chaos that had broken out when they realised the boys were missing, with everyone involved in a frantic search of the house. Leah said that she noticed the rear door was ajar and yelled at the other kids to go and check outside. They rushed out, believing that the boys might have wandered towards the creek at the rear of the property. Suddenly, one of the older children yelled out, 'The twins are in the pool!'

They all rushed to the pool area, Leah jumping into the water first, followed by the oldest boy. Together, they got the boys out and carried them inside. Leah and Larry commenced CPR, and the boy rang 000 for an ambulance.

'They took so long to get here,' Leah said,

Geoff thought, *Enough is enough – don't torture yourselves.*

Leah got the clothes the twins were wearing at the time and handed them to Geoff. He looked tearfully at the green Santa jumpsuits and disposable animal-print nappies. She asked if he could get rid of them, and he went to the car and placed them in brown paper bags, which he labelled and sealed. On his return, he commenced his examination of the pool area and, in particular, the gate. He took measurements, more photographs and notes, and found that the problem had been with the gate's cheap, inappropriate hinges. Larry told Geoff that he had put them on a couple of months ago. The other kids would often stand on the bottom rail of the gate to open the latch. This would have placed stress on the hinges, resulting in the closer latch not engaging; hence, the twins merely pushed the gate open.

Geoff wrapped up his examination and told Detective Malligan that he felt it was time to leave. The duty officer had already returned to the station, leaving the investigators to finish their work, and it was now time to leave the family in peace. The others left, allowing Geoff to spend some quiet time with Leah and Larry, during which he suggested counselling. He told them to think about it and said that he would possibly see them in the morning. He asked Leah if there were any special toys she would like the boys to have on their journey to Sydney. She said that Jayden never slept without his 'dum do', a dummy. Geoff's heart sank, as his own son, Thomas, wouldn't sleep without his 'doody'. He took the dummy and drove back to Temora Hospital, where he placed the dummy with the boys and left instructions with the contractor to make sure it went to Sydney with them. The contractor loaded the little bodies into the purpose-built VW combi van, to be taken to Sydney in the morning. As Geoff watched the van drive away, he was relieved that he wouldn't have to go to the post-mortem. From the hospital, he drove straight to Temora police station, where he set about completing the paper-work. Afterwards, he sat in quiet reflection behind the crime-scene wagon's wheel, before the lonely drive back to Wagga.

Geoff walked through the door of his house at 4 a.m.; all was quiet and the house was in darkness. He went straight to the kids' rooms and checked on Emily and Tom, before sliding into bed and snuggling up to Jocelyn. He lay awake, thinking about death and trying to come to terms with his own grief.

When morning came, Geoff quickly got up, showered and was gone by 7 a.m. He couldn't bring himself to discuss the events of the previous day with Jocelyn and she didn't push for details. They held each other tightly as he kissed her goodbye. He didn't want to bring this grief into his home. He was instead keen to get away to the relative sanctuary of the office, where he could look after such mundane daily tasks as the roster and the overtime forms and job book.

At about 8 a.m., Geoff got a call from Duty Inspector Winson, who wanted the latest on the drownings. Geoff briefed him with the full story and an outline of what he'd done at the scene. The inspector told him that the police media department had rung, putting them on notice that reporters and crew from Channels Seven and Ten were flying to Temora, along with various members of the print media. He asked Geoff if he could liaise with the police media section on behalf of the patrol

'Can you call them right away?' the inspector asked.

'Why can't one of the duty officers do it?' Geoff replied.

'Sorry, mate. Deputy Commissioner Jarrett is coming to check the station and discuss future changes within the force today and you've been nominated by the boss. Nothing I can do about it.'

Geoff reluctantly picked up the phone and rang the police media department, which gave him the bad news that every man and his dog was on its way. The media were likely to converge on the house at 11 a.m., and the relatives needed to be warned. There'd been a number of drownings on the eastern seaboard that week and water safety was a topic on everyone's lips. *Nothing like a child drowning; even better if it's twins.* It made Geoff sick. What in hell was he going to do? Then he thought of Greg Cox. Together, they hatched a plan over the phone. They decided that Greg would do an interview for the media, on the basis that the press was coming anyway, so that they should at least try to control the situation. Geoff spoke briefly to Leah, then hightailed it to their house, his adrenaline pumping.

When he arrived, there were cars everywhere. He rushed inside and was quickly introduced to a number of friends and relatives of the family, who were all gathered in the lounge room in support. Greg and Elaine soon turned up, and Greg, Larry, Leah and Geoff then discussed their plans. The parents couldn't understand why the media were there, and they were terrified. Geoff explained the situation as best he could, outlining what they would do and apologising for the ugly mess. He assured them that they just had to band together and they'd get through it. When the media turned up, Larry and Leah were to gather the kids and go down to the back shed, while Greg and Geoff marshalled them out the front. The plan was to take them to the side of the pool, position them at the fence, and let the media get their precious footage. Greg would do an interview and, hopefully, the press would then leave the Groths in peace. Geoff went outside with Greg. Finally, at 11.20 a.m. all was ready, and he gave the message that the family should head down the back.

As the day's heat intensified, Geoff began to sweat and become agitated. He took the media contingent to the side fence and watched in disgust as they filmed their footage. It seemed to take forever and his patience was decreasing by the minute. Greg then did a series of interviews in front of the pool, and just when Geoff thought the ordeal was almost over, the media demanded more time to get better angles with their footage of the pool. Geoff snapped, and a few unpleasantries were exchanged. The last straw was when the photographer from the Wagga paper spotted the family down the back and wanted to get a photograph.

'Take that fucking photograph and I'll jam your camera right up your arse. I've been fair to you and now you're shitting on this family. Piss off and give these people some privacy!' Geoff yelled.

It was at least another thirty minutes before he eventually got rid of them all. Their final request was for a photograph of the kids. When the last member of the media finally left, Geoff was frazzled, frustrated and angry. He looked down at his sweating hands and saw they were shaking. He returned to the house and watched through the windows to make sure the media was gone, before he walked down to the shed to let the family know it was safe to return. They were hot, thirsty and distressed. The house was full of people, solemnly wandering about with the continually ringing telephone in the background.

Leah asked Geoff if he could talk to the other kids, as she was worried about them. He took them all to one of the bedrooms, where the kids asked a lot of questions. He did his best to answer carefully and honestly, and encouraged them to talk freely about the twins and about their feelings. Afterwards, he asked if they would like to say a prayer. They said they would, and Geoff asked them to all hold hands and close their eyes. He said, 'Think of Jayden and Stewart for their next journey. God give Jayden and Stewart peace, and God give the family strength. Amen.' The simple words hung in the air as the tearful children filed out of the room.

Back in the loungeroom, Geoff talked to the relatives, and learned that Larry's dad was dying of cancer. Just as he was thinking how unfair this was, his mobile rang. He had to go to Young regarding a fatal farm accident. Geoff told Larry and Leah that he would have to go, but would return later; he didn't say where he was going. Before he left, Leah asked if he could get in touch with a counsellor, as she was particularly concerned about their eldest boy. He told her he would do his best, said goodbye and let himself out, feeling the midday heat as he walked to the car.

Geoff drove cross country to Young, his mind flooded with images of what he'd just left and of those he might be about to see. A wave of exhaustion hit him; it was hot, his eyes felt heavy, and he focused all his energy on warding off a deep sense of dread. He headed out of town to a cherry orchard, the scene of this latest tragedy.

The detective in charge was waiting out front, and explained to Geoff what he knew about the elderly man's death. He'd lived on the property with his daughter, who was the person who had called for help. The man's body had already been removed and taken to the morgue. The two men walked to where an abandoned car sat idle among the cherry trees. The runaway car had rolled down into the orchard, dragging the elderly man with it when he had leaned through the window in an attempt to stop it. He was crushed when the car pinned him against the cherry trees.

After having a look at the scene, Geoff approached the investigation in his usual manner: taking a number of photographs of the scene, of the car and of the point of impact. It was relatively straightforward, taking him about an hour to complete his notes and measurements and draw a plan. He then went to the Young morgue, where he examined and photographed the body. The man's injuries were consistent with the scenario he'd been given and he was satisfied that there was nothing suspicious about the death. He thought to himself, *Here is a man in the twilight of his life and the twins were only at the beginning of theirs.* He just wanted to get back to Temora to finalise everything with the Groth family.

On the way back, Geoff made several calls in an attempt to get the state health department to provide the Groths with counselling. He was finally transferred to the boss of the right department, who was prepared to help. He said that he needed a written briefing, which he asked Geoff to fax to his home that night. Geoff was relieved he could offer the family a ray of hope that would help them deal with their pain and suffering. He went to the Groths' place and got the necessary information for the counsellor and told them to expect a call in the morning; it was now 6 p.m. He finally walked in the door of his home at around 8 p.m., and immediately prepared and faxed the counsellor's briefing notes to him.

Geoff then sat silently looking at his son sleeping, and having a beer to steady his nerves. Exhausted, he finally showered and went to bed about 11 p.m., but then tossed and turned restlessly. The ring of the phone jolted him upright at 1 a.m. 'There's been a fire; you're needed right away,' the caller said.

Dragging himself from bed, Geoff dressed and went to the scene. Almost on autopilot, he investigated: shining his torch around the blackened scene, taking photographs and establishing the point of origin of the fire. Stumbling through the charred remains and inhaling the toxic fumes that were wafting about only heightened Geoff's sense of unease. It was 3.30 a.m. when he finally returned to bed; this time he fell into a deep sleep until he woke abruptly at 6 a.m. He was completely exhausted, but got ready to go back to work for another day of carnage.

Shortly after arriving at the office, the police media rang to thank him for what he'd done at the Groths' house the day before. They wanted to let him know how pleased they were about the cooperation between the police and the media; they'd apparently had appreciative calls from a couple of television stations. While he was grateful that at least they made the effort to call, he felt that the whole farce should never have happened. That morning he also heard that the Groth boys' post-mortems had been rescheduled for the following day; this only served to heighten his anxiety, as he was keen to hear the official cause of death.

The next day, Dr Cala, the duty pathologist, rang about 2 p.m. and confirmed that the cause of death was drowning. Geoff had been glad when he heard that Dr Cala was the duty pathologist, as he thought he was a great bloke and a wonderful doctor. Having witnessed many of his post-mortems in the past, he knew that Dr Cala would respectfully and empathetically do what had to be done. He rang Leah and told her the news and advised her that the boys' bodies would be back in town later that night. She let him know that the counsellor had rung and a session was planned for

Saturday. She thanked him for his support and told him that the funerals would be on the following Tuesday.

Over the weekend, Geoff couldn't get the boys off his mind. He was sullen and self-absorbed, and didn't want to open up to Jocelyn. In any case, he thought that she found the drownings too upsetting to talk about. He wouldn't have blamed her if she did feel that way, but he preferred to shield her, anyway.

Geoff was pleased when the personnel inspector called to say that at 2 p.m. on Monday there would be a debrief with a private psychologist, John Flockton. He thought that was a step in the right direction, particularly for Scott and Phil. He didn't need it as much as they did, or so he thought.

The debrief was held at the hospital and took an hour and a half. As the session progressed, Geoff realised it wasn't a suitable forum for him to express how he felt. There were many people present and the atmosphere was impersonal, the discussion being pitched more towards the group as a whole rather than to individuals. Geoff was teary during the session but didn't feel comfortable revealing his feelings in a room full of strangers. As well, he feared that what he had to say would only traumatise the others further, and he even thought his input might make them angry. At the end of the session, those present talked about going to the funeral the following day, work permitting. John encouraged them to attend. Geoff thought that John did a good job with the session, considering the number of people there and their diverse duties, but felt that, overall, the debrief was only a clinical exercise.

At the funeral the next day, Geoff, as he had done at Emily's schoolfriend's funeral, wore his uniform as a mark of respect. He parked near the church and watched as a steady stream of mourners filed in. He saw a newspaper photographer standing across the road, and anger rose in him as he wondered when the press would leave the Groths alone. Larry, Leah and the kids arrived and were ushered into the tiny church, which, by now, was filled to capacity. Geoff followed them in, and immediately focused on the two tiny caskets surrounded by stuffed toys and helium balloons. The cleric, who had driven from Canberra at the family's request, commenced the service. He had baptised the boys and now he was burying them. He told those gathered about the boys' love of their mother and of how they would waltz around her to 'From This Moment On'. That was the cue for the usher to play the song but, unfortunately, the wrong one started playing. Geoff moved quickly to the CD player, and changed it to the right song, which echoed around the church. Larry and Leah gave him grateful smiles. As he glanced around the room, he saw eyes constantly being wiped, and people with their heads down whispering the song's lyrics. Holding his emotions at bay, Geoff quietly sang along too.

When the service was over, everyone gathered around as the two tiny caskets were placed in the back of the hearse. Geoff stood waiting at an intersection closest to the cemetery, a lump in his throat. As the cortege passed, he saluted the boys. Once at the cemetery, he stood at the back of the congregation and his mind flooded with memories of the tragic series of events. He could hardly breathe. His whole body seemed to feel the torture of knowing those two beautiful boys were gone. Once the service was over, he was talking to one of the ambulance officers when Larry caught the officer's gaze. He gave him a huge smile and then turned to Geoff, and put his arms around him in a long embrace. 'We're so happy that you could make it. Please come back to the club and meet our families,' he said.

Geoff was humbled, feeling that, after all, he had only done what

he was paid to. When they got to the club, Larry introduced Geoff
around to those of his relatives he'd not yet met, and they all shook
his hand and thanked him. He was a trifle embarrassed, yet proud.
He soon bade farewell to Larry, Leah, the kids, Greg and Elaine.
As he was walking out, Leah's uncle, whom he'd met at the house
on the day the media had gathered, grabbed him and gave him an
emotional bear hug.

On the slow drive back to Wagga, 'From This Moment On'
came on the radio, and Geoff started to cry. He knew he had once
again crossed a boundary and become emotionally involved, but he
wouldn't have had it any other way.

Over the weeks leading up to Christmas, Geoff was in contact with
Larry and Leah over various matters and sometimes he'd call them
just to see how they were. It was difficult for him to get the twins out
of his mind, particularly on Christmas Day. He didn't talk about it
with Jocelyn, as he didn't want to ruin her Christmas, although he
knew she was thinking of the tragedy as well. On Christmas morning his thoughts went straight to the boys. While he was watching
his children gleefully opening presents, he felt a sense of worthless-
ness as he thought of the twins and their presents lying unopened
under the tree. He called Larry and Leah to wish them well and tell
them he was thinking of them; it was all he could do.

Geoff got the photographs of the drownings back a few weeks
after Christmas. He opened the package with dread and flicked
through the images; he could hardly stand looking at them. He'd
never felt this way before and it secretly worried him. He quickly
put the photographs in the brief with his notes, and sealed the envelope. He knew he'd have to face the photographs again during his

preparation of the brief for the Coroner but, for now, he preferred to worry about it later.

January went by in a blur of call-outs and little rest; the whole month Geoff single-handedly rushed from one job to the next. Each one made him more depressed as he got further behind. He had to produce what felt like countless briefs of evidence, each fifteen to twenty pages long, some requiring scale plans. He left the Groth one until last. He started it several times but as soon as he'd lay the photographs on the table and start to compile the evidence, he'd feel physically sick. After several attempts, he took the brief home and forced himself to face it. He'd hoped Jocelyn could assist him, as sometimes she'd help him caption photographs and proofread reports, but this one was too close to home and she didn't want to see any part of it. Eventually he completed the brief and, relieved, handed it over to the officer in charge.

Around May, he received a file containing a letter of appreciation to him from the Groths that they had written back in January. The letter would have meant so much more if he had received it when it was written; instead, he was disgusted that it could have been misplaced and treated with such insensitivity. He wanted to contact the Groths but he couldn't bring himself to do it, which made him feel weak and useless. He knew that if he could just see for himself how they were recovering from the tragedy it could make all the difference, but it didn't matter how badly he wanted to visit the Groths, he couldn't. Jocelyn offered to write to Larry and Leah on Geoff's behalf, which he felt was better than making no contact at all.

The closure Geoff craved would never come, even though he knew he had been a help to the family. Every year on the anniversary of the Groth twins' drownings, his thoughts still spiral into a dark place.

14

LOSING IT

In the heat of January, two weeks after the Groth twins' deaths, over a single weekend Geoff attended the deaths of four elderly men. Each time the phone rang, he jumped and grabbed the receiver with a shaking hand. Temperatures were reaching the mid-forties during the day and only dropping to the mid-twenties at night. The heatwave in the area was killing the town's old people, and each time one of these lonely deaths occurred, the body would decay for days before anyone noticed the victim was missing. Geoff was called to investigate one death after another as bodies were discovered in stinking hot houses. Three elderly men were found in their beds and the fourth had literally melted into his lounge chair. All the dead were badly decomposed, flyblown and in advanced stages of maggot infestation.

On arrival at the scenes of these deaths, Geoff was bombarded with blowflies and air that was barely breathable. One of the bodies had blown up to almost twice its size as it fermented in the locked-up house. A dog had been trapped on the premises for days on end with its dead master and was barely alive. Geoff scanned the room, taking in the piles of books, papers and magazines stacked around the body. He negotiated the mess while conducting the examination and taking photographs. He struggled to manoeuvre the dead weight of the man in the confined space among the clutter. It made no difference that the deceased was in an advanced state of decomposition; Geoff still had to examine the scene to eliminate the possibility of suspicious circumstances. He checked every part of the house and closely checked for signs of an intruder or foul play. Gagging from the stench, he took regular breaks outside. Not knowing how long the man had been decomposing, he checked the use-by dates on food stored in the fridge in an effort to estimate the time of death.

Finally, Geoff called the government contractors to assist with removing the body. The youngest contractor called to the scene was so repulsed that he rushed from the house dry-retching. He refused to return and help with the body, leaving Geoff and the remaining contractor to get the man onto the stretcher and out of the house. The deceased's skin was so stretched that any movement sent bursts of putrid fluid running to the floor. Geoff constantly dry-retched as he and the contractor ferried the body out into the street. Finally, they loaded him into a steel trunk in order to contain the dripping body fluids.

The following Monday morning, Geoff showed up at the morgue for the four post-mortems of the elderly men. When Doc Lennon arrived, he commented on the advanced state of decomposition of the four bodies. The morgue was filled with the stench of rot, and maggots were spilling out onto the floor and writhing about like a mass of worms. When it came time to perform the autopsy on the most badly decomposed man, Doc Lennon announced it was the worst case he had ever seen. He went on to explain that the body was at the point of decomposition immediately before the full degradation of the body cells. The smell was so bad that Geoff wore a full plastic protective suit. He knew from experience that no amount of washing could ever rid his clothing of the foul stench once it had settled on the fabric.

Later that day, Geoff prepared his overtime forms for the four call-outs he'd attended over the weekend. He attached a letter and faxed it with the paperwork:

If I ever see another fucking flyblown dead body it will be too soon!

This cry for help received no reply.

Since he attended the alcohol treatment program at St John of God, Geoff's drinking had been under control, but things once again started deteriorating. He lost a lot of weight and was still taking briefs of evidence home just to keep up with his workload. He was sinking into depression and isolating himself at home.

Geoff was regularly having disturbing dreams that included people parachuting and falling to the ground. He'd be falling along-side them but also watching from above, and stopping just prior to hitting the earth. He'd investigated an incident where a para-chute had failed to deploy, killing the victim on impact and leaving a crater in the ground. This repeatedly featured in his dreams, in which he could clearly see the imprint of the body. He also dreamed of being a passenger on planes and gliders, and heading straight towards the ground but stopping before the final impact. Joce-lyn would shake him awake, desperately trying to calm him as he screamed for help.

Sometimes when Geoff was driving his car, everything would

seem to start happening in slow motion and he would see the vehicle skidding towards a post or a tree. The sound of sirens would trigger flashbacks, and he'd suddenly start to feel shaky and nervous. Cartoons upset him; he especially detested the Road Runner character, which triggered in his mind frightening images of falling over a cliff. At times, he'd lose it when a tragic news items flashed across the television screen. He would explode and start yelling, 'Turn it off! Turn the fucking thing off!'

One night in winter, Geoff was working late in the office; things weren't good at home and he was in a dark mood. There was strong wind and heavy rain, and the thunder and lightning added to his feeling of foreboding.

Geoff was standing out the back of the station having a cigarette when suddenly he heard a light plane flying overhead. He looked up but the plane was out of view; it was coming from the north-west and sounded as though it were flying too low. *That'd be right; another bloody plane crash*, he thought. He listened to the sound of the engine fading in the distance, all the time feeling uneasy. He then thought obsessively of the plane crashing and he began to fear that perhaps this was an omen. After a few minutes, he realised that it had flown over and that things seemed to be all right. Relieved, he walked back into the station and returned to his work. About an hour later, he heard over the police radio that a light plane had crashed in a paddock at Golambo Hill, south-west of Wagga and just a short distance from Wagga Airport at Forest Hill. Those first on the scene were calling for crime scene to attend.

Visions of the two prior plane crashes Geoff had attended came clearly to him; he could see the bloodshed. The weather was almost identical, with the rain, fog and wind, and he knew he now had to go through it all again. Geoff set off for the scene, all the time wishing he could just go back to the office where it was safe and warm. He was fighting with himself, half his mind assuming the responsibility of the impending scene and the other half dreading it.

As he approached, he was directed to the entrance of a local property. He passed many emergency service vehicles parked along the roadway leading right up to the entrance gate. There were groups of people standing about. It was chaos. Annoyed, he pulled up and spoke to a constable waiting at the gate.

'Who's in charge here?' he barked, and continued, 'Let's get some order and a sense of who's doing what.'

'The boss is speaking with the property owner. Access is through a private property over there and by four-wheel drive only. The firies have already gone in; there's nothing anyone can do. All on board are dead,' the constable told him.

Two senior police were placed on guard restricting vehicle access. Judging by the number of people milling about, there was already trouble with crowd control.

Geoff went to find the officer in charge, who was with the property owner. At the homestead, the three men spoke briefly about access and then set off, with the inspector and the property owner in front and Geoff behind. The vehicles rattled and bumped along the makeshift track during the fifteen-minute journey, driving through paddocks and rough terrain until the crashed remains of the Italian-made Partenavia twin-engine plane came into view. The aircraft had obviously disintegrated into several pieces as it slammed into the southern side of the hill. The wreckage was strewn across the hill's peak and then along a path down the northern slope. At this early stage, it was assumed that the plane had come in too low on approach to the airport and, in the foul weather, crashed into the side of the hill, causing both the pilot and passenger to be ejected.

Geoff surveyed the scene by torchlight. Torn-off arms, broken legs and torsos lay scattered about. He'd been told earlier that the security express plane had been on its final leg of a regular mail run between Albury, Corowa and Wagga. From what he could see, the cargo included pathological specimens, bank records and mail. Amongst the debris were jars containing bloodied fluid and body organs. Although some of the jars were intact, several of the specimens had spilled on impact. The contents of the jars mixed with the remains of the crash victims' bodies. He saw next to a vial of blood a number of medical documents that were obviously meant to accompany the specimens to the laboratory. Geoff tried to distinguish between the victims' body parts and the pathology specimens but gave up, leaving it till later. Mixed with the body organs was mail that had been scattered over a wide area around the crashed plane; it blew about in the wind as he stepped around the body parts while searching the scene.

Geoff stood for a moment, rubbing his hands together in an attempt to alleviate the cold; there was so much to do and so much he'd rather not think about. *There's stuff strewn from arsehole to breakfast. This is total shit; just another fucking day in my fucked-up life.* There was nothing he could do in the darkness, and he instructed that the scene be guarded until first light.

Geoff and the duty officer then stood together in the darkness discussing what needed to be done, rain dripping down their faces and off the ends of their noses. Geoff heard a noise in the distance and shone his torch in its direction. Glowing in the dark were the distinct red pupils of a fox's eyes; they darted to one side and then back again as the animal crept closer to the plane. Next, the light picked up the outline of the fox's bushy tail, trailing behind its body as it slunk along.

'Look, over there,' Geoff said, pointing the torch at the fox as it darted back and forth. 'It's going for the bodies. Quick, scare it off; we need to get a tarp and cover the remains before it drags them away!'

The duty officer ran back to the car and ordered tarps over the radio, while Geoff grabbed what he could from the back of the four-wheel drive. He managed to find a sheet of plastic, which he threw over part of the remains. Twenty minutes later, the rescue squad arrived with tarps, and the men got to work covering what they could in an effort to protect the bodies from the hungry vermin as well as from the elements. Geoff strapped a tarp over the first torso, then found the other one and repeated the process. Afterwards, he assigned two local police officers the job of watching over the scene and keeping the animals away during the night.

When the Coroner arrived he walked through the scene with Geoff inspecting the damaged plane and noting the point of impact and the bodies' positions. They discussed Geoff's desire to start the examination the following morning and the Coroner agreed it would be best to leave it until first light. All the vehicles being driven from the scene slid over the slippery surface, which seemed to have deteriorated since they'd travelled over it a short time before. In the rear-vision mirror, Geoff saw the two local constables warming themselves by a makeshift campfire. *It's going to be a long night*, he thought.

Back at the office, Geoff angrily plonked himself into his chair; sighing, he began completing the job book and tying up loose ends. The heated room did nothing for him; he was chilled to the bone. When he got home he went straight to bed. He was tired but sleep didn't come easily with the thought of what lay ahead the next day; he had a series of nightmares filled with body parts and blood. He left the house at sunrise and the rain was still teeming down.

On arrival, Geoff was told that the original access to the scene was no longer viable; the night's rain had saturated the ground and it was now too boggy even to get a four-wheel drive through. They went to a neighbouring property and asked if access to the crash site was possible. It was, so they set off over a series of paddocks towards the crashed plane. Geoff asked the officers on duty watch whether the foxes had been back. It was obvious that the more experienced of the constables was unsettled. He told Geoff that they'd had a terrible night, constantly being startled by the sounds of the foxes encroaching on the scene. Standing in the darkness with only his torch and gun to protect the bodies had taken its toll. He went on to explain how the sounds of the foxes and vermin attacking the tarps had rattled him. He'd scare one fox off and then another would creep up; it happened over and over, forcing him to let off a number of warning shots. He was a mature man, who had formerly worked in the RAAF, but this showed Geoff that even the most seasoned and hardened officer could be deeply affected by working in such horrific conditions. Later, the constable would go to Geoff, saying that he couldn't get the scene from that night out of his mind.

In light rain, Geoff set about dividing the scene into a grid, running string lines in a methodical pattern across the entire area. He also got to work photographing the entire scene, taking shots from different angles and showing the positions of the body parts in relation to the plane's fuselage. Next, he drew a sketch plan detailing the site topography, and the resting place of the plane, the debris and of those killed. Representatives from CAA and BASI worked alongside him in a coordinated effort.

When all examinations were complete, Geoff prepared two body bags to take the shattered remains of the thirty-three-year-old pilot and twenty-two-year-old passenger, who'd decided to accompany his friend at the last minute. Wearing gloves and a full protective suit, Geoff commenced collecting the pilot's torso, carefully picking up each body part along with torn flesh and bone. He picked up small portions of body matter, placing them inside the bags beside the main body parts. As rain soaked the ground, he heaved the larger parts into the bags with great difficulty. Next, he walked the entirety of the scene, collecting specimens of other body matter and placing them in separate jars. The intact ones would go to the appropriate laboratory but the spoilt ones would be disposed of at the morgue rather than being left for wild animals to scavenge. Finally, the two body bags were conveyed to the government contractor, who was standing by his vehicle to receive the bodies for transportation to the morgue.

Geoff followed the bodies to the morgue and, upon arrival, booked in each bag and their contents. The bags were then placed on trolleys and unzipped, and each body searched for items of identification. As Geoff looked in the pilot's clothing, he felt something inside one of the pockets. It was a number of photographs: glamour shots of the pilot's wife. He carefully placed them in an envelope and itemised the property in his notebook.

Outside, Geoff was met by the hospital grief counsellor, who requested a viewing for the pilot's wife. Geoff felt sweaty and agitated as they discussed the procedure. He now had to return to the morgue and prepare the body; this was a job that clearly wasn't his responsibility but, as usual, he was lumbered with it. He covered one side of the pilot's face with a sheet and tucked it under the head, rolling the face to one side and allowing the covered cheek to rest on the table. He wheeled the trolley to the viewing window and waited.

A short time later, Geoff met the pilot's wife and gently explained the nature of her husband's injuries and what the viewing would entail. He told her that her husband's injuries were such that full identification would not be possible and that she would only see the area of his face that was not disfigured. Finally, he handed her the photographs he'd retrieved from the body, which she gratefully accepted, and guided her to the viewing room. Geoff stepped out of view while she said her final goodbye.

The following day, he returned to the morgue to attend the post-mortems with Mark Sykes, who got to work fingerprinting both of the deceased for identification purposes, as neither body was suitable for full visual identification. He methodically held each hand in his rubber-gloved one while he rolled ink over the fingers and pressed them to make impressions on a radioed form. The pathologist then started his examination, opening the body cavity, removing organs, weighing them and setting them aside for analysis, while Geoff took photographs. The procedure was repeated for the second body, with organs, blood and urine lined up in containers on a steel trolley for transportation to the appropriate laboratory. Finally, the cavities were sewn up, and the bodies washed down and wheeled over to the storage facility, where they were put into their separate refrigerated compartments.

Back in Wagga a few days later, Geoff received a phone call from the officer in charge of the crash investigation.

'I've been talking to the pilot's wife and she wants to see the photographs of the crash. I need you to bring the photographs and meet me at the house, and explain to her what happened at the scene,' he said.

'No, the photographs are too graphic – all it will do is upset her. I'm not doing it,' Geoff replied.

The officer in charge was firm, saying, 'She has every right to see them and if you don't bring them out, I will.'

Throughout the investigation, the officer in charge had spent a lot of time explaining things to the pilot's wife and generally giving her support; they had developed a rapport and he'd done his best to keep her up-to-date with information. Geoff, resigning himself to the job, set a time and date for the two men to meet at the family home. Geoff didn't want to face it; to see relatives suffering the trauma of losing a loved one was bad enough but actually to stand by and explain the details of each photograph was something he particularly dreaded.

On the day of the visit, he sat down with the pilot's wife and explained what had happened and what each photograph showed. It was confronting but afterwards he accepted that at least the family now knew the details of how the pilot had died, which would lessen the impact of their revelation at the coronial inquest. He didn't realise that the pilot's wife had no intention of discussing with family members the details of the horrific nature and extent of her husband's injuries.

At the inquest a few months later, Geoff entered the witness box to give evidence. He was shocked when the barrister appearing on behalf of the pilot's family went on the attack. He asked a number of questions about why the bodies had been left in the open overnight, where the bodies were found and what state they were in. He openly criticised Geoff's decision to leave the bodies at the scene until the following day so that he could examine the scene in daylight.

Geoff was initially evasive, giving only the bare facts in an attempt to avoid talking about the gory details in front of the family.

They were sitting in the back of the court, hanging on every word. While he struggled to find the right words, the barrister insisted he answer the questions. Nerves set in and Geoff felt unsure; he'd never felt this way in an inquest before. He tried desperately to focus and defend his decision to leave the bodies at the site overnight, but his words came out in bursts and disjointed sentences. The barrister raised his voice and demanded that Geoff just answer the question. Geoff blurted out the horrible truth in a rush, his mind in a blur. Just as he'd feared, the family members began to sob. His heart raced and his voice faltered. He saw in the family's faces that something wasn't right – these people hadn't known! The pilot's sister burst into floods of tears at hearing the shocking truth. Geoff couldn't contain his emotion when he saw her distress. He took a deep breath but could feel tears welling. Shaking and gripped with fear, he was losing control.

The barrister, seemingly oblivious to the emotion in the court, continued his questioning, asking Geoff over and over why he'd left the bodies of the two victims at the scene. He accused Geoff of being callous and said that clearly, from the families' point of view, he'd made the wrong decision. Geoff tried to explain the importance of his examining the scene in daylight and again began to struggle with his composure. He couldn't believe that after trying his best to do everything right, spending time with the pilot's wife, and even cleaning and preparing the body for viewing, he was being criticised. He finally cracked, breaking down and sobbing in the witness box.

The Coroner, Sev Hill, warned the barrister to respect the witness. He then addressed the court, saying that obviously they had heard some criticism of Detective Bernasconi, and that he wanted to make the point that he'd conducted many inquests in which the detective had been involved and that he had always known him as a man of great expertise, who had made the right decision on this occasion. Mr Hill added that he had never before seen Detective Bernasconi suffering from stress during a cross examination.

Geoff was shocked by his breakdown in the witness box. From that moment on, things changed. He now couldn't be sure he wouldn't lose his composure again. In the past, he'd cried occasionally but his emotions being out of control was something new. Still, though, Geoff was unaware of how close to going under he really was. Later, the Coroner mentioned to Geoff's superior officer what had happened but, surprisingly, not a single formal inquiry was made. The senior investigator involved in working on the Golambo Hill plane crash, who wasn't in court that day, rang Geoff and inquired after his health, but nothing else was done or said at that time about Geoff's emotional state.

The following August, the Coroner released his findings – that bad weather and pilot error were the cause of the crash. He commented that during cross examination he had seen Geoff 'losing it'. He also mentioned that he'd dealt with Geoff for over fifteen years and had never before seen him like this. After this, Geoff was called into the inspector's office and asked if he was all right. He told him that he was, because, deep down, he was hoping it was an isolated incident. Nothing else was said and it seemed that the whole episode was forgotten, but Geoff clearly wasn't okay. He was now barely functioning and just couldn't seem to get on top of things.

A week after seeing the inspector, Geoff was in the forensic vehicle on an errand when an urgent call came over the radio for assistance at a domestic dispute. Believing he was the backup car, he rushed to the scene; however, when he arrived, he realised he was the first one there. Immediately he sensed that, without prompt action, a siege could develop. An agitated man was bailed up inside the house with his wife, threatening her with a knife. Geoff approached the house and negotiated with him. After a short time, the man surrendered himself and the knife.

During the incident Geoff had secured his gun and handcuffs in the crime scene vehicle, as wearing appointments during forensic examinations could interfere with the collection of evidence by getting in the way of wearing protective clothing. When he'd arrived at the scene he'd reacted instinctively, and hadn't considered the possible effect of approaching the situation unarmed. Afterwards, he was gutted to learn that a weapons instructor, who'd arrived at the scene shortly after the incident was successfully resolved, had made a complaint that Geoff should be disciplined for not having worn his gun. There was an investigation and consequently Geoff was put under intense scrutiny about his actions on the day, and asked to justify having attended the scene without his gun and handcuffs. He was now possibly facing a neglect-of-duty charge. He felt that he was just never quite good enough in the eyes of the hierarchy, and his paranoia grew as the investigation went on. The last straw came a few days later, in the guise of a missing exhibit.

Around the middle of 1998, Geoff had attended an aggravated break and enter where a man had broken into an elderly woman's house in Gundagai. She was bashed, threatened with rape and subjected to property theft. On the night of the attack, the offender was found in a paddock at the rear of the crime scene. He was wearing a blood-soaked shirt, analysis of which determined that it carried the same DNA as the victim's and only one in seven million people had that same DNA. The exhibit had been sent to the division of

forensic medicine at Glebe, and after all examinations were concluded, it was secured in the Sydney district crime-scene unit's
exhibit room at the Sydney Police Centre. Geoff then took the shirt
back to Wagga, where he'd secured it in the crime-scene unit exhibit
storage area, awaiting transportation back to the station where it
had been originally.

On the day of the offender's trial, Geoff was investigating a murder at Tumbarumba and had the only exhibit-room key. He was
asked to locate the exhibit when he returned and hand it over to an
officer involved in the case, who would take it to court. When Geoff
finally returned and entered the secure exhibit area, he couldn't find
the shirt and realised it had been sent to Tumut police station. He
explained this but no one listened, preferring to lay the blame on
him and maintain he was the last person to have possession of the
exhibit. It got back to Geoff that there were rumours that he had
been negligent and lost the exhibit. Obviously, word had got around
about the incident at the Golambo Hill plane crash inquest. He was
disgusted and hurt at being treated this way. He was adamant he'd
brought the exhibit safely back from Sydney and handed it over to
the fingerprint expert, who had conveyed it to the officer in charge
at Tumut, but the Tumut staff were saying they didn't have it. For
now, though, he was blamed for the shirt having disappeared and
for the ensuing disruption to the court proceedings.

The defence counsel argued that without the blood-stained
shirt the prosecution case was weak. The judge agreed and the trial
was aborted. The next day, both the local and the Sydney news-
papers had a field day blaming police for sloppy work and careless
handling of the exhibit. The headlines read: 'Lost: Evidence vital to
trial' and 'Police bungle leads to jury discharge in elderly woman's
bashing case'. It seemed that someone was going to have to pay and

that it was going to be Geoff. Comments such as 'We will find who is responsible and charges will be laid' horrified him; everyone knew that he worked in the crime-scene unit, so the comments obviously referred to him.

Geoff was even more shocked when the local area commander instigated an internal inquiry, leading to him being questioned at length. He strongly protested his innocence but it would be another twenty-four hours before the shirt was finally located at Tumut police station. On the day the shirt was found, two days after it had allegedly disappeared, Geoff was with Derek Bullen, the local police chaplain, from whom he had sought pastoral care. The local area commander told Derek that the shirt had been found and asked if his apologies could be conveyed to Geoff.

By this stage, though, Geoff was fearful, paranoid and extremely depressed. Suicide had begun to seem like a way out, and he had thought about being the one to give them a crime scene to look at. He constantly toyed with the idea of going down to the river at Wiradjuri reserve and hanging himself from a tree. *Who will they blame then?* The apology had come far too late. Geoff was furious that he'd been hung out to dry and, to his mind, it was unforgivable.

Derek suggested to Geoff that he take some time off. He went home with an armful of paperwork for what was supposed to be a two-week break – certainly not what Derek had had in mind. In effect, Geoff would merely be working from home. Altogether, he had about a dozen Coroner's statements to prepare. Some were for fires he'd investigated but most of them related to deaths, several of which were of people he knew. By this stage, Geoff had been professionally involved in at least twelve such deaths. Adding to his stress was the headline in the local paper: 'Police no longer shirty over missing evidence'. The journalist who wrote the article lived across the street from Geoff. He couldn't understand why he hadn't simply asked him what the facts were. Once again, Geoff felt betrayed, and that even his neighbour had it in for him.

At home the day after the exhibit was found, Geoff was looking at the mound of papers in front of him and the scores of photographs strewn over his desk when his mind just went blank. He simply didn't know where to start; he tried to sort the paperwork in order of urgency but couldn't think straight. He was paralysed with fear and then he began to shake uncontrollably. Suddenly, he was curled up in a ball on the loungeroom floor, wrapped from head to toe in a doona, his whole body shaking. He lay there having bursts of uncontrollable bodily tremors until Jocelyn found him, totally incoherent, when she arrived home from work.

Realising Geoff was in serious trouble, Jocelyn decided to get him professional help. They discussed the nightmares he was having and the exhaustion he felt. And then there was the recent occasion when he'd sat in a chair all day reading the same page of a book. Jocelyn hadn't been able to believe it when she got home to see Geoff with a cold cup of coffee on the table next to a chair in which he'd obviously been sitting all day. He admitted that the day had passed in a blur, without him having any awareness of time and of how long he'd been sitting there.

Jocelyn finally said, 'You've got to do something about the way you are. I just can't handle you like this.'

Geoff knew she was right but was incapable of making a decision; he knew that he had to put his life in others' hands.

The next day Jocelyn helped Geoff make a call to St John of God Hospital in Richmond, the centre for PTSD, where he believed he could commit himself to live-in depression and anxiety treatment. He then rang the duty officer and advised him that he wasn't doing too well and would be going into hospital. Jocelyn helped him fill out all the paperwork relating to his illness and his request to be classified as hurt on duty. There was a knock at the door and Geoff opened it to see Inspector Ken Finch, who, when they couldn't find Geoff's gun at the station, was worried that he might be suicidal.

'It's where it's always been,' Geoff told him.

'Where's that?' Ken asked.

'My handcuffs and gun are stored at the bloody station, with all the other duty officer's weapons!'

The inspector immediately did a complete backflip, saying, 'Oh well, we were just a bit worried that you had your weapon here and that you might do yourself harm.'

Geoff was incensed. It seemed to him they cared only about the safe storage of departmental equipment.

'Fuck me! Are you going to go down to the shed and take all the rope out of there, or turn off the electricity, or take all the knives out of the kitchen? Because if anyone knows how to kill himself, it's me,' Geoff said bluntly.

'Oh, don't be like that; calm down,' Ken answered.

Ken was clearly uncomfortable with the situation and it dawned on Geoff that he was merely doing what he'd been instructed to do. With that, he left. There was no follow-up or offer of assistance, and Ken's visit was pretty much the last time Geoff had anything to do with the local command or his immediate supervisor. The command had stripped him of his gun and handcuffs without any formal notification. To Geoff, this was the ultimate humiliation and the beginning of the end.

15

ST JOHN OF GOD

Geoff travelled to Sydney and saw Dr McGrath at St John of God. He described his work and the impact it was having on his mental state. While he was talking, his whole body trembled uncontrollably. He told the doctor that his wife felt he was going downhill fast, that he couldn't sleep, was having terrible nightmares and couldn't stop shaking. Geoff asked if he could go back on the medication he'd been prescribed some fifteen months before and had stopped taking. Dr McGrath agreed to prescribe Luvox. He also told Geoff he believed he was suffering from post-traumatic stress disorder and suggested he consider attending the PTSD management course at the hospital's Richmond centre. The doctor gave Geoff a medical certificate and sent him home with a referral to see a visiting PTSD specialist at a private Wagga hospital.

When Geoff got home, things didn't improve. The medication didn't work as well as it had before and he fell even deeper into a depressive state. Finally, Dr Reinhardt, the PTSD specialist, was due to attend the Wagga hospital on a Vietnam veterans' consultation day and Geoff made an appointment. Dr Reinhardt formally diagnosed him with PTSD and major depression. She suggested he apply for the next PTSD treatment course at St John of God, which was due to start the following month.

In the meantime, Jocelyn was struggling with Geoff's erratic behaviour. On one occasion, she asked him to collect Emily from school as she was working late. Around 3.30 p.m. that afternoon, the school called Jocelyn to say that Emily was still there and could she pick her up. Jocelyn rang everyone she could think of trying to locate Geoff, but no one had seen or heard from him. When Emily and Jocelyn finally got home, she found him fast asleep on the kids' trampoline in the backyard. She was furious and demanded to know why he hadn't gone to the school as planned. Geoff simply shrugged his shoulders and said, 'Oh well.'

This type of behaviour was completely out of character for Geoff; he had always been so organised and punctual. Now, though, he seemed to have no concept of time or commitment and, it seemed, he was incapable of completing the smallest task. When Geoff finally left for the PTSD treatment course, Jocelyn was relieved and thankful that, hopefully, he would finally get the help he needed and in time life would return to normal.

During his first twenty-one-day hospital stay, Geoff learnt a lot about his symptoms and about how they'd developed after his constant exposure to so many traumatic scenes over the years. He learnt about what causes stress and how the body and mind react to it, and the basis of hyperarousal, anxiety and depression. They explained to him the nature of PTSD and how the body reacts when the limit of its exposure to stress is exceeded. The events that may trigger PTSD include natural disasters, violence, being in or witnessing an accident, and ongoing exposure to trauma. Geoff had experienced all these to an accumulative degree. Next he discovered and began to understand the signs of PTSD, which include withdrawal and the feeling of being on an emotional roller-coaster, having intrusive memories and thoughts, nightmares or recurring dreams about an event, as well as flashbacks, panic attacks and insomnia. These could be triggered by anniversaries, people, places, smells, sounds, sights or tastes. The key to coping seemed to be developing resilience.

Geoff realised he should have been equipped with knowledge of stress, but was only now learning about the impact on him of constant exposure to trauma. He also realised that the pressure of work, including court appearances, and the resulting exhaustion from working long hours without a break had been key ingredients in his eventual collapse. All those years spent working alone without adequate rest or support, combined with the traumatic nature of the scenes he examined and the stress of dealing with grieving relatives, was too much for anyone to cope with; he was horrified at the degree to which he'd been left exposed. It explained a lot about the feelings he had been struggling with, especially his profound sadness about those who'd lost their lives. This had led directly to his depression and thoughts of suicide.

Geoff now understood why he had begun to feel angry with those he perceived to have been responsible for the tragedies or to have failed to act and therefore allowed these terrible events to happen. His feelings that these events were unjust had led to anger and frustration. This flowed over to his disillusionment with police management and his belief they could have prevented his illness if they had protected and supported him. In fact, the department's lack of support was one of the key triggers. Geoff understood that his alcohol and tobacco use were ways of avoiding the painful emotions relating to his ever-increasing workload. Finally, he had become overwhelmed by life in general and was no longer able to cope with certain things.

Geoff now began to see the benefit of recognising his responses to stress, talking with a therapist and joining a support group. He knew he needed a plan for coping, and that monitoring his physical health, allowing himself to grieve after events and letting himself feel emotions, rather than turning them off as he'd been taught, were all key factors to ensuring ongoing mental health. He had to learn to let go of destructive thoughts and feelings, including obsessional thinking, avoidance, guilt and self-loathing, and learn to take one day at a time. He also realised the importance of not relying on alcohol to mask his emotions. He now understood that he had used alcohol to numb his distress going right back to the Carrafa family car accident in 1984.

Geoff had to learn to challenge his feelings of helplessness and regain control of his future. He had to focus on looking after himself, rather than caring for others as he'd done for so many years. He needed to learn to relax physically, using imagery and meditation, eat and sleep well, have regular exercise and find enjoyable activities to do. It especially hit home with Geoff that he no longer played the guitar or enjoyed music as he once had. He hoped he could rediscover his love of music and somehow find peace in playing it as he had before his trauma had become too much to cope with.

Geoff understood for the first time that he was sad but not bitter about what had happened to him during his career in the police force. He now didn't blame anyone but was deeply disturbed by how much he'd changed over the years; it had happened so gradually that he hadn't noticed. Above all, he wished someone had prepared him for forensic work, or at least educated him about ways to care for himself. Geoff wanted his old self back but, at this stage, working on fixing himself seemed like another burden. He was now learning how to deal with the many horrific incidents he'd seen over the years, but he still had so much grief to work through that it was almost like trying to climb Mount Everest with bricks on his back.

Foremost in Geoff's mind was, despite everything, his love of the job; he still saw himself as a forensic investigator and hoped to achieve the promotion he'd worked so hard for. During his hospital stay, he decided to apply for sick leave and have his condition classified as hurt on duty. Although Geoff was beginning to realise he was suffering from a mental illness, he still couldn't see the degree of damage he'd sustained, and had every intention of returning to work. At the end of three weeks, he packed up and discharged himself without letting Jocelyn know, and proceeded to hitchhike home.

The first Jocelyn knew about Geoff's impending return was when she saw him walking up the road as she stopped at the local service station to buy milk on her way home from work. She couldn't believe her eyes when she realised it was Geoff, who looked dishevelled and spaced out. She was even more horrified when he admitted to hitchhiking all the way from Sydney to Wagga.

At home that evening, Geoff curled up under the doona again and lay on the loungeroom floor as though he were in a cocoon. Emily asked what was wrong and Jocelyn tried to explain to her in simple terms that Daddy wasn't well and that they should just leave him alone. The next day, Geoff sat in a chair staring off into space. Jocelyn began to panic as she realised that he was still on the brink of total collapse.

Over that weekend, the family all went to a fair at the local racecourse, where Geoff spotted a woman pushing a pram. He looked inside and saw the baby asleep but he thought it looked dead.

He turned to Jocelyn and whispered, 'You'd better get me out of here – that baby looks like it's dead!'

Jocelyn looked over and said, 'It does too. Come on; let's go.'

They quickly left.

Geoff struggled to come to terms with his reaction to the sleeping baby, and couldn't convince himself it hadn't been dead. He was still hoping to return to work but, on the other hand, didn't feel like he was getting better and simply didn't know what to do. The next day, Geoff demanded Jocelyn accompany him to their solicitor's office, where he signed over power of attorney.

At home, he again tried to tackle the large pile of unfinished Coroner's briefs, but it was all too much and he retreated under the doona again. Jocelyn came home to find him curled up in a ball, shaking and crying. He was saying he was no good and that she was better off without him; he was clearly distraught and potentially suicidal. Seeing Geoff's paranoia firsthand destabilised Jocelyn. The fun-loving man she had first met was gone and she couldn't see him ever returning. She convinced him to allow the social worker from the hospital to come to the house. They talked for a couple of hours until Geoff finally said he would go to the Wagga Base Hospital. Jocelyn got in touch with the Police Association and they agreed to organise the first possible flight from Wagga to get Geoff back into St John of God Hospital at Richmond. Geoff spent the next two days heavily sedated on a cocktail of drugs; he can't remember being taken to the airport or getting onto the plane.

Scott Coleman and Mark Sykes were in touch with him and did the best they could, but both men were struggling with their own stresses. Scott's wife was slowly dying and he was trying to cope with this, as well as the demands of a young family and working long hours. Likewise, Mark, as the only local fingerprint investigator, was dealing with his own exhaustion and workload. It was no secret that Geoff was hospitalised, but he received no word from his local area command, nor did the physical evidence section in Sydney offer any assistance. It seemed that, now more than ever before, he was on his own.

Two days later, Wal Taylor, Geoff's solicitor from the police association, was at Mascot Airport to meet Geoff and take him straight to St John of God Hospital. Geoff again paid for his treatment through his private health insurance and this time stayed for seven weeks.

During this time he had a number of visitors, including his mother, whom he hadn't seen for around eight months, as she was living in Tweed Heads. When she walked in the room and saw him, she exclaimed, 'That's not my son!' Geoff was stunned at his mother's reaction, as he had thought he was getting better, and was consumed with guilt for distressing her, as she was unwell.

He also had a number of visits from the police association but no word from forensic services in Sydney until just before his discharge in December. The officer in charge visited with his wife, and left after a quick chat and a wander around the grounds.

During this time, Geoff had heard through his colleagues that there was the threat of transfer to Sydney, which only served to heighten his anxiety and fear. He was waiting for a call to show him he was valued but the only call he received was from his local area command. It was the shift supervisor, who called Geoff's mobile and promptly rattled off the details of a suicide scene he wanted him to attend. Geoff was stunned; it appeared the sergeant had no idea he was in hospital. When he told him, 'I'm in the nuthouse,' the sergeant apologised and hung up.

Finally, Erik Oates and Wal Taylor from the police association arrived and plonked a pile of hurt-on-duty and medical-discharge papers in front of Geoff. Initially he was dismayed that his career with the police was over, but he soon came to realise any hope he had of returning to police duties was gone. The discharge papers listed his injury as post-traumatic stress disorder. In the section describing how the injury or illness occurred were the words 'exposure to crime scenes, particularly while performing crime scene duties for thirteen years, compounded by repeated "revisiting" of crime scenes through preparation of reports, brief preparation and court attendance, together with the emotional drain of dealing with and consoling victim's families'. Likewise, the medical discharge papers were marked with 'post-traumatic stress disorder' and Geoff simply wrote, 'I am unable to discharge the duties of my office due to post-traumatic stress disorder.'

Just before Christmas, while Geoff was still in hospital, he received a card in the mail from the Groth family. On hearing that Geoff had suffered a nervous breakdown, they had sent him their best wishes. This card gave him great comfort. It showed what a compassionate family the Groths were and, in a sense, it made him realise how lucky he was, as, even though he was ill, this was nothing compared with their loss.

Meanwhile, Jocelyn was struggling at home with all the things that Geoff had once done. Scott and Mark were keeping in touch and giving her emotional support, but they were now running the office with one less person, as had been the case when Dave Frost was off sick due to stress. One day, Jocelyn ran into one of the government support officers who worked at the Wagga police station, and he asked Jocelyn if there were anything she needed or that the local police could assist her with while Geoff was in hospital. She mentioned that the lawns needed mowing. The next day, an internal memo was sent around the station asking for volunteers to form a lawn-mowing roster to help Jocelyn out. She then received an angry call from the station telling her to ring the police association if she needed help in the future; it was pointed out, in no uncertain terms, that this sort of assistance was *not* the local staff's responsibility. Jocelyn was furious. The police association had already done enough by helping to get Geoff into hospital, and it didn't seem right that the local station should fob her off like this. She was sure that most of the staff there didn't feel like this, but if they were told not to help they had to follow orders. She found out later that the man who had sent round the internal memo had been hauled over the coals for trying to assist.

Geoff himself was taking life one day at a time, continuing his therapy and trying to get on top of things. He still found it difficult to focus on his recovery, as, in his work, he'd always been the one who picked up the pieces. As well, for the first time he was talking about the way he had felt after attending scenes at which countless people had lost their lives. He spoke particularly of those cases involving people he knew and of how difficult it had been to be placed in an investigative role when he really needed to work through his own feelings of grief. Geoff realised he had to count his blessings and learn more about himself. He knew, too, that he had to learn to change his negative thought processes. By this time, he'd become cynical and less tolerant, especially of the media and its focus on high-profile cases. He felt strongly that those who didn't get the attention suffered the very same way as those who did, and yet, it seemed, nobody gave a shit about them. He now had to learn to value life while living with pain, guilt and death.

The breakdown of his and Jocelyn's relationship was foremost in his thoughts. It was during this stay in hospital that, with his brother's help, he made the glass-topped coffee table memorial dedicated to Jocelyn and the kids. Jocelyn helped by finding the newspaper clippings he'd kept of all the investigations he'd attended over the years. His 'reflection' table was his way of dealing with every tragedy with which he'd been involved over the past decade.

The next step in Geoff's recovery was a memorial service in the St John of God Hospital chapel to commemorate his career and to honour all the people who had lost their lives. He would finally get to say goodbye and he also wanted to thank his family for all the sacrifices they'd made throughout his police career. Jocelyn helped put the order of service together, and a program with special readings and music was prepared. Jocelyn and the kids travelled to the hospital for the service and enjoyed this special occasion that helped Geoff heal the many wounds of the past. The service concluded with the words:

A thing is complete when you can let it be . . .
Let there be more joy and laughter in your living . . .
Every end is a new beginning.

And finally, one of the most profound aspects of Geoff's recovery was his facing his demons through cognitive behavioural therapy. A scale monitoring his level of distress was used to track his progress. Geoff learned that emotions, thoughts and behaviour are connected, so that how you feel, what you think and what you do are all related, and distress is a result of certain thoughts. Such thoughts can be controlled by examining them in a realistic way. One example of such a thought for Geoff was his belief that his not being able to cope meant he was a failure. He realised after working through this thought process that, in fact, he had done a good job and simply reacted normally to abnormal situations.

Geoff's therapist encouraged him to write his thoughts in a journal. Once the journal was finished, he read it over and over in an attempt to permit himself to grieve and let go of his experiences. As he wrote his thoughts down, his memories of what had happened years ago flowed onto the page with ease and accuracy. Finally, he felt a sense of release after having allowed himself to express feelings he'd harboured for over a decade. In one such entry, he wrote:

During my admission to St John of God Burwood I have explored that very issue of recovery and vowed my future dealings would take that into consideration with my clients. Unfortunately they came thick and fast; I had been a police officer for over twenty years and a Forensic Crime Scene Examiner for sixteen years. Over that time I had been involved in the investigation of approximately 1200 deaths. Those deaths ranged from murders, suicides, fatal motor vehicle accidents, domestic accidents and unnatural deaths. The deceaseds varied in age from foetus to 100 years old. I always found dealing with the deaths of infants and children cut the hardest. Parents lives shattered, siblings devastated and other relatives offering clumsy support.

It is difficult enough for relatives to accept the death of a child let alone deal with the enormous intrusion of a forensic and police investigation. Acumen and diplomacy, honesty and compassion are essential criteria towards professionalism, never more apparent when the death takes place in the home.

It had been my unfortunate privilege to intimately deal with many deaths involving children over the years; in fact one in particular led me to meet my dear wife and friend. We have shared numerous ones since including a preschool classmate of our daughter.

My exposure to tragedy had been well established and in later years few things shocked me, the main legacy being caught in the moment of time with relatives at their most vulnerable and not seeing the inevitable recovery that takes place over time.

After writing about the Carrafa family accident and then the sadness he felt after the drowning of the Groth twins, Geoff wrote about what had become of the job he'd loved so passionately.

Reform the police, the Royal Commissioner said. There's no room for a bent and crooked cop. Society expects more from those in blue. Join in the transformation – corruption we will stop. Honesty will be the foundation on which to build – strive for a strong and committed majority. Looking after our people, our greatest assets, those that serve our first priority.

Over twenty-one years I've served, sixteen behind the lens, a thousand deaths and nightmares along the way, the Carrafa family of six, countless triples and doubles, murders, rapes and suicides both night and day. The Enngonia riots entrenched into my memory. The Groth twins, the Frost and Miller babies, to name just a few. Hours, days and weeks isolated from my family doing my job, proud to serve as part of the crew.

The demons of death became too much. Time to admit my frailties and take the first steps, seek some help, I told myself, confident I was valued, for the new age of truth encouraged those who wept. The weeks go by with not so much as a call, perhaps they just wish to give me space. The wheels were turning full circle as I slept, my future publicly discussed, their plans gathering pace. We'll find a spot in Sydney to hide him, the good news passed to my colleagues then to my wife while I'm trying so desperately to come to terms with the chaos in my life.

A teacher once told me that when one door closes another door opens, I'm determined to make use of that class and now my career door has slammed shut, they can shove the job fair up their arse.

16

THIS FINE OFFICER

After spending Christmas in hospital, Geoff was finally discharged from St John of God and went home on 31 December 1999. He was now heavily medicated on antidepressants, and antipsychotic and sedative medication, which included Effexor XR, Zyprexa, Valium and Normison. Ironically, in early January 2000, he received notification that he'd successfully passed the assessment for promotion to commissioned officer, that being the rank of inspector or above.

A couple of days later, the police medical officer (PMO), Dr Tom Norris, recommended that Geoff be medically retired from the force. Even though the PMO had recommended this course of action, independent doctors' reports still had to be submitted prior to a final decision being made. Over the next nine months, the NSW Police sent Geoff to visit a number of doctors in Sydney and he was required to go over the entire painful story of the events leading up to his illness again and again.

Geoff also continued to see Dr Reinhardt but things weren't improving at home. Finally, in February, Jocelyn and the kids left. Geoff was devastated – he'd lost everything he'd worked so hard for.

Jocelyn was also struggling with her own sense of loss; in many ways, she had developed secondary PTSD from the impact of living with Geoff. She had had to watch helplessly as her husband deteriorated while trying to cope with her own distress over the deaths of friends and associates. On top of that, the mere fact that through Geoff's work so many tragic incidents had become part of her everyday life had taken an incredible toll, and she was determined to have a normal and happy life again. Jocelyn never lost her deep feelings for Geoff but she just got to the stage where she could no longer live with him. For the sake of her own sanity and to protect the kids, she finally decided to go her own way.

With Jocelyn gone, Geoff turned to family for support. In particular, his brother, Victor, and his eldest daughter, Kate, from his marriage to Annette helped him get through this terrible time. Kate's parents had divorced when she was around six years old and, at that age, she didn't understand the nature and impact of her father's work. It wasn't until much later, when she was about fifteen and Geoff was hospitalised for the first time, that she began to comprehend. She realised that her father was sad when he began turning up at her school during lunch to see her. Kate saw him crying a lot and during this time he confided in her that he thought nobody understood what he was going through and that, in some cases, they didn't believe there was anything wrong with him. This made her grow up pretty quickly. As well, Geoff told her that something happening to her would be his worst nightmare – yet more baggage for her to carry in her teenage years.

After Geoff was released from hospital, he wrote Kate a letter saying that he was sorry he hadn't been there for her and for her older brother, Scott, while they were growing up but that he wanted to try to make up for lost time. It wasn't until Geoff filed a civil claim against the NSW Police in 2002 for the injuries he'd sustained that Kate really understood what he'd endured. She felt sick to the stomach when she realised what he'd had to see and deal with in his work as a crime-scene examiner, and was distressed by the unfairness of this happening to such a giving and loving person. She came to the conclusion that it was no wonder her father changed over the years. When Kate saw the reflection table that Geoff had made in hospital, it brought tears to her eyes. *How could he have done all that and how did he cope?* she thought. Kate's biggest relief after Geoff was treated was the fact that he was no longer a policeman; enough was enough.

Over the next fifteen months, Geoff went back to St John of God Hospital for three more sessions of in-patient care. He was still learning to live with depression, deal with intrusive thoughts, and cope with his continuing sleep difficulties. He was desperately trying to move on with his life but he realised the damage was so deep that his recovery would be a long and complex journey. It was around this time that he met his new partner, Leonie, and once again enjoyed the fulfilment of a new relationship.

Meanwhile, Geoff's medical discharge was still being processed. His psychiatrist at St John of God, Dr Reinhardt, submitted a medical report. In it, she wrote:

I first assessed Mr Bernasconi on the 13th of September 1999. He was a 43-year-old man, living with his second wife and children, aged five and two, on sick leave from his work as a police officer.

He presented with recurrent intrusive thoughts, nightmares and flashbacks that related to incidents which had occurred during his police service. These arose spontaneously or could be triggered by reminders of the traumatic events, [for] example, TV reports of accidents, sirens. He also described anxiety episodes characterised by sweating, palpitations, agitation and hyperarousal.

He had become so overwhelmed by his distress that he felt increasingly depressed and at times suicidal. He stated that throughout his career he had been exposed to numerous distressing incidents where he witnessed death and was filled with helplessness and horror. The impact of these was increased by the fact that, being in a rural community, the victims were often personally known to him. A number of incidents stand out as being particularly distressing and prominent in his re-experiencing symptoms.

Mr Bernasconi is a very compassionate man, who has been particularly concerned about the impact of tragedy on surviving relatives.

On examination, Mr Bernasconi was a fit-looking man, appearing younger than his stated age, in casual clothing. He was agitated and tearful, but pleasant and cooperative, with good eye contact.

He is no longer able to perform duties as a police officer even in a restricted capacity. Because police work is associated with reminders of his traumas, he is likely to decompensate if exposed to these triggers. I recommend that he should be medically discharged from the police force.

Dr Malcolm Dent, consultant psychiatrist, also submitted a report setting out his findings, dated 29 June 2000. It stated that he saw Geoff for assessment over one and three-quarter hours. He had seen Dr Reinhardt's report and acknowledged the diagnosis of 'post-traumatic stress disorder and major depression'.

He noted that Geoff was a very pleasant, courteous man, who was clearly intelligent. He found him to be well in control of his emotions and his actions during their meeting. He stated that Geoff was initially very apprehensive, and once he started giving his history, the stress that lay beneath his controlled demeanour became apparent. Geoff became upset, holding his head down at times and dropping his voice in volume.

Dr Dent stated that Geoff didn't show any sign that he was manipulating the situation or that he was exaggerating any of the information. His emotions were clearly genuine.

During the interview when he was describing the Carrafa accident and the Groth twins' drowning, Geoff was obviously distressed, flat in voice and manner, and very sad. He told Dr Dent that he was continually flashing back as he recalled these episodes. He told the doctor that: 'If I go to do a job, I sit down and explain my role, why I'm there, to seek out the truth and facts, and any questions they have I'll try to answer.' Dr Dent noted that it seemed to him Geoff had provided very sensible and appropriate psychological support to the families of the victims.

It became apparent to the doctor that Geoff put a defensive moat around himself to isolate his emotions and avoid emotional contact with others, a very common phenomenon in those with PTSD. Technically, it's called inhibition of affect, but many sufferers think of it as an emotional moat with the drawbridge up and them inside their own defended castle.

It was clear to Dr Dent that this was a significant element of Geoff's behaviour, and that Geoff's association with a number of veterans, particularly Vietnam veterans in the St John of God program, had assisted Geoff in dealing with the gross inhibition of emotions common to PTSD sufferers. The group program encouraged people to vent their emotions and to talk about their feelings. Geoff said that 'if there's a bit of hurt in recounting it, I will wear it [because] every bit of gain is a bit of gain ... I'm trying to break the moat mentality. I don't want to remain angry with the police service and would prefer to help others.'

Dr Dent also identified very clear physiological symptoms of anxiety: pins and needles in the hands and legs; profuse sweating, latterly wetting the bed; tremors (at the time of the assessment somewhat improved); and an inability to be quiet and still. These symptoms had been present over a number of years, but Geoff had managed to keep going, at considerable cost to himself, his family and his job.

The doctor noted that Geoff estimated he had improved around 50 per cent through the program and treatment at St John of God, largely through removing him from stimulus to flashback, recapitulation or aggravation of his PTSD.

'That's not to say I haven't [had suicidal feelings]', Geoff told Dr Dent, and these occured especially over the twelve months leading up to August 1999 when he experienced the evolution of his condition into major depression: loss of weight, loss of appetite, chronic insomnia, pervasive helplessness and hopelessness, withdrawal from others, isolation of emotion, severe feelings of depression and despair. Some of these symptoms may have been present in the period before this but they were often of a temporary nature.

Dr Dent acknowledged that there was no past or family history of nervous disorders, that is, nothing of a constitutional or genetic nature to indicate any vulnerability to such a disorder. He also spoke to Geoff about his plans for the future. Geoff's goals were 'no more front line! I'd like to work with people on a voluntary basis, for example, juvenile offenders or people in aged care. I used to love playing the guitar and singing and I'd like to do some entertainment for old people.'

The doctor concluded that the diagnosis of chronic PTSD with co-morbid major depression was beyond doubt. Geoff's history indicated an irrefutable cause based in his work with the NSW Police. The doctor said:

I must comment upon the exemplary nature and sensitivity of this fine officer in the discharge of his duties over the years. However, he is now quite incapable of discharging his duties as a Sergeant of Police because of these mental disorders. It is also quite improper to consider he would be capable of fulfilling any duties of a lesser rank that would otherwise be reasonable for him to perform. That is, he is not fit for either full duties or light or restricted duties; this is because of the severity and chronicity of his mental disorders.

My view is that he is unlikely ever to be able to work again in a job for which he is reasonably qualified by education, training or experience . . . I do not believe he is fit for any work outside the Police Service, and this is on a permanent basis. He will be fit for voluntary work on an occasional part-time basis in the areas he is seeking to pursue; I suggest such wishes or actions are indications of the man's essential worth of character, but if he is exposed to any risks or reminders in his daily activities . . . this will create an enduring chronicity and enduring vulnerability.

The doctor noted the trauma and stress Geoff had experienced in his job was of the kind that no one in the general workforce would ever be exposed to, and that his future life should be one of peace and freedom from risk and stress. Geoff's work had permanently impaired his mental health and cost him his families and two marriages.

I believe he's paid a very high emotional price (including the loss of his career) because of what I consider (having interviewed this excellent man) to be an unduly high standard of personal attitudes to proper service and assistance of those with whom he's been involved as the sufferers or victims of severely traumatic events.

I believe he needs the ongoing treatment that is set in place with his psychiatrist and his counsellor. He needs to remain on his medication; this may be a very long-term supportive proposition. My experience in dealing with severely traumatised war veterans indicates there may be many years of intervention and support to get them to a very limited state of being able to cope and manage, but never at any stage re-exposing them to any stressor.

I think if he is able to do that and have that allowed him, then he will be able to provide particularly empathic support to the aged and youths by way of counselling. There is somewhat of an attitude in clinical psychiatry that the best healers are often those who have been the most severely wounded, and I think aspects of this will apply to Mr Bernasconi.

A further number of doctors' reports were submitted that all came to the same conclusion. Geoff was officially discharged from the NSW Police on 29 September 2000, retiring medically unfit, hurt on duty. Shortly afterwards, a letter of thanks was published in the *Wagga Daily Advertiser* under the heading, 'Thanks, Geoff'.

Sir, Good luck, Geoff. Geoff Bernasconi was and will remain one of the finest policeman to grace the city of Wagga. He is a true gentleman and a true professional. I have had the misfortune on several occasions to assist Mr Bernasconi, from a fatal motor vehicle accident to the disappearance and death of my father. On these occasions I found Geoff to be honest, competent and extremely thorough and dedicated. The job Geoff was required to undertake was, as is imagined, a difficult one, yet through his nature he was able to instil a level of ease and confidence in what were difficult times. I for one wish Geoff all the best in the future and have no doubt he will succeed at whatever he puts his hands to. Signed, Mario Frisoli

Shortly after his retirement, Geoff took on a cleaning job with the Turvey Tavern in Wagga. He worked in the mornings for twenty-two hours per week. Before long, the tavern increased his duties so that they included cleaning and fixing poker machines. Once again, Geoff felt overloaded. He quickly realised that he wasn't coping and resigned four months later.

After having a demanding job for so many years, Geoff suddenly had nothing to do; it seemed that finding a balance in his life after police work was not going to be easy. He needed something to do that would keep his mind active but wouldn't place him under stress. As soon as he felt overwhelmed, the old anxiety and depression would return. It was almost like his body had a built-in memory, immediately identifying when he had too much to do with not enough time to do it, and he'd feel his adrenaline start pumping. He was still learning how to turn such feelings into a positive response and finding ways to relax. He was learning to recognise his triggers and discovering ways of coping, such as pacing himself. When he felt depressed, he would rest and listen to soothing music until his mood lifted.

Geoff was slowly working through the feeling of failure he had related directly to his early retirement. Eventually, he managed to accept that he wasn't a failure – he'd just retired a few years early. But he still needed to work out what he would do now. With this in mind, he renovated his kitchen. This gave him a project and he could also work at his own pace; he found he was quite good at this type of thing and had a sense of accomplishment when the job was finished.

Geoff came to realise that some days were better than others. He often visited the cemetery, where he would wander among the headstones, reflecting on his situation and giving thanks he hadn't ended up in one of these graves. He was sad to think that those who committed suicide hadn't been able to confide in others or seek help; he was glad that he'd been able to do this. Even though Geoff had thought of suicide on occasions, he had known he could never take that step because he'd seen what it did to the deceased's families, and he could never do that to his kids.

Geoff enjoyed working in the garden. To help him deal with his grief, he decided to build a memorial garden at the back of the house; it would be a place he could go to reflect. He constructed a pond, which he dedicated to the Carrafa family. He erected a sign 'Carrafa Pond' and whenever he felt bereaved, he'd sit there and spend a little quiet time reflecting. He also erected a bird bath under his bedroom window, with a sign saying 'Alex' in memory of Emily's little schoolfriend who'd died of a cerebral aneurysm before falling from a tree. Next to it, he built an archway in memory of 'Jesse Lise', Dave's granddaughter who'd died of cot death.

That Christmas, Jocelyn and the kids were with Geoff to celebrate the festive season. The year before, he had been in hospital and the family had missed out on the traditional Christmas celebration, and they were going to make up for this. Some time after the separation, Jocelyn had found a new partner, Ian, and moved to Townsville with the kids. She soon remarried and later had another child, a daughter. Geoff realised he had to move on. He was thankful that he continued to have a close relationship with Jocelyn; they still cared deeply for each other and kept in touch regarding the children.

When Jocelyn wandered out into the front yard, she was surprised to see how intricate Geoff's memorial garden was; she lingered at each stage and took in its significance to Geoff and to his recovery. It was obvious that he found great solace in spending time reflecting at the memorials he'd built so carefully. It seemed that he now had his own special place where he could grieve.

17

FIGHT FOR JUSTICE

By late 1999, Geoff had realised that he would never rebuild his life to the degree he'd hoped he would. He was still suffering bouts of depression and paranoia. After treatment with Dr Reinhardt, he began to understand how profoundly his work had affected every facet of his life and, worse still, that the effect was longstanding. Geoff initially sought advice from Walter Taylor of the police association in relation to his rights regarding his hurt on duty claim and his pension entitlements. In February 2000, Geoff was advised that he had a potential common law claim, based on a New South Wales Court of Appeal decision, *State of New South Wales v Seedsman*. He was given advice on bringing a claim against the NSW Police Service for compensation and referred to a firm of solicitors, Oates and Smith.

Up until this point, Geoff had not thought of his injury as having been caused by the police service's conduct. He had thought of his condition, although initially he didn't know what it was, as part and parcel of the stress of being a police officer, and wasn't aware that the police service could have, for example, provided debriefing, counselling, and job rotation, and monitored his psychological health, which could have prevented him suffering an injury. Once Geoff had decided to make a civil claim he was informed of the three-year statute of limitations, that is, a claim had to be filed within three years of the person becoming aware of their injury. Geoff's injuries went back to 1984, when he'd attended the Carrafa family accident scene, but he only became aware that he had a psychological illness after having treatment at St John of God and reading Dr Reinhardt's psychiatric assessment.

With his solicitors' assistance, Geoff then embarked on the painful task of writing an affidavit setting out the history of his work with the NSW Police and the culmination of exposure to trauma that ultimately led to his developing PTSD. In January 2002, his solicitors filed a notice of motion for extension of time, and the following month a claim was filed in the District Court giving notice to the NSW Police that Geoff was seeking compensation for his injury. A number of documents were exchanged between Oates and Smith and the solicitor of the defendant, the state of New South Wales, until late February 2002, when Geoff's solicitor advised him of the possibility of serving an offer of compromise on the defendant. This meant settling the matter out of court for an agreed sum.

Geoff was advised that the offer of compromise would be less than the full value of the claim, which probably meant that if the matter were settled he would have to agree to accept a smaller amount in compensation; however, he would probably be awarded almost all his legal costs. Ultimately, this would save him about half his legal costs, should the matter go on to a full hearing in which his claim succeeded. However, he would have to be prepared to accept the agreed sum of money as full and binding settlement.

Geoff considered the benefits to his mental health of making the offer of compromise. The matter would be finalised and he wouldn't have to revisit the incidents he'd listed in his affidavit during court proceedings. Giving evidence would undoubtedly cause him further distress and, in addition, there would be the stress for his family members who would be witnesses. He realised he'd already put them through enough over the years, and just wanted the case settled and over with. He was still struggling with day-to-day activities, let alone being able to deal with court proceedings. However, he was determined to fight for justice and, hopefully, raise awareness of the mental and physical effects of forensic work. In March 2002, Geoff signed the paperwork signalling his desire to proceed with the offer of compromise. In it, he stated,

I hereby authorise and instruct you to settle my claim in the sum of $150 000 plus costs arising out of my employment with the NSW Police Service.

I authorise and instruct you to enter a verdict in respect of my claim against the State of NSW in the District Court of NSW for verdict for the Plaintiff in the sum of $150 000 plus costs.

I understand that when verdict monies are received I will be given an itemised account of costs and disbursements.

I understand from the settlement that the following amounts will be deducted;

Medical expenses which are unable to be ascertained. I understand that I am content that they are not in access of $15 000 which is the amount outstanding that has been approximated for medical treatment which I have received to date.

Social security payments which cannot be ascertained. I note you have not had payments from the Department of Social Security and therefore the refund due to the Department will be nil. I understand that should the refund be in excess of this I will be still liable under commonwealth law to pay that amount.

Other reductions (example, litigation lending, irrevocable authorities re debts to previous solicitors, banks, building societies etc.).

Legal costs and disbursements have been approximated by my solicitor to be no more than $15000, however I settle my case upon the understanding that should they be more I will be responsible for any additional costs or disbursements.

I understand that I may be liable to repay the monies by way of treatment expenses which the NSW Police Service has paid on my behalf.

I understand that from the settlement I will receive not less than $125000 clear in my hand provided the deductions are as set out above.

I understand that changes to the Social Security Legislation may require me to repay any benefits I have received in the past whether by way of pension, unemployment benefits or sickness benefits and I may be deprived in the future of ongoing social security entitlements. I understand that all efforts will be made to minimise my liability in this regard; however, I settle my case acknowledging the above.

I understand that should there be any monies repayable to Medicare I will be responsible for the payment of these expenses.

It has been explained to me and I understand that this settlement is in full and final settlement of all my rights at common law in respect of my psychological injury, yet I will still be entitled to a hurt on duty superannuation allowance.

Shortly after submitting the offer of compromise, Geoff, to his shock and disappointment, received notice that the state of New South Wales had rejected the offer of settlement. It appeared that the NSW Police did not in any way accept responsibility for Geoff's work injuries, even though they had pensioned him out of the police service as hurt on duty. It seemed that they would defend the matter in full. Geoff was then served with a document from the defence containing numerous pages of questions regarding all facets of his police work. In total, he had to answer 163 questions, many seemingly trivial and irrelevant to the case. Having to do so almost made Geoff physically sick from stress. Almost a year later, on 28 February 2003, the state of New South Wales filed notice of grounds of defence. Geoff realised the matter would go to a full hearing at the Sydney District Court on a date to be set. It was some three years since he'd been discharged from the police and he still couldn't see that there would be any way out of this nightmare for some time to come.

Affidavits were filed at the District Court on 5 February 2004 and the trial set down for the following December. The extension of time for which Geoff had applied was granted, and his Honour Judge McLoughlin in the civil jurisdiction of the Sydney District Court heard the matter. Geoff and his family travelled to Sydney and sat through the description of the details of each and every tragic event he'd attended through his twenty-three years of police service. Over the ensuing two weeks of the hearing, Geoff had no option but to face facts and come to terms with the physical and emotional transformation he'd undergone over years of exposure to trauma. The evidence described the impact on his health and the slow decline in his quality of life. At times, it all felt like a delusion; he couldn't believe he was sitting in court and that his career had ended like this.

The court heard that Geoff was claiming damages for psychiatric and psychological injuries sustained during his employment as a police officer, which related to his attendance at crime scenes, dealing with victims of crime, and investigating the physical circumstances of incidents and crime, as well as related duties. He was exposed to an unsafe work environment and unnecessary risk, causing him to suffer PTSD, major depression and nervous shock. Geoff alleged that the nature and conditions of his work had caused his injuries, and that his employer did not provide appropriate warning or education about recognising symptoms of this condition. As well, he was not given the benefit of debriefings, which could have reduced the impact on him of his work, or given regular psychiatric assessment. None of the evidence was contested nor a single witness called on behalf of the defence, except for a brief appearance by a psychologist attached to the welfare section. Finally, the defence conceded that Geoff's psychiatric injury was foreseeable and that the injury was, in fact, PTSD. However, they denied the injury was work related!

Judge McLoughlin commented that Geoff's alcohol consumption was a result of what he'd been exposed to in his work and the NSW Police's negligence. He felt that Geoff's condition was foreseeable given his extensive workload, and that had it been monitored and managed, his symptoms could have been reduced, therefore avoiding his current plight. He found that the effects of stress from the work Geoff had described were well documented and the NSW Police were well aware of them. This was evident from the general information available on how to deal with this type of stress. In addition, the service was aware that organisational intervention in the form of support and training was essential to police officers coping with stress. He found that Geoff's exposure to stress was significantly greater than that suffered by ordinary serving police officers, and that by the 1980s he should have been provided with critical incident stress debriefing, which would have assisted in identifying symptoms of PTSD as a reaction to exposure to traumatic incidents. The NSW Police were particularly aware of the need for proactive measures, he said, given a police culture that discouraged officers from admitting to what they saw as weaknesses.

They failed to implement and monitor access to counselling, debriefing sessions and senior officers' managerial decisions relating to supervising the effects of stress. Work systems and training programs on stress management and awareness, similar to that learned as part of police procedure and criminal law, should have been included. There should also have been in place an employee assistance program, peer counselling programs, operational policies that reduce stress, and professional counsellors to assist the officers and their families. The management program should have been improved, including greater supervision in order to enhance communication and decision-making, and workplace environment issues – including physical work space, quality of equipment and compensation packages – should have been addressed.

Judge McLoughlin found that it was because of these failures that Geoff was required to work long hours without assistance or suitable work practices in a highly traumatic environment without adequate counselling or debriefing. That he was under stress was obvious in 1984 and he should have been evaluated by a psychologist. As well, annual assessment of his work environment and psychological state should have been implemented. By the mid-1980s, or at least by 1992, the police force should have been aware that a number of elements cause stress to police officers, including continual exposure to people in pain or distress and the worst problems and elements of society, inadequate direction from supervisors, insufficient training, irregular shifts and long hours. Officers of normal fortitude and personality are at risk of developing PTSD and this was evident in the police service's failures to manage exposure to numerous traumatic incidents. The judge noted that Dr Reinhardt had mentioned in particular that Geoff was a very empathetic man, with great concern and compassion for the people involved in the incidents he had investigated, and that his caring nature and strong sense of altruism and devotion to duty had made him function more effectively in his role.

The judge found that the NSW Police failed to adequately warn that performing crime-scene work could lead to psychological or psychiatric injury. As well as not providing training to identify the signs of PTSD and preventable measures, specific training on how to deal with the graphic nature of forensic work, and with bereaved relatives and distressed victims was also not available. Due to his work commitments, Geoff was not given opportunities to attend stress management workshops. The three debriefing sessions he attended were inadequate and impersonal and did not cater to his emotional needs, nor did they occur within a reasonable timeframe after the events.

The diagnosis of PTSD with depression had been accepted by the commissioner of police, as was the fact that this condition was a result of Geoff having been hurt on duty, rendering him unfit to discharge his duties. Judge McLoughlin accepted the doctors' reports confirming the diagnosis of PTSD, that both Geoff's marriages ended due to the impact of PTSD as a direct result of the work he was engaged in, that it was the reason he lost the career that he was so passionately committed to for many years, and that his incapacity was permanent.

The judge said that psychological deterioration had been evident in Geoff from about 1994 and there had been episodes of psychological reaction even prior to this. If he had been assessed regularly by psychologists at least annually from 1988, his deteriorating condition would have been discovered much earlier than 1999. The judge accepted that Geoff did not know of or understand his psychological injuries until October 1999, when he was advised by Dr Reinhardt that he should be discharged from the police service. Therefore, he was within the timeframe allowing for an extension of time to pursue a civil claim.

Judge McLoughlin accepted that, in all likelihood, Geoff would have gone on to work at the level of inspector, having passed the assessment centre process that made him eligible for promotion and acted in positions at this rank on a number of occasions. He found that in-patient treatment was likely to continue due to the level of Geoff's injury and that this increased the likelihood of him having little social interaction. The judge found that depression significantly affected his ability to enjoy life.

Judge McLoughlin awarded Geoff $785 217.69. On 8 August 2002 an offer of compromise was rejected by the NSW Police, and so costs were awarded on a solicitor/client basis. It was finally over.

Geoff wasn't in court when the judgment was handed down but instead spent the day sitting by the grave of one of the people he'd come to know in death. His head in his hands, he sat in silence. His thoughts touched upon the profound effect that this death and so many others had had on him, his regrets about the past and his wish that he'd been supported in the work he so loved. Under the circumstances, the gravesite was the most comforting place he could be. He didn't yet know his battle for justice was over but, in any case, it made no difference. For Geoff, the damage was done and no amount of money could turn back the effects of time.

18

LIFE GOES ON

On that evening in June 2006, Geoff and I sat and talked for hours. During the night, his daughter Kate arrived. Geoff left the two of us to talk alone for a while so I could understand how she had felt growing up with a father so affected by his work. While she was talking, I was particularly struck by how the effects of PTSD impact on the families of sufferers and, in particular, the children.

After dinner, Geoff and I talked until after midnight. At one stage we were trying to remember the names of our colleagues from the Diploma of Applied Science in Forensic Investigation in Canberra, 1993 to 1996. Geoff disappeared and, after a short time, returned with a photograph of our graduating class. We were both shocked to see how many of the people in it had since been struck down with PTSD; in fact, there weren't many in that group of thirty who were still serving with the NSW Police.

Finally, exhaustion hit us both and we decided to leave the rest of our conversation until morning. It was a bitterly cold night and, as I prepared for bed, I took a small dose of Ativan, an antidepressant that would settle my nerves and help me to sleep. Those days I rarely took it but this was one occasion I knew I needed it. It would be impossible for me to empty my mind of the images Geoff and I had talked about, but I was determined to process the information without fear. I knew that Geoff's descriptions would trigger memories of experiences of my own, but by now I wasn't frightened of these images and thought this would be a test of how far I'd come in my own recovery. That night, images flashed across my mind and I woke often and felt the chill in the air, but I also told myself that it was all right and that I was safe.

In the morning, Geoff and I continued where we'd left off, discussing and debating every facet of his work as a crime-scene examiner. By midmorning neither of us could go on – we were both physically and emotionally exhausted. We agreed that I would probably return to Wagga over the next year or so to fill in any gaps, but at this stage I had plenty of material and was keen to get home and start this project.

Just before I left, Geoff asked me to wait a moment and disappeared behind a door leading under the house. He wanted to show me something. A few minutes later, he returned with an array of exquisite guitars. He lined the instruments up, showed me each one and described its history and sound qualities. It was wonderful to see that his love of music had returned; he wasn't yet playing again but his guitar collection told me that he was rediscovering a pleasure that had been lost to him for years.

Afterwards, Geoff led me through the hall on our way to the front door, and paused at a framed certificate on the wall. I saw it was his police service discharge certificate. It said:

Certificate of Service

This is to certify that Geoffrey Paul Bernasconi was a member

of the New South Wales Police Service from 23 January, 1978
until 29 September, 2000 having attained the rank of Detective
Sergeant and having been awarded the following decorations:
National Medal.

The certificate was signed by Commissioner Peter Ryan. I sighed
as I realised the irony of his last day of service being Police Remembrance Day.

As I headed back to Sydney, I thought about how I was going to
write this book. One thing I did know was that, just like my first
book, *Crime Scene*, this was a story that had to be told. Here was a
perfect example of how an excellent man could, due to his police
work, be reduced to a shadow of his former self. I always like to
think that whatever an experience, good or bad, it can be learned
from. I knew it was imperative that police working in rural areas
had the opportunity to understand what could happen to them.
I was passionate about warning those who chose a forensic career
of the dangers of performing such a role year after year without
adequate training, counselling, rotation, backup and debriefing.

Both Geoff and I loved our work but the end result for us had
been the same. Geoff had told me that his colleague (and a former
colleague of mine) Scott Coleman had recently succumbed to PTSD
and was now on long-term sick leave. The illnesses of Geoff's boss,
Dave Frost, of Geoff and of Scott marked more than forty years of
PTSD in workers in the same office. This appalling waste of the lives
of such fine and committed men had to stop.

A week or so after I got home, a package arrived in the
mail. Inside it, I found a bundle of old newspaper clippings and

information relating to Geoff's career. Most of it was water damaged and covered in mould, but it contained information going back twenty years. Over the next year and a half, I spent many hours sifting through the clippings, letters of appreciation, cards and doctors' reports. They were an interesting snapshot of Geoff's life and outlined what a truly remarkable man he is. I was beginning fully to recognise the many qualities he displayed as he loyally discharged his duties throughout his career.

Geoff and I had many discussions over the phone, and emails flew back and forth about information I needed. I saw his health improve, deteriorate and improve again as he struggled with the ebbs and flows of his debilitating illness. We spent many hours talking things through, as people with similar experiences do. I shed my own tears as I wrote the harrowing stories of those poor victims and their families, and of other people who came into Geoff's life. The hardest thing was writing about his emotional response to the Shania Twain song the Groth twins had loved to dance to. By that stage, I felt the full brunt of Geoff's emotional collapse and allowed myself to grieve in a way that would never have been possible for me in previous years. I often lit a candle and said a prayer both for the victims and for Geoff as anniversaries occurred, and I incessantly talked things through with my partner, Ken. I realised that Geoff's story would be hard to read, but in life there are so many lessons to be learned and I, for one, have learnt many on this journey.

In October 2007, I made the trip to Wagga again. This time, Geoff and I met early in the morning and sat outside by the pool. He was packing up and preparing to move house; he hoped that this new start would be a fresh beginning for him and I hoped this too.

Typically, I had many questions to ask and Geoff dutifully answered each one as I probed every facet of his life. We spoke for four and a half hours straight. This reflected our work ethic from our policing days, when we could work on a project for hours without a break. The only difference now was the exhaustion we felt after such a long session. Gone were the times when we could work on pure adrenaline for days, forgoing sleep and food to get the job done; now we both gave in to the need for rest after pushing ourselves to the limit.

The next morning, Geoff came to the hotel where I was staying to have breakfast with me. We talked for another hour or so, filling in gaps from the day before, and discussing where the book was leading and what would happen next. Afterwards, he took me on a tour of Wagga, showing me where he'd lived. He drove me past the police station and crime scene units old and new. He also wanted to show me the scene of a motorbike accident he'd not spoken to me about before, in which two young men had been killed. As we sat by the side of the road, Geoff explained how a fire engine with lights and siren blaring had, while rushing to a fire scene, crossed to the wrong side of a major road where it led under a railway bridge. The fire engine careered over a slight rise in the road, and as it came down the other side, a motorbike came out of the dip and they collided head on. The young men on the motorbike were killed instantly.

Geoff described the families' grief; one of the men who was killed was the second child in his family to have been killed tragically. But the most distressing part of the story for Geoff had been his reaction to the accident. When he arrived to investigate, he saw it had happened right outside the unit in which he was living at the time. He sat in the back of the four-wheel drive, holding his head in his hands. *How am I going to live here now?* he thought. The accident had happened right outside his bedroom window so that he would daily be faced with the scene. This was yet another indication of the difficulties Geoff faced every day of his working life; he just couldn't seem to get away from the constant reminders.

Geoff then drove me into town, as I'd arranged to meet Jocelyn who had moved back to Wagga. Although she and I had talked on the phone and exchanged emails on many occasions, we still hadn't met, and I was looking forward to putting a face to the voice. He took me to her workplace in the main street of Wagga and introduced us. Then he said goodbye and left us to it.

In a local coffee shop, Jocelyn and I chatted away about all sorts of things: family life, children and work, and, of course, touched on the book and Jocelyn's involvement in its story. All of a sudden, she stopped talking and urged me to look out the window.

'Quick – see that lady there,' she said, as she pointed to a woman wearing a red blouse.

I looked at the woman as she walked past, going about her business.

'It's the poor lady who lost her two sons. One of them was killed on a motorbike under the railway overpass,' she said.

Amazed, I looked again: it was the mother of the boy killed in the accident, the scene of which Geoff had taken me to just that morning. It brought home to me the proximity of people in country towns. I told Jocelyn how Geoff and I had just visited the scene of the tragedy, and we both sighed in disbelief.

I asked Jocelyn if she could read part of the manuscript in which I'd described her life with Geoff. I knew this might be uncomfortable but it was important to check that I'd got the story right, both its factual details and the picture I'd drawn of her life with Geoff. She read silently for a few minutes and then looked up and said,

'Yes, that's pretty much how it was.' We chatted for a few more minutes until it was time to leave; Jocelyn had to go back to work and
I had a long trip back to Sydney. As we parted, I promised I'd be in
touch and we went our separate ways.

Later that day, I received an email from Jocelyn saying how preoccupied she'd been for the rest of the day after reading details of
her life in the manuscript. I knew how she felt, as I'd struggled with
my own doubts when writing *Crime Scene*; it's difficult to reveal the
innermost workings of your life to others. I assured her that it was
imperative she was comfortable with all the details I included in the
book about her time with Geoff; she would have the final say over
what would be published, and it had to be right both for her and
for her family. The amazing thing was her strong desire to help tell
Geoff's story. Like me she felt that it had to be told, and she had the
strength of character to see it through. Now that we'd met, I'd seen
the kindness and compassion that shone through her deep-green
eyes and realised I'd been in the presence of a remarkable woman,
who'd somehow come through her journey with Geoff without any
regrets or other negative emotions. Yes, she'd been angry at times
about the treatment Geoff had received during his working life and
about the lack of assistance when the chips were down, but there
was no hint of bitterness or self-pity. In fact, it was obvious that she
still cared deeply for this fine man who was the father of her two
children, and they were remarkably close.

Over the following two months, I did nothing but write, as this
project became an obsession. My usually full-time voluntary work
with the Police Post Trauma Support Group took a back seat as
my friends and members of the group realised I simply had to get

the bulk of this project finished before Christmas. I still followed up on emails and phone calls from serving and retired police who needed assistance, but this had to be done after my writing ended each day, and I found myself working harder than I had since I'd been diagnosed with PTSD. Something I'd learnt over the years was to pace myself: get adequate sleep, keep alcohol consumption to a minimum and try to find time to exercise. It had only been recently that I'd discovered the benefits of prayer, which seemed to allow me to sleep soundly at night, something with which I'd struggled for years. I also started going to Mass regularly and renewed my faith in God. It wasn't that I'd ever lost my faith but, with being so busy, I had simply lost touch with the church. I now had a local parish – somewhere I could go to reflect on the past and, in God's love, grow in the future.

After a short break over Christmas, I pushed on with finishing the book. On Australia Day 2008, I was invited to Gunning, Crookwell and Taralga in the Upper Lachlan Shire to act as their Australia Day ambassador. Ken, the kids and I headed off down the highway to Gunning in separate cars so that I could continue on to Wagga afterwards for one last interview with Geoff and Jocelyn.

On Sunday 27 January, I arrived in Wagga just before lunch. This time I met Geoff at his new home. He was still unpacking but had settled in and was enjoying his new surroundings with Leonie.

Geoff and I got to work quickly; by now we were both used to the routine. He answered my incessant questions, while I flipped through pages of the manuscript, jotting down notes. As we spoke, I noticed a photo of Kate with her new baby son, Riley. Geoff had mentioned a few months earlier how excited he was about the birth of his first grandson and it was lovely to see this picture of the contented baby in his mother's arms. I could see the pride and love in

Geoff's eyes when he looked at the photo; they were no longer filled with sadness. For a minute I forgot why I was there, preferring to savour the moment. It made me realise what this story was really about – not only life's struggles but also its joys.

A week earlier, I'd asked Geoff over the phone if he could take me out to Old Nubber station to visit the memorial to the Young plane crash victims. I realised that this might be difficult when he told me he wanted to ring the Clark family first and let them know we'd be coming. I didn't want to disturb the family and started to think it might be best if I went there alone. Geoff and I talked this through, and he told me that the memorial was about an hour from Wagga and, in fact, on the road back to Sydney. I decided to go home that evening and visit the memorial on my way. Geoff drew a rough sketch, mapping out the roads leading to Wombat via Cootamundra along the Olympic Way. We then checked it on the map, and Geoff described what the memorial looked like and what landmarks to look out for along the way. Before I left, Geoff and I chatted about the future. He mentioned that he'd like to help out at the local old people's home and work with the youth at Sunflower House, a local mental health facility. As well, he was, of course, now a devoted grandfather. Leonie and Geoff came out to my car with me, and we stood chatting for a minute, before hugging each other and promising to keep in touch.

I then headed off to Jocelyn's place for her to have a last check through the story before I continued on to the memorial. I got lost and found myself sitting outside the cemetery – rather fitting, considering. I rang Jocelyn, who offered for Ian, her husband, to come and guide me to their house. We had a laugh about this when I finally arrived, and it was nice at last to meet Ian, Emily, Thomas and Hannah. Jocelyn and I sat at the kitchen table and discussed the story before I asked her to read a number of chapters. I kept my eye on the clock, as I didn't want to get to Old Nubber station in the dark.

Jocelyn made comments as she read and I jotted down notes and made adjustments. At one stage, she looked up and had tears streaming down her face. This brought tears to my own eyes and I quickly offered her an apology.

'Don't be sorry,' she replied. 'It's all right. It's just that some of this is upsetting as I know the people involved, but I'll be okay.' She went back to her reading. Sometimes she dabbed at her eyes but at other times she had a little chuckle. Afterwards, she said, 'See – you managed to make me both laugh and cry.'

It was a defining moment; I knew I was on the right track.

At 5 p.m. I said I'd have to go, as I still had a long drive back to Sydney. Ian kindly offered to drive me out to the Olympic Way so that I wouldn't get lost. Jocelyn and I hugged each other, and I again hit the road. After around ten minutes of following Ian, he waved me on and I was now on the main road to Wombat.

The countryside was mesmerising in its beauty, yet unforgiving at the same time. I imagined Geoff driving along this same road on the night he headed out to the Young plane crash. I could imagine his dread alone on that wet night as he anticipated what waited for him in that lonely paddock. I passed Junee and Cootamundra, and finally saw the turnoff to Wombat; shortly afterwards, I saw a large sign on the left indicating the Old Nubber schoolhouse. I turned into the dirt driveway and immediately saw the stone memorial, standing alone in front of seven trees on the hillside. The sun had almost set by the time I parked and walked to it.

Around a large rock lay bare earth on which cattle had slept. I stood and read the plaque.

These 7 trees were planted in memory of Alanda Clark, Jane Gay, Prudence Papworth (died 12th June 1993), William Caldwell, Stephen Ward, Brynley Baker [and] Wayne Gorham who were tragically killed in a plane crash near Young on 11th June 1993. They were planted by Alanda's family on her 17th birthday, 22nd July 1993.

I stood there and reflected on Geoff's career, and on my journey with him that was now coming to an end. I thought of all the tragedies that had brought me here and of the talks he and I had had over the past year and a half. We'd laughed and we'd cried, but ultimately we'd worked towards resolution. The events we'd talked about seemed so long ago but the present was the product of the past. Geoff had mentioned the trees at the memorial, and wondered if they'd grown; indeed they had but the drought had made the earth dry and hard. I uttered the words 'From dust we came and to dust we return,' before saying a prayer for the victims and their families. Then I gave thanks for the grace and dignity with which Geoff had treated those who lost their lives. I stood under the largest tree and looked up into the sky. An eerie wind swept through the branches, but, as I stood back, there was no sound. Long shadows were forming along the paddock; the day had almost passed. I laid my hand on the trunk of the smallest tree and it was still warm.

EPILOGUE

I hope that by telling Geoff's story, others who have suffered will no longer suffer in silence. It is Geoff's hope that by sharing his story he can help create positive change in the way forensic police are cared for and that things will be different for the next generation. As I am, he is still passionate about his work but regrets how it changed his life.

My voluntary work with traumatised police began after *Crime Scene* was published in 2005. The very night the book hit the shelves, I began to receive emails and letters from people of all walks of life – police officers and their friends and families, military personnel, mums and dads, school children – expressing their shock at what it's really like to work in the emergency services. In writing about my life I'd tapped into the emotions of others who'd had similar experiences or knew someone who had suffered the effects of trauma. I didn't set out to make people cry but I'd touched on a subject that affects all of us at some stage of our lives; death and grief are things that we all have to deal with. One of the things that struck me as I started talking to others who'd been exposed to trauma was the lack of education they'd had on how to cope with its emotional effects. Policing has always been and always will be an occupation that deals with death, and I'd like to think that in the future young people will be better prepared for this facet of their work.

My good friend Suzana Whybro and I had spent countless hours discussing our feelings and our responses to our illness. Like Geoff and me, she suffered from PTSD as a direct result of her crime-scene work with the NSW Police. She developed the illness about a year after I did. Luckily for us both, we already had a strong friendship that had begun when we worked together at the Sydney district crime-scene unit during the early 1990s. Through our common understanding of the effects of trauma, we were able to support each other. Many times either one or both of us cried during our regular phone calls and meetings when we were on sick leave. Waiting for our employer to make decisions about our future was the loneliest and most degrading time of Sue's and my careers. I did receive a weekly phone call from the section commander inquiring after my wellbeing and I appreciated this immensely. But I was starting to understand that most injured police did not have the luxury of a weekly call or a colleague and mate to lean on.

Sue and I met with another former crime-scene examiner and rescue squad operator, Rob Foster, who was also off work with PTSD. We talked about the emptiness one feels when one is on long-term sick leave and threw around ideas of how we could help ourselves. Our morning-coffee conversation ended up lasting a whole day; we had so much to say to each other and talking with someone who truly understood seemed to fill the emptiness inside. I asked them if they thought I should ring all the retired police with PTSD I knew and invite them to the local RSL club for coffee. Sue and Rob thought it was a good idea, so I called eight former colleagues and made a time and date to meet. To my surprise they all turned up, and, again, morning coffee became lunch and then afternoon tea. Two of the members were a married couple; they were both retired from the force and dear friends of mine from my old policing days at Campbelltown. Paula, who was known affectionately as 'Big Bird' and who'd helped me on my first day in the force when I was posted to Campbelltown in 1985, and her husband, Paul, were now in my life again. It was obvious that we all needed the support of others who understood this dreaded illness.

After a couple of meetings we decided to advertise in the *Police News* and invite serving police to join us. At this time we called ourselves the Law Enforcement Post Trauma Support Group, as we couldn't use the word 'Police' in our name without the police commissioner's permission. The day our advertisement appeared in the *Police News*, I started to receive emails, and Rob took many phone calls from police asking for help and wanting to join our group. We decided that the meetings would take place on the third Thursday of every month at the Campbelltown RSL club. The next step was advertising, so we came up with some words and I asked my cousin, Jane Canfield, who ran a business design company, to create a brochure. My husband's company, CEO Global Logistics, paid for the first 500 copies, which were quickly distributed throughout the state. By then our meetings were being held in a private room in the club, who had kindly waived the room-hire fee, and were starting to have a set agenda.

I was amazed at the response from retired police, some of whom had been out of the force for fifteen years, who seized the opportunity to join our group. The common themes in their reasons were feelings of abandonment and isolation and difficulties in finding understanding and acceptance. Bob Walsh, a retired senior sergeant who'd worked in both city and country policing, made contact. Although he'd never been diagnosed with PTSD, he'd suffered his share of trauma while serving in the force and now wanted to assist the group.

Each meeting saw new members walking through the door: some were shaking and heavily medicated; others needed help to walk from their cars. The kindness I saw members showing their former workmates was uplifting. From the earliest meetings, we invited those present to talk about their experiences, which often touched upon thoughts of suicide. It was obvious there were many distressed people in the room, which I found difficult to process afterwards. However, I'd been discussing the group's development with my psychiatrist, Dr Selwyn Smith from St John of God Hospital in Burwood. He was a great source of information and support, and I'd often ring him for advice. He guided me through the ups and downs of learning how to steer the emotions of those at our meetings. Slowly, I came to understand my own response and learned to empathise with, but not absorb, my fellow sufferers' distress.

There continue to be many tears shed during the meetings, especially when new members introduce themselves and tell their stories. But we have learnt to keep these sessions on track, and although it can be tough to hear about someone else's struggles, we have managed to allow our members to be heard without further traumatising those present.

At just about every meeting I saw a familiar face come in the door. It was both heartening to see old acquaintances and distressing to see how their careers had ended. We soon started having guest speakers to talk about such topics as relationships, substance abuse, self help, sleep disorders, and secondary PTSD in children and spouses. Deborah Chivers came on board as the spouse coordinator.

Deb took on the role with enthusiasm and quickly developed a good rapport with those in need.

At the end of the first year, I received a telephone call from Cath Allen, the state coordinator of the Police Peer Support Network. One of her peer support officers – in fact, my old buddy Roger, with whom I'd attended a fatal car accident on Father's Day in 1985 – had told her about our group and she rang to introduce herself, find out more about us and offer assistance. Cath then came to one of our meetings, and spoke to the group about peer support and welfare issues and protocols. She brought with her pamphlets on the employee assistance program (EAP) and other services available from within the force, and answered questions.

In December that year, Cath invited me to be a guest presenter at the annual Police Peer Support Conference in Bathurst. Bob Walsh came along for support and stood at the back of the huge auditorium while I gave my presentation. As he commented later, you could have heard a pin drop as I explained in detail the slow progression of my PTSD and the formation of the Law Enforcement Post Trauma Support Group and the assistance it offered. I was thankful that yet another barrier had been crossed and that the group was slowly getting acceptance from within the ranks. This presentation led to many emails from and referrals of injured police who required assistance from our members. It was heartening to see the police culture of not talking about such issues slowly slipping away.

Meanwhile, I was contacted by one of the police chaplains, Reverend Melissa Baker, who had read *Crime Scene*. After we discussed the group, she indicated her desire to get involved and soon afterwards applied to her senior chaplain for permission to assist our members. I immediately saw the benefits of Melissa's work: she gave our members counselling, support and pastoral care, and much comfort was derived from her mere presence at meetings.

With the many and varied inquiries coming from all over New South Wales, I could see there would be a need to develop regional and country branches. It wasn't long before people were travelling from all over the state to attend our meetings; Al Lukes, Glen Hannah and his partner, Lyn, would get up at 3 a.m. to drive from Wauchope so that they could arrive on time. Within a few months, they started the mid-north-coast branch at Wauchope. We were then faced with challenges in coordinating these new groups as they developed. I couldn't believe the exciting progress that seemed to happen almost every day; it gave us confidence, as it reinforced the importance of what we were doing.

It was now time to form a committee and vote in office bearers. Bob looked after this and suggested registering our name, applying for an Australian Business Number, and becoming a benevolent society and registered charity. This would enable us to apply for funding, which was important as it was clear from the amount of phone calls made and kilometres driven to attend meetings that it wouldn't be long before the committee members were acting at great financial cost to themselves.

The biggest issue at this point was the group's name; we now saw the benefit of being known as the Police Post Trauma Support Group (PPTSG), rather than using the American term 'Law Enforcement'. Bob wrote a letter to the police commissioner, Ken Moroney, asking permission. I was aware that this application would go through the legal branch and I just couldn't face this process, as I feared some of its members would not support our request. I was glad that Bob had the fortitude and ability to do so. Before long, we had confirmation that our application was approved. My eyes filled with tears. We had finally received recognition from the top cop and our existence was now acknowledged in a positive way.

Bob, in his wisdom, had invited Commissioner Moroney to attend a meeting and a few weeks later we received a letter accepting this offer. The meeting he would attend would take place in June 2007. A couple of weeks before it, Bob organised for us to meet with the former police commissioner, Tony Lauer, who was now on the board of the Police Credit Union. We explained to him how the PPTSG worked and he asked how we were funding it. He was appalled when we told him that we were using our own funds and immediately offered to make inquiries with the Police Credit Union about the possibility of their making a donation. Afterwards, Bob and I discussed Tony's receptiveness and how positive the meeting had been; it was yet another step towards acceptance.

We then focused on our upcoming meeting with Commissioner Moroney. I invited the senior chaplain, Father Barry Dwyer, whom I'd spoken to about PPTSG on many occasions, to attend. He had also been present when I spoke at the Police Peer Support Conference and so was well aware of the group. My good friend and mentor Dr Roger Peters accepted our invitation to be guest speaker. His work as a specialist in PTSD and as a psychologist to over 3000 police over the previous twenty years certainly gave him the credentials to help make this meeting a success. I hoped that the commissioner would see the good work we were doing and, in turn, allow those present to be heard and validated.

Around forty serving and retired police were in attendance at the meeting. After giving Commissioner Moroney an introduction to the group and its history, Roger began his speech. Part way through, he mentioned a similar support group that he'd been involved with in 1985. He produced a plaque with the NSW Police badge attached and an inscription that read:

Presented to Dr Roger Peters in appreciation of your contribution to the NSW Police Force from the Hunter support group, 1985

He then turned the plaque over and read from another inscription attached to the back:

The Hunter Police Support Group first met in 1985 but was effectively banned by the NSW Police Department in 1987. This plaque has also been retained in memory of one of the group's first members, Detective Sergeant Anthony White, who took his own life in 1988.

The atmosphere in the meeting was one of shock. I had no idea what was coming next when Roger turned the plaque around again and read from a second inscription on its top:

Rededicated to the Police Post Trauma Support Group and Esther Mckay, June 2007

I couldn't contain my emotions and cried quietly as Roger approached and handed me the plaque. As I looked around the room, I saw tears flowing; the significance of this dedication was obvious. Not only were we running a professional and compassionate support group but we now had the approval of the very department that had previously seen fit to ban this type of initiative. It showed the change in attitude of police management from ignorance to acceptance. I was saddened to think that others who had attempted to help themselves all those years ago were looked upon as a rogue group of troublemakers when, in fact, they were simply seeking solace from others who understood the illness.

It was now time for Commissioner Moroney to answer questions from the floor, and they flowed thick and fast. Again, tears were shed. Commissioner Moroney was visibly affected and answered each question with great sincerity. Before the meeting concluded, the commissioner pledged his full support and then offered an initial donation of $2500 to the main Campbelltown group, with the offer of the same amount for the mid-north coast and other groups as they formed. We were elated to receive our first injection of funds.

It was now time for lunch, and Roger and I sat with the commissioner for the next half hour and discussed the many issues that had been raised. As we talked, a line of those who wished to have a few minutes in private with the commissioner began to form. Roger and I moved away, and one by one each member of the support group sat and spoke with him. Finally, at 3.30 p.m., it was time for Commissioner Moroney to leave but first he handed me his card with his direct phone number and email address on it. As he did so, he invited me to contact him at any time about any issue relevant to the PPTSG members and assured me that he would attend to it immediately.

After the meeting, Commissioner Moroney sent an internal memo to all senior executive staff about his concern at what he'd seen and heard at the meeting. It now seemed that the issue of trauma in policing and improving conditions for our injured police would be addressed. Two weeks later, the commissioner sent me an email inviting me to attend the upcoming state executive group meeting and address the deputy and assistant commissioners about the PPTSG, our work and any areas of concern. Now I could be a voice for those who could not speak for themselves and, in time, hopefully some of the system's inadequacies could be rectified. At the meeting, I spoke for ten minutes and made the most of my time to explain our history, aims and objectives. Commissioner Moroney explained that since attending the group's meeting, he'd instigated an internal review of the sick leave process, and said that when that review concluded, there would be one into the external sick leave policy.

In October 2007, I was awarded the *Daily Telegraph* Pride of Australia Medal for Community Spirit after Bob Walsh nominated me for the voluntary work I do with the PPTSG. When my name was announced, I was disbelieving but elated. Bob Walsh was sitting at the back of the room with my husband, Ken, when it was announced, and his huge smile brought tears to my eyes. I accepted the award not just for me but for all those serving and retired police who selflessly commit to community service and who have suffered trauma in the line of duty. In my acceptance interview, I spoke of the hard work that so many members of the PPTSG do behind the scenes. Without the members themselves and all the committed volunteers, our group would not have been possible. It was an amazing day of celebration. My husband was proud of me, and no one can fully understand the support he's given me over the years, despite the countless nights I've been in my office assisting police who are in crisis and all the other times my work has taken me away from my family. He has never complained and has constantly encouraged me to continue to help others. Above all, the medal gave the PPTSG credibility and exposure; it's one thing to be accepted by other people who suffer from this illness, but it's totally different to be accepted and honoured by the general public.

It was now time for Commissioner Moroney to retire and I asked him what would happen when the new commissioner, Andrew Scipione, took the reins. He urged me to introduce myself to him and, hopefully, open the lines of communication. Soon afterwards I wrote to Andrew Scipione, and he replied promptly, inviting me to attend his office for a meeting. In October 2007, he, Superintendent Graeme Waldron and I spent close to an hour discussing the PPTSG and its future goals. I found Commissioner Scipione to be open, warm and engaging. He spoke of his desire to support the group and offered assistance on the same level as that of Commissioner Moroney. I was relieved that the PPTSG would continue to move forward with the assistance of the NSW Police.

True to his word, Tony Lauer had broached the subject of funding with the board of directors of the Police Credit Union. In August 2007, I received an email from Trevor Kerrison, General Manager, Marketing and Human Resources, pledging the credit union's support and offering a cash donation. I was once again elated, and in October went with Bob Walsh to their head office in Sydney, where Trevor presented us with a cheque for $3500. He also offered a fundraising golf day and advertising in their magazine urging police to donate to our group. This financial assistance came at a particularly good time, as the money the police force had donated had just about run out. We were now afloat again, able to pay for committee members to attend branch meetings in the country, financially assist our two new branches at Wagga and the Northern Rivers, cover auditing and insurance costs, and reimburse telephone expenses. Most importantly, we could pay to have our own website, which can be found at pptsg.org.au. Those suffering in silence can now access information in the privacy of their own homes.

There are many people working quietly behind the scenes assisting police in need; the PPTSG is available twenty-four hours a day and already we have helped save a number of lives. It is a tribute to police camaraderie; it's wonderful to see each member not only seeking help for themselves but helping others. This typifies the lesson I learnt about the police family on my first day at the Goulburn Police Academy in 1984: that police always look after police. This type of support has only been possible because the previously taboo subject of police officers suffering from trauma has come out into the open; generally, police are no longer afraid to ask for help and they often then help others. Over the past two years, I've reconnected with many former colleagues, some of whom I hadn't seen for ten or fifteen years. Just as I felt when collaborating with Geoff while writing this story, it feels as though we were working together only yesterday, as our friendship and loyalty have always continued. When I see how far we've come, I feel that same pride I felt on the parade ground at the police academy more than two decades ago. Policing gets into your blood in a way that only those who've experienced it can understand. It's what brought Geoff and me together, and sustained us through this journey.

As the writing of this story finishes, a new chapter begins for Geoff. When we last met for dinner in Wagga, he excitedly mentioned he'd started a new job. That very day, he'd begun a new career as a wardsman at a local hospital. He looked great in his uniform and it was inspiring to hear him happily chatting about the future. Well done, Geoff; I am proud to call you colleague and friend.

ACKNOWLEDGEMENTS

My greatest pleasure in writing this book was working with Geoffrey Bernasconi, who offered himself to me with warmth and honesty. Thank you, Geoff, for suggesting I write your story, and in doing so making a profound contribution to raising awareness of and removing the stigma associated with mental illness. Excerpts from Geoff's journal written in St John of God Hospital were most valuable and are acknowledged in the chapters 'No Man's Land' and 'The Groth Twins – From this moment on'. I'd like to extend my heartfelt gratitude to Jocelyn Mason for baring her heart and soul as the book progressed, and for assisting with research materials and historical documents. I'd also like to thank Geoff's daughter Kate for allowing me to explore through her personal experiences the secondary effects of PTSD on children.

I'd especially like to thank my mother, Valerie Ross, for editing the manuscript, constantly assisting me with specifics of the written word, and patiently guiding me through the difficulties of writing about trauma. To my husband, Ken O'Brien, my love and gratitude for supporting me throughout this project and for constantly discussing each phase, offering constructive ideas and keeping me focused. My beautiful children, Robert and Alice, thank you for your enthusiasm and laughter, which helped keep things in perspective.

I thank Roger Peters, my dear friend, who has constantly offered guidance, friendship and laughter, no matter what time of the day or night. His knowledge and professionalism in the area of PTSD have been invaluable, and I particularly thank him for writing the foreword and reading the first draft. I'd also like to thank Gary Moffitt for providing me with important information regarding fingerprinting, and Senior Constable Mark Butler for assisting me with facts relating to the Police Peer Support Program.

Thank you to Suzana Whybro for reading through the first draft and extending your never-ending friendship and kindness. Peta O'Shea, thank you for your instincts, love and humour; you are a constant source of revelation. Laurell Magnusson, thank you for your sisterly love, regular encouragement and counsel. Rochelle Jackson, fellow author and friend, your encouragement gave me the confidence and stamina to push on; thank you. I'd also like to thank my friends and former colleagues from the Police Post Trauma Support Group, who inspire and motivate me to write about trauma and its effect on police. And to my extended family and friends whom I'm blessed with, thank you.

Thank you to my wonderful friends from Penguin Books, Ali Watts and Belinda Byrne, who advised, supported and encouraged me from beginning to end. This project would not have survived without your words of wisdom and gentle guidance in the right direction. Sarina Rowell, my editor, thank you for doing such a wonderful job in polishing the book. It's been a pleasure to work with you and I appreciate all your hard work. And, finally, thank you to Anne Rogan of Penguin Books and the wonderful Penguin team, from the Art Department to Publicity.

Geoff Bernasconi and his daughter Kate on his last day of service,
29 September 2000, ironically Police Remembrance Day